Financial Update
2020/2021

Pearson

At Pearson, we have a simple mission: to help people make more of their lives through learning.

We combine innovative learning technology with trusted content and educational expertise to provide engaging and effective learning experience that serve people wherever and whenever they are learning.

We enable our customers to access a wide and expanding range of market-leading content from world-renowned authors and develop their own tailor-made book. From classroom to boardroom, our curriculum materials, digital learning tools and testing programmes help to educate millions of people worldwide — more than any other private enterprise.

Every day our work helps learning flourish, and wherever learning flourishes, so do people.

To learn more, please visit us at: www.pearson.com/uk

Financial Update
2020/2021

 Pearson

Harlow, England • London • New York • Boston • San Francisco • Toronto • Sydney • Dubai • Singapore • Hong Kong
Tokyo • Seoul • Taipei • New Dehli • Cape Town • São Paulo • Mexico City • Madrid • Amsterdam • Munich • Paris • Milan

Pearson
KAO Two
KAO Park
Harlow
Essex CM17 9NA

And associated companies throughout the world

Visit us on the World Wide Web at:
www.pearson.com/uk

ISBN 978-1-83961-623-5

Printed and bound in Great Britain by CPI Group.

CONTENTS

The Supply and Demand Test   1

Commodities   8

Practice Questions   16

The Market and the Allocation Of Resources   19

Competition and Contestability   26

Quasi Markets   53

National Income Accounting   60

Output Gap   69

History and Industrial Structure   75

The Locational Conveyor Belt   84

Consumption and Debt   85

Labour Demand   87

Labour Supply   90

The Coordination Problem   96

Participation   107

International Political Economy   109

The Politics of the Low Wage   114

An Unemployment Problem?   117

Inflation   125

Aggregate Supply and Demand   129

Income Multiplier   138

Housing   140

International Trade   153

Trade Protectionism   156

Economic Associations   168

What is Money?   172

Monetary Policy Instruments   175

Qe Arguments   182

Negative Interest Rates   184

Exchange Rates   189

Changing Vehicles   201

Market Failure-Externalities   205

Market Failure-Demerit Goods   208

The University of Lincoln does not necessarily agree with views expressed in this *Update*.

HOW TO USE THIS UPDATE

Financial Update 19/20 **covers a period from mid-June 2019 to May 2020**, and is compiled to provide case studies and information on topical issues in the financial environment for Business, Finance and Economics students.

There are many welfare diagrams for level one, two and three students, plus discussions of macro and micro policy and a long introduction related to simple supply and demand analysis. Housing features strongly. Moreover, there are several topics concerning the use of numbers for levels one, two or three. Increasingly, the emphasis is not to provide information, but assist in the utilisation of information.

New(ish) topics include Quasi-Markets (level 2) and International Political Economy (level3 IBM).

Although there are numerous references to the Corona virus, the reality is we hope much of the old way of life will return or that the new form will follow many, but not all rules and relationships. Much of our theory will not apply during and immediately after the Virus period.

Read the Financial Times/ Use FT.com

THE SUPPLY AND DEMAND TEST

Supply and Demand analysis is one of those elements an undergraduate Business Studies student MUST grasp. Price and quantity decisions are featured in strategic management, marketing, management, accounting and finance. The bluff of putting an × in the middle of some text and hoping that that will do merits nothing. By considering how you apply theory to a case study, your tutor discriminates between those who understand a topic and those that do not. Knowing that something occurs directly after something else should be distinguished from knowing WHY that something occurs directly after something else. The 'no idea student' will bluff; the 'descriptive student' will identify a process without demonstrating a solid grasp of the underlying causes; but the 'analytical student' will MAKE it CLEAR that they have an understanding of a process that guides the relationship between these phenomena.

Let us begin with a basic issue and see how we can apply theory to a case. One example is the nature of property markets, which is featured later in this text. We will assume the forces of supply and demand determine both rents and house prices. Moreover, in this discussion we can talk about elasticity.

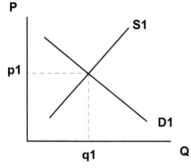

Here, we have the standard product of our analysis, the equilibrium or market-clearing price. At this price, the number of units fabricated by the collection of small producers is equal to the number of units that consumers as a whole wish to acquire. Sadly for the non-engaged student, this is as far as it goes.

How can an increase in price come about? From the figure left there are three possibilities: the demand schedule shifts right; the supply schedule shifts left; or price rises for non-market reasons. Why might the demand shift right? Here, we consider those factors that affect the consumer group, such as their preferences, their number, their wealth, etc.. Why might the supply curve shift left? Here, we consider those factors that affect the producer group, such as their costs, profit preferences, etc.. Why might price rise otherwise? Here, we consider non-market factors, such as government regulation on a price minimum, say price of alcohol.

When is it that there is a move along a schedule, and when is there a shift? A change in the price level will lead to a move *along* a demand or supply schedule. Otherwise, with a change in conditions there is a shift. When answering a question on prices, demand and supply mechanics should be illustrated and this key issue ought to be addressed.

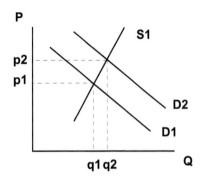

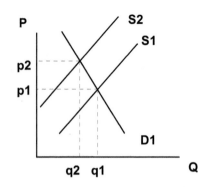

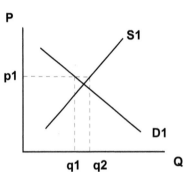

It gets more complicated when one turns to elasticity. We will discuss arc elasticity where the change in quantity demanded or supplied is reflected in the slope or gradient. As a guide, the shallower the schedule, the greater the adjustment in quantity (sensitivity) to a given change in price. As you can see, the four diagrams below are arranged to show a common shift in the supply schedule – conditions change for producers.

For a shift to the left, supply conditions have hardened. Say for example, firms face a higher employment tax. One could consider whether this is passed on to the consumer. Let us assume that the tax shifts the supply curve upwards. Of the four, which figure reflects the tax being absorbed entirely by the consumer?

Fig1

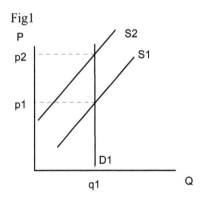

Fig2

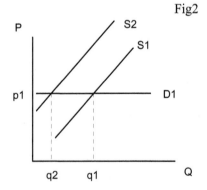

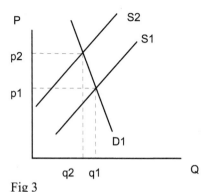

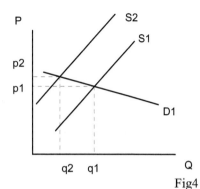

Fig 3   Fig4

With Fig1 there is no change in quantity at all and in Fig2, there is no change in price. These are logical extremes. The vertical demand curve reflects a good where its demand is not sensitive to a price change. Fig3 shows that it takes a large change in price to alter consumers' demand. Fig4 entails a small change in price provoking a large change in quantity demanded. Fig2 is an extension of that line. An infinitely small change in price leads to large change in quantity demanded.

Commonly, you are expected to relate these to a formula. Here, price elasticity of demand entails the % change in the quantity demanded divided by % change in price. The negative sign reflects the downward sloping demand curve.

$$P\varepsilon_D = (-)\frac{\%\Delta Q_D}{\%\Delta P}$$

❑   With Fig1, the change in quantity is zero. As a result, the % change in Q_d is zero. Thus, the good has zero price elasticity of demand or is perfectly inelastic.
❑   With Fig2, the change in price is zero. As a result, the % change in P is zero. Thus, the good has infinite price elasticity of demand, or is perfectly elastic.
❑   Figs 3 and 4 are in between. Fig 3, the steep schedule, is described as relatively inelastic and the formula generates a value between 0 and –1. Whereas Fig 4, the shallow schedule, is described as relatively elastic and the formula generates a value between –1 and –∞.

Try calculating: Original quantity $q_1 = 40$, $q_2 = 20$; original price $p_1 = 4$, $p_2 = 5$
       %Δq = 100×(20–40)÷40 = –50%   %Δp = 100×(5–4)÷4 = +25%;
–50% ÷ +25% = –2 (not a % but value).   Which figure would this reflect? –2 is in the range –1 to –∞, suggesting the demand curve is shallow and is described as relatively price elastic.

To answer the earlier question, all the tax is paid by the consumer when the demand curve is vertical (zero - perfectly inelastic).

Focusing on the slope of the supply curve, there is a corresponding set of figures.

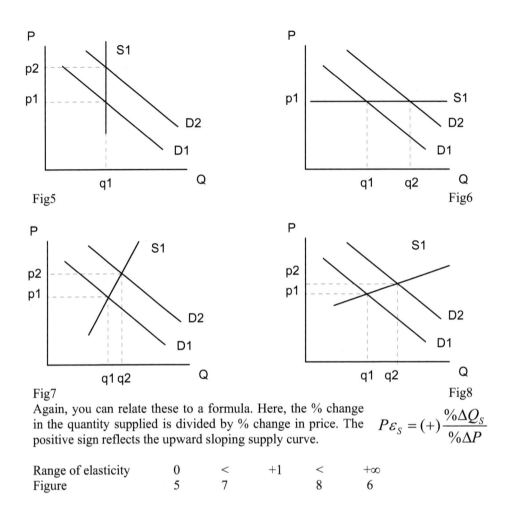

Fig5

Fig6

Fig7

Fig8

Again, you can relate these to a formula. Here, the % change in the quantity supplied is divided by % change in price. The positive sign reflects the upward sloping supply curve.

$$P\varepsilon_S = (+)\frac{\%\Delta Q_S}{\%\Delta P}$$

Range of elasticity	0	<	+1	<	+∞
Figure	5	7		8	6

Uses of the concept of elasticity of demand

Price sensitivity is a very important measure in Economics. As the exchange rate changes relative prices, the goods must be price sensitive to make a devaluation of the currency worthwhile. It can be successful if the price elasticities of the imported and exported goods sum to over one. This is bound up with the next point; elasticity and revenue are related. Depending on whether the demand curve is elastic or inelastic, a given price change results in different revenue changes. If the good's demand curve is steep, a raised price increases revenue.

In Marketing, a focus is market segmentation. In Economics, this is known as price discrimination. Here, the market is segmented into distinct groups, each with different price sensitivities. The groups that are relatively price insensitive are charged a higher price for, essentially, the same product as the others. Using data mining techniques, Accenture has been able to identify which spare car parts in a manufacturer's range customers are less price elastic. Using this, at least seven car and truck makers charge an extra $415m/yr. As this is monopoly rent (charging more than marginal cost), this broke European competition rules. Although trivial, appearance matters. It advised Mitsubishi to raise the price of a 'silvery model badge' from €14.42 to €87.49. The point is that margins on cars can be 10% but spare parts could be nine times that. However, price hikes are avoided where insurers pay attention. Securite Reparation Automobile (SRA) measures car parts inflation and publishes this in the hope it will exert downward pressure on parts inflation.

The caché associated premium brand is, in part, based on the quality, price and the exclusivity. How it is sold and who sells it matters. Although it seems wasteful Burberry burned bags, clothes and perfume. In 2017, unsold merchandise worth £28.6m contributing greatly to the total of over £90m over five years. Richemont (Cartier and Montblanc) spent €480m on watch buy-backs recently over two years. This avoids the grey market and the discounters that might devalue the brand – keeping the brand from becoming cheapened – but is wasteful and socially-useless.

So, having suggested that the slopes of the demand and supply schedules are important considerations when answering a question, what influences these slopes?

Factors affecting price elasticity of demand
- If there are close substitutes, in the event of a price change, it is easier for consumers to switch from one product to another … so the slope will be shallower with more/closer substitutes.
- The consumer's income relative to their necessary expenditure is important. If there is little discretionary expenditure, consumers will tend to be more penny-wise…. this implies that the demand curve will be shallower.
- If the good is an essential, the demand curve will be steeper.
- Luxury goods are ones that are nurtured over years. A luxury product's image is handled carefully and reinforced through heavy advertising. The advertising should reduce the influence of substitutes, so one would expect that the demand curve is steeper.
- Information is key: consumers make choices on the basis of relative prices. Where price changes are easily noted and where consumers are more sophisticated about prices and alternatives, the demand curve will be shallower.
- Time is a factor. In the very short-run, consumers have little time to respond to a change in price. It takes time to find and become comfortable with alternatives.

Factors influencing elasticity of supply
- The element of time is perhaps even more important in supply. In the very short-run, there is no scope to respond to a change in demand. Some perishable products must be sold that day so will have elasticity of supply of (close to) zero e.g. perishable fish on Friday. In the short-run, some factors are fixed whilst the variable costs of labour and raw materials can be altered. As the period of analysis is extended, there is greater scope to adjust these fixed factors. A farmer cannot

increase the crop easily during the year, but can plant more in the next season. As all factors of production are variable, elasticity of supply tends to be greater in the long run. Thus, with an extension of the time frame, the supply curve is shallower.

❏ Cost of attracting factors of production into the firm/industry influences price sensitivity. It depends on the price sensitivity of the factors of production and how easy it is to substitute one factor for another. The easier it is to draw in labour from other industries without wages rising, and the more readily the producer can replace capital with labour, the shallower supply curve for the product is.

❏ A further factor is elasticity of demand for substitutes in production. The demand for the resource may vary as a result of a change in the demand for any one of its alternative uses. Steel may be used for making motor vehicles, fridges, ships, etc.. As demand increases for cars so the amount of steel made available to the motor vehicle industry will increase, increasing the price elasticity of supply of steel for ships.

Cross elasticity of supply
Cross elasticity of supply measures responsiveness of quantity supplied of one good to a change in price of another. **Substitutes in production** are goods for which producing more of one requires producing less of the other. An example is producing butter and milk or cheese. If the price of butter rises, then the supply curve for cheese must shift to the left. In order for the producer to meet the higher demand they would supply less cheese at any given price. Substitutes have a negative cross elasticity of supply – as the price of butter rises, the supply of cheese falls.

$$CX\varepsilon_S = \frac{\%\Delta Q_S{}^A}{\%\Delta P^B}$$

Complements in production are pairs of goods that are by-produced, such as mutton and wool. If the price of wool rises, to produce more wool, the number of sheep needs to be increased - hence the supply curve for mutton shifts to the right. Complements have a positive cross elasticity of supply - as the price of wool rises so does the supply of mutton.

To summarise, the sign tells you whether the two goods are complements or substitutes and the value indicates whether the goods have a weak or strong relationship. For example, mutton and wool are complements so their CXεS will be positive. As they are strong complements, the numerical value will be high. Butter and cheese will have a negative CXεS. As they are strong substitutes, the numerical value will be high.

substitutes	0	>	−1	>	−∞
complements	0	<	+1	<	+∞

Cross elasticity of demand
Cross elasticity of demand measures responsiveness of quantity demanded of one good to a change in price of another. If the two goods are unrelated, there will be no response. However, if they are related, the change in the price of the other good will *shift* the demand curve under consideration. If the two goods are **substitutes,**

$$CX\varepsilon_D = \frac{\%\Delta Q_D{}^A}{\%\Delta P^B}$$

they will have a positive cross elasticity of demand. As the price of good *B* increases, consumers switch from purchasing good *B* to good *A*. This shifts the demand curve for good A to the right. If the two are **complementary** goods, they will have a negative cross elasticity of demand. As the price of good *B* increases, consumers reduce their demand for good *B*. As good *A* is purchased in combination with good *B*, this shifts the demand curve for good *A* to the left.

Butter and margarine are substitutes so their CXεD will be positive. As they are strong or close substitutes, the numerical value will be high. Shoes and shoe-laces will have a negative CXεD. As they are strong complements, the numerical value will be high.

| **complements** | 0 | > | −1 | > | −∞ |
| **substitutes** | 0 | < | +1 | < | +∞ |

Income Elasticity of Demand

If the good is not affected by the income of consumers, the good have a zero income elasticity of demand. However, if the consumers' income does affect their demand for the good, the demand curve will *shift.*

$$Y\varepsilon_D = \frac{\%\Delta Q_D}{\%\Delta Y}$$

If the good is classified as inferior, it suggests that as consumers' income grows, their demand for this good falls; they purchase a more expensive version, perhaps. As income rises, the demand curve for this good shifts to the left. YεD is negative.

If the good is classified as normal, it suggests that as consumers' income grows, their demand for this good increases. As income rises, the demand curve for this good shifts to the right. YεD is between 0 and 1. If the good is classified as luxury or superior, it suggests that as consumers' income grows, their demand for this good increases as above but the response is disproportionally high. As income rises, the demand curve for this good shifts to the right. YεD is greater than 1.

We could use elasticity as an indicator: shoppers are getting richer. At a time of a price war, sales of supermarket own-label budget goods fell by 24.5% in 2016Q1 relative to 2015Q1. Premium foods, such as taste the difference, rose 4.4%. Indeed, the ONS found that household expenditure in 2014 was 5% greater in real terms than in 2012; £547/wk vs. £507.

In September 2017, the EU was apologising for a dual food quality issue. With lower incomes, Eastern European consumers cannot afford the same quality foods. In response manufacturers cater for this. The Tulip Food Company sells luncheon meet in Germany and the Czech Rep. The former bought a pork meat version whereas the latter were sold mechanically separated poultry meat instead. This was just one of 15 brands sold in the Republic with a differential quality. Inferior versions are sold in low income countries and normal, in high.

Veblen coined the phrase 'conspicuous consumption' to recognise the way that elites often wanted to demonstrate their prowess and superiority by marking it through lavish consumption. Rather than different, the Sutton Trust in January reported that the modern elites consume these items more often. For example, 29% of those after tax incomes are £200k+ would go to the opera often. But this is only a minority. In the survey they used, 44.2% HH with income of £200k+ lived in London (35.9% of £150-199k; 33% of £100-149k).

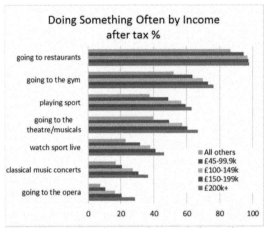

From this set of results one can see what is income sensitive/ a luxury good. There is a relationship between wealth and cultural consumptions: those with highest HH incomes after taxes are more likely to 'watch sport live', to be 'playing sport' and 'go to the gym' than others.

COMMODITIES

A Swine of a Problem
The Dept. of Agriculture (USDA) predicted that global supply growth of pork would outpace demand in 2018, sparking 'fierce competition and lower prices.' The fall in US hogs and cattle prices is contributing to the change in American diets by boosting supplies of pork and beef. Restaurants were seizing on the increases to promote hamburgers instead of chicken, while grocery stores featured pork. What resulted was Americans lost their taste for chicken.

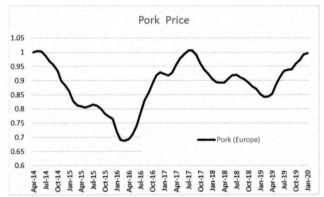

In late 2018, an outbreak of African Swine fever in China raised alarms. The ASF virus, endemic to Africa, is fatal to pigs and has no cure. The current wave of cases began in Georgia in 2007 and spread to parts of Eastern Europe and Russia before, in August, reaching China. China had half the world's pigs @ 430m and its 1.4bn population consume 55m tonnes of pork, annually. By January, pork prices were up by 116% and it was estimated to have lost 100m animals over the year, importing the shortfall in the teeth of a trade war. The year to November saw a jump of 63% in imported pork. Australia exported 81% more beef over the period. Importantly, this displaced exports to other countries. Overall, exports of Australian beef grew by just 7%. Oddly, Australia got lucky. The price of beef would have fallen due to the draught in Australia driving prices down. In the graph above you can see pork prices in Europe. As substitutes in consumption a rise in pork price should drive up the price of chicken. This was the case from mid-2019. However, market movements offset each other. Domestically, in Brazil, an exporter of meats, saw inflation. UK pork producer prices grew by 12% whilst in Europe they increase by 40% over 2019. Chicken was affected by a downturn in the restaurant trade and the Corona virus. The price drop pushed producers to slaughter chickens driving price down further. To ameliorate the situation, China released 30,000t of frozen pork reserves and increase imports.

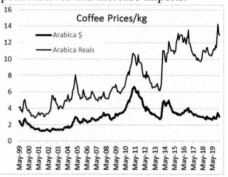

Rebuilding the herd from the 40% drop in 2019 led to piglet prices rising in China to a record Rmb84.

Stirring Coffee
Volatility in the coffee market is leading to a crisis in production. Despite Nestlé using coffee as one of four priority growth areas, falling benchmark prices over four years for Arabica coffee is making production uneconomic. An ICE futures price of $2.05/kg is below the $2.65-3.31/kg Central American growers need.

Grower	1p
Processor	0.4p
Transport	0.3p
Exporter	0.2p
Roaster/margin	8p
Milk	10p
Cup&napkins	18p
Staff	63p
Shop/Rent	88p
Tax&small costs	38p
Profit	25p
Total	£2.49

A £2.49 cup of coffee contains only 9.9p in actual coffee, and only 1p goes to the grower.

A fall in the Real against the Dollar makes Brazilian coffee more competitive. With a record harvest of 62m bags, the supply curve shifts right, depressing world prices. A plunge in global coffee prices in the spring and summer months of 2019 to their lowest levels in 13 years has begun to trigger a massive shake-out in the market. With increasing use of mechanization and other new technologies, the world's top two coffee producers, Brazil and Vietnam, are achieving productivity growth that outstrips rivals in places such as Colombia, Central America and Africa, who are increasingly likely to be driven to the margins, unable to make money from coffee. Some are already turning to alternative crops while others are abandoning their farms completely. In Colombia and Central America, coffee is typically grown on hillsides where mechanization is more difficult, and hand-picking cherries has kept production costs relatively high. Average yields in Brazil over the last decade have increase by more than 40% to about 1.5tonne/hectare. Vietnam's grew by 18% to around 2.5t/htr. Guatemalan and Honduran growers are increasingly abandoning farms and Colombian farmers' peak harvest was in the early 1990s. Central American productivity declined by 3% to 0.6t/hr, whilst Colombian grew by 12%, productivity is about 1t/htre.

Cocoa

In July, Ivory Coast and Ghana, which together produce more than 60% of the world's cocoa, introduced the $0.4/kg living income differential (LID) on cocoa future prices for the 2020/21 season, in a bid to ease pervasive

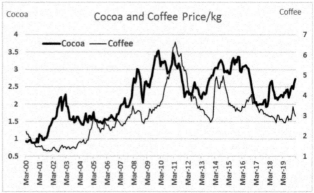

farmer poverty. However, by October it was under review. Chocolate makers Barry Callebaut, Mars, Wrigley, Nestle, Hershey's and Mondelez all supported the LID. The new scheme was undermined by chocolate makers scaling down purchases and negotiating discounts on other parts of the price. The buyers use a country premium, or 'differential', which covers bean quality differences and is a key element in the cocoa price. Ivory Coast beans, some of the highest quality available on the mass market, lost out as the industry stockpiled before the LID was implemented, causing an upward price move. The October review amounted to little as contracts were signed but buyers were able to buy without a differential. In 2015, the costs breakdown was estimated as follows:

Prices in Dollars ($)	Sells/kg	Costs	Profit	Final sale%
Farmers income	1.874	0.664	1.21	6.6
Inland Transport	1.971	1.874	?	0.5
Taxes/MarketingBoard	2.745	1.971	?	4.2
InternationalTransport	2.793	2.745	?	0.3
Costs port of arrival	2.993	2.793	?	1.1
InternationalTraders	3.038	2.993	0.15	0.2
Processors&Grinders	4.434	3.038	2.11	7.6
Manufacturer	10.858	4.434	8.77	35.2
Retail & Taxes	18.917	10.858	4.73	44.2

The farmer got 6.6% of the final value. It was estimated that a necessary farm gate price/kg to move farmers out of poverty was, for Ivory Coast: $3.166 and for Ghana: $3.116.

Supply of Oil

In June 2018, a new constraint depressed West Texas Intermediate crude (WTI) relative to benchmark Brent. Infrastructure constraints in the shale-rich Permian basin kept WTI below Brent crude. Pipelines were overwhelmed as production continued to hit new highs of 10.9mb/d. Typically, Permian barrels went to the Gulf Coast for refining or export, but those pipelines were at full capacity. More oil started to flow to the storage hub of Cushing, Oklahoma, where US futures are priced. For the week ending June 1st 2018, pipeline utilization from Cushing to the Gulf Coast was about 92%, up by 3% and 4% on April and May, respectively. The price differential hit $11.57, the largest since March 2015. The average monthly price differential can be seen in the graph left. The differential grew over the rest of the year.

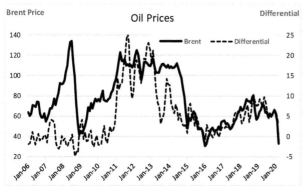

In January, Occidental bought one of the largest hedges against an oil price fall. This was to protect Occidental's dividend to shareholders leveraging to take over rival Anadarko Petroleum for $38bn in 2019. Provided by the Bank of America Merrill Lynch and Citigroup, it covers 110m barrels of oil, or 300,000b/day, each for 2020 and 2021. Occidental receives a max of $10 above market price if below $45/b.

- $45 is the price minimum (put option)
- $55 is the min price Occidental will receive for 300,000b/d (put option)
- $74.09 is the max price Occidental will receive for 300,000b/d (call option)

The hedge meant the firm could sell the oil at a minimum of $55 a barrel in 2020, even if crude prices fell below that, to a limit of $45 a barrel; but the company's selling price was capped at $74.09, and it would lose out on any revenue earned from oil prices rising beyond that mark.

Occidental capped revenues for 2020 and 2021 but only got downside protection for 2020 - a lopsided deal sometimes referred to as a naked hedge. Limiting future revenue without getting a guarantee against falling prices is unusual in the energy sector. A Put option allows the holder to sell oil at a certain price (at a given time). The Call option allows the holder to buy oil at that price.

Storing Up a Future
After failure to agree a production cut amongst the OPEC+ (includes Russia), Saudi Arabia decided to raise oil production. The price war in oil that started 9th March pushed oil prices to around $19/b at the end of March. Let us examine different portions of the market. One would expect that with a shift in demand for petrol to the left as fewer people travel, the oil price (derived demand) would fall. One would also expect that with Russia and OPEC at each other's throats, the price of oil would fall also due to increase supply. Even if there was a production war, with the Corona virus affecting crews, the tankers may not leave port.

Well, the bit in the middle is interesting. Rational expectations tells us the demand for oil will rebound. Arbitragers buy in a cheap and sell in an expensive market. Speculators could buy at a cheap time and sell at a more expensive. But they need somewhere to store the oil once it is out of the well. As oil supplies increased, Goldman Sachs estimated that demand would fall 26mb/d or about 25% of global demand. There was a scramble for Very Large Crude Carriers (VLCCs). The slump in spot oil prices stretched the future six-month gap to a record $13.95/bl, prompting traders to hoard oil. At least 20 VLCC were chartered for $40,000-80,000/day to store crude for 6-8 months. Vortexa estimated that about 57mbarrels were afloat. Six-month charter rates for VLCCs jumped to about $120,000/day [or $10.80/barrel]. Thus, the profit in each bit of the market is squeezed out by other market. In March, Donald Trump ordered the Department of Energy to fill the Strategic Petroleum Reserve to the top but the April 2nd a bid to buy up 30m barrels fell through due to lack of funds. On 29th the DoE announced that Chevron, Exxon Mobil, Alon and 6 others agreed to rent space to store 23mb to others.

As production is cut, as refineries are shut down the excess crude, supplies will dissipate. Two Texas shale producers, Pioneer Natural Resources and Parsley Energy, requested at the end of March that the Texas regulators to curtail oil production. Oil in Midland, Texas, was sold on that day for under $10/ barrel. The idea was to prevent foreign oil imports from the Middle East entering the US market. On 20th April the price of WTI became −$37/bl. With May futures about to expire rather than take delivery of the oil and incur storage costs, traders paid others to take oil off their hands. At the end of April, with the price of WTI at $12/bl, Chesapeake Energy, a US fracker, was preparing bankruptcy filing. Following the glut of gas it was focusing on oil production when a Saudi-Russian energy price war began.

Gold Demand

World Gold Council reported at the end of April one of the substitute markets off-set another. A collapse in jewellery production in 2020Q1 led to a drop in gold demand of 208 tonnes relative to 2019. However, exchange traded funds (ETFs) storing gold on behalf of investors, mainly in the United States and Europe, added a 298 tonnes ($16bn) to demand. There is a dash for commodities when investors are frightened. Oil would be

Tonnes	2020Q1	2019Q1	%Δ
Jewellery	325.8	533.4	-39
Technology	73.4	79.9	-8
Electronics	59.0	63.5	-7
Other Industrial	11.2	12.8	-13
Dentistry	3.2	3.5	-9
Investment	539.6	300.5	80
Bar and Coin	241.6	257.6	-6
ETF& Similar	298.0	42.9	594
Central Banks +	145.0	157.0	-8
Total	1,083.8	1,070.8	1

another home but that was disrupted by the price war. The supply of gold, including scrap fell to 1,066.2t, down 4% from 2019. LME gold price between January 2019 and March 2020 rose 23%. As gold can be both a consumption and an investment asset, with so many falling on hard times in India, consumers sell rather than buy jewellery. Gold consumption fell there 36% to 101.9t, but scrap gold supplies rose 37% to 119.5t in 2020Q1.

Staple Harvesting

In May with the price down from $200/t to $30/t Washington State Potato Commission was giving away russet potatoes. Normally, they would be turned into french fries and hash browns. However, with the July harvest looming, a combination of supply chains failing and closed restaurants, schools and hotels, thousands of tonnes were sitting in warehouses. 90% of Washington potatoes are processed for food service, nearly half for international markets. With exporting constraints and price below costs, you could store, lower price or give them away. With unemployment and poverty soaring, the last might be the best solution.

Also, in May reports emerged that India's wheat harvest could reach the 107.1m tonne mark worth >$26bn would prove a test case of harvesting in lockdown. The Food Corporation of India (FCI), India's state grain stockpiler and largest buyer purchases wheat from farmers at a guaranteed price. Wheat stocks at FCI warehouses on April 1st were 24.7m tonnes. If forced to purchase 37 to 40m tonnes of wheat in mid-2020, the warehouse could be full by June. The government will struggle to export much of that, as the fixed domestic prices have pushed Indian wheat prices about $35 a tonne above the world price of $199.

Farming is a marginal activity. Nearly 85% of India's farmers own less than five acres of land. The backbone of the harvest is an army of 5,000 labourers. With lockdown, only 10% were available. Half of their income of around $394.72 comes during the wheat harvest. India's growers are ill-equipped to hold on to such volumes for long so that dearth of workers affects what is brought to market. Only 10% of the usual number farmers bring crops to wholesale markets. This affects seeds and fertilizer sellers as fewer growers can afford to buy materials for the next round of planting window that begins in June. The lockdown has severely hit India's more than 7,000 wholesale food markets, which are the only channel for getting food supplies to the populous. Buyers extended their wheat procurement period from the usual 20 to 30 days to more than two and a half months.

Segmenting the Market
Elasticity is associated with price discrimination. The necessary conditions for price discrimination are:
- The firm is a price maker – this would exclude small (perfectly competitive) firms;
- Markets can be separated – the firm can prevent reselling or arbitrage between the high and low priced markets;
- Customers in each segment have different price elasticities – the higher price is charged to the customers with the least price sensitivity.
In effect, price discrimination is designed for the firm to extract some, or the entire consumer surplus available.

There are three types of price discrimination
❑ First Degree: is where the firm sells to customers the same good at different prices. The price reflects what that someone is willing to pay, such as individual haggling or an auction. In June 2016, the exploitation of personalising product was reported in the FT. Digitised Printing allows Heinz to sell a 50p tin of tomatoes for £2 or £3 as a 'get well soon' can.

❑ Second Degree: is where the price per unit varies with volume. The lower price is a 'reward' for greater the volume (bulk purchase discount). Here, one should keep in mind the supersized food portions, such as popcorn cartons in cinemas. This value-for-money larger unit is responsible, in part, for the obesity crisis in the western world. In the diagram right P_1 stands for the price of a normal portion. This is the profit maximising quantity (MC = MR at Q_1). However,

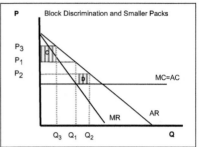

assuming constant average costs, the food monopolist, by offering a larger version, the supersize, can increase profit by area D, at Q_2, which is a lower price per unit but requires a larger volume to be purchased/ consumed.

An alternative analysis focuses on the impecunious. P_1 may be prohibitive for some poorer consumers. To lower the outlay, a price discriminator may offer smaller unit to sell, Q_3, charging price P_3. It also appropriates more consumer surplus (area C). An example of this is the pack of 10. As they made smoking more affordable for young smokers, in October 2013 Euro MPs voted to prohibit the sale of packs of 10 cigarettes. Also, smaller packs provide an easier route for a lapsing person to return to smoking. In May 2016, this became EU law.

The Sunday Times found that some groceries sold in smaller sizes in Poundland were more expensive per unit than in supermarkets. Kellogg's cornflakes sold at 40p/100g whereas a full sized box in Sainsbury's cost 26.7/100g. Milk available in 2litres for £1 was sold in 4pint units in Asda for 89p. Perhaps this is an economy of scale or perhaps it is price discrimination, but this penalizes the poor.

❑ Third Degree: is where the market is segmented by some characteristic and a different price is charged in each segment. For example, there may be some cosmetic repackaging of the product. 1st and Standard class rail tickets or air flights fit into this category. The train or plane arrives no quicker for both groups, but the 1st class passenger is granted special privileges or superior conditions of passage. Other forms of segmentation include peak and off peak (mobile) phone with free minutes per month. Euro Disney was revealed in July 2016 to be engaging in geographical discrimination, charging French customers €1,346 when UK (€1,870) and German (€2,447) visitors were paying more for the same services. This charging is possible as most French visitors' book through Google.fr.

Petrol

Whilst crude dropped from $50 to $19/barrel, UK petrol prices fell in March by their monthly largest margin since October 2008. The RAC reported that 9.18p came off the average price of unleaded in the month. The price of diesel was down by nearly 7.9p to 117.8p/ltre. It was the supermarkets announcing unprecedented single price cuts on

23rd March that contributed to the overall monthly price drop. Morrisons announced a 12p /8p cut in petrol/ diesel. Asda topped that with a drop of 14p.

Unleaded	2nd Mar	31st Mar
UK	122.72	113.54
NI	121.01	107.3
SC	122.45	111.42
NE	121.76	110.76
WA	121.96	111.02
YH	122.8	111.95
SW	123.52	113.03
NW	123	112.83
WM	123.8	113.8
EE	123.92	114.09
SE	124.64	115.39
EM	123.89	115.08
LON	124.17	115.87

The regional average prices for unleaded fuel, within regions they can vary by as much as 35p/ltre. This could be due to 3rd degree price discrimination – Londoners pay more than they should. Other possibilities:-

- A small cost relates to distance to transport the fuel. More remote a filling station, the more expensive the deliveries. Economies of scale also matter. Low volumes but with fixed costs, force smaller forecourts to charge a higher price.
- Joint provision of supply: Supermarket fuel stations are typically 3-4p/ltr cheaper than the UK average in part because they can use fuel to promote the rest of their business and attract more shoppers.
- Convenience when time is a factor. Motorway service stations tend to charge higher prices because motorists have to use them unless they are prepared to leave the motorway.
- The main driver of petrol prices is how much competition there is and whether there is any competition from supermarkets. Supermarkets, although with only around 15% of forecourts, tend to drive prices. So the local monopoly issue is similar to airlines with the low-cost rival; where they are absent, the price is higher.

Today, large on-line retailers, such as Amazon and Walmart, go as far as intra-day price changes on the most popular items. The discrimination can depend on shopping habits by country. Borderfree finds that Canadians tend to shop in the evening after work, Australians tend to shop in their lunch hour, and Russians tend to shop all day long.

A long standing form of third degree price discrimination hit the headlines in 2016 – gender discrimination. Cases revealed included:

- Bic at tesco.com: a pack of 10 twin-bladed men's razors on offer at £1 Or pack of 8 twin-bladed lady razors at £2.
- Levi's original version started at £75 for men in a mid-blue wash, and £85 for women.
- Clarins cream for men £29/50ml and £44/50ml for women.
- M&S plain 100% cotton vests (pack of 3) for men £12.50 or £6 for a single female one.
- Nike's football studs for men £29.99 but for women from £125.
- Argos blue scooter was £5 cheaper than a pink one.

Following the Times report in January 2016, Boots, Argos and Superdrug vowed to review sexist pricing. Bic though was saying that pricing was a retailers' issue. Tesco argued there are 'additional design and performance features.' But is this just too simple? This occurs in the US, so not a UK repressed cultural issue. The New York Department of Consumer Affairs found that female versions were, on average, 7% more expensive than male. This was over 800 products. Women are much more careful shoppers than men, better able to scrutinise adverts and pricing gimmicks. It may be that there is a Veblen dimension; women perceive more value in the more expensive products

In the table below, are relative costs of haircuts in US$. Female haircuts are *not* universally more expensive. The UK has similar prices to Ireland. Chinese women face similar costs to Indian. But Indian men pay less than all the others. Is this discrimination, or a reflection of value? How does that operate in China?

One would expect that DVD sales would decline, as storage and players become issues for the next generation. Economies of scale would be lost and the actual physical cost would make DVDs just a high priced alternative for the oldies, but they ae not. A new release digital film can be as little as £3.49. The pricing of individual titles and formats varies

$	Women	Men	Ratio
USA	73.33	17.5	4.19
UK	49.34	18.5	2.67
Ireland	43.25	15	2.88
China	13.1	14.4	0.91
India	13.5	2.72	4.96

according to retailers' trading and licensing deals with content owners. One explanation is the need to shift the stock out of a warehouse. If it has not sold as well as they had hoped, a film studio may have done a deal with Amazon to shift the physical stock at a discount.

	DVD	Download
Blue Jasmine	£4.92	£7.99
House of Cards series 1-3	£16.99	£44.97
Breaking Bad series 1-5	£28.71	£53.94
The West Wing series 1-7	£39.99	£104.93
Friends series 1-10	£45	£129.99

Impatience coupled with price discrimination could be another. Young adults not used to owning a physical copy are more interested in instant gratification; they want to see the next episode now and are willing to pay the price. This does not work so well with bundled episodes or seasons. The packaging or storage costs make a DVD an expensive option. Here, the higher price is either a two part tariff, in that you need to buy a DVD player. Alternatively, it is 3rd degree price discrimination; segregating the market on those who prefer digital delivery. BPI reported that physical music consumption was down 9.3% in 2016 when streaming was up 67% by volume with similar market share (41% vs 36%).

PRACTICE QUESTIONS

Unfair Competition
The FA cup games between Manchester United (MU) and Cambridge United (CU) highlighted strange finances and something not quite right about an essay title.

'Assess the contention that Cambridge United, when visited by Manchester United in the FA cup, should raise the gate price.'

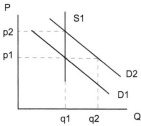

The basis of the essay is the notion that, in the very short-run, there is a fixed capacity. This price elasticity of supply is then zero. CU has a capacity of 9,000. Also, the two clubs have a different fan following. CU had annual turnover in 2013/14 of £1.6m and MU earned £433m. So, the travelling fans could dwarf the normal number through the turnstiles.

We assume that CU would price to fill the stadium. With a vertical supply curve, a shift in the demand curve to the right, should lead to a higher ticket price. One would expect the larger MU travelling fan base would increase the demand for tickets at CU above the normal home game. You should construct diagram as above to illustrate your grasp of S, D & elasticity.

If the ticket prices do not rise to p_2, as some might view this as exploitative, undermining the loyalty that CU may be relying upon, there would be excess demand for tickets (q_2–q_1). This could be resolved by ticket touts, extracting consumer surplus, or by a queue. Here, we are assuming a market determination. If we view CU as a monopoly, pricing may be based on revenue maximization. This may not lead to pricing to fill the stadium.

The reality about the visit is actually counterintuitive. CU is better off playing away. Under FA cup rules 45% of gate receipts should go to the opposition. Cambridge would receive £1.25m when they played away. The home game though, after they had passed over the 45%, would leave them with less than a normal home game against Stevenage. Fewer local consumers than normal could see the adverts around the ground. Anyway, national advertisers keen to take advantage of the 7m TV viewers would replace many.

Peak Load Pricing[1]
In April 2016, Delhi banned the use of 'surge pricing.' This is where the Uber and local taxi apps manage excess demand by raising price when demand for services outstrips supply. This rise in price may be six or seven times the base price. The licences issued by the Local Authority control the number of standard taxis and autorickshaws. The LA also regulates fares. The number of private taxis has surged.

In an effort to reduce the amount of pollution emitted by vehicles, private vehicles can only use the road every alternate day depending on the licence plate of the vehicle. This should boost demand for taxis. Let us again consider this case using microeconomics.

---

[1] FT 22 4 16 Delhi puts brake on 'surge pricing' among taxi apps p19

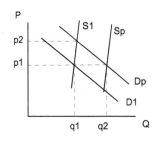

'Should taxi drivers raise price at peak time?'

The basis of the essay is the notion that, in the very short-run, there is almost fixed capacity. This price elasticity of supply is low. It is not vertical, rather than taxis, the taxi services can increase: they could travel more quickly to their destination. Having said that, because peak times may correspond with peak traffic, slowing services down, it could more than off-setting this. Ignoring that congestion element, normal demand = D1. At peak times (say the school run) the demand curve shifts right to Dp. Through the app, knowing both the demand and supply, Uber respond to this increase by pushing up price from base at p_1 to p_2. If services could be scheduled to reflect the peak load, price need not rise. This requires more taxis to be on the road, shifting the supply to the right (Sp).

If the taxi fare did not rise to p_2, as some might view this as exploitative, there would be excess demand taxi services (q_2–q_1). This could be resolved by a queue.

Upon it emerging that Tottenham would meet Liverpool in the Champions League final on 1st June 2019, return tickets on budget airlines, normally available for around £100 pounds, rose to as much as £1,500, while nightly hotel rates in Madrid soared from €100-150 to over €1,000. Unlike the taxi issue, travellers juggled two inflated prices.

In the World Cup match between England and Colombia in July 2018 pub chains took advantage of the increase in demand. Stonegate Pubs charged up to 50p more for a pint in some of its 690 pubs; Yates in Manchester charged an extra 20p on drinks; Walkabout in Colchester added 25p; and the Clock House in Harlow, 50p. Let's analyse this with a question. 'Should Pubs Raise Prices when England Play?' Using our supply and demand analysis we have two elasticity issues and two shifts. First, once supplied to the pub, the cost of each pint of beer remains the same but that additional bar and door staff are needed. To make life easy, it will be assumed that the additional costs are paid for by the additional charge – the gap between P_2 and P_1. Price elasticity of demand is treated as high under normal conditions. The normal quantity consumed over the evening is q_1. The British Beer and

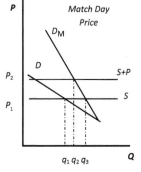

Pub Association expected England fans could consume an extra 6m pint during the evening, suggesting the demand curve would shift to the right. However, overcome by the urge not to miss too much, fans are less likely to worry about the price and shift pub, so the demand curve D_M would be steeper. If price does not increase, consumption rises to q_3. The price hike shifts the supply curve from S to $S+P$. If the elasticity is less than unity, $(P_2 - P_1)q_2 > (q_3 - q_2)P_1$, so revenue increases. This may tick-off the regulars, but the revenue bump may be worth it. In effect, this looks like a tariff diagram with a branded product that is advertised.

Economies of Scope
The theory of economies of scope states the average total cost of a company's production decreases when there is an increasing variety of goods produced. Economies of scope relate to complementary products while focusing on core competencies. For example, a taxi can carry both passengers and goods more cheaply than having separate vehicles, one for passengers and another for goods. In this case, joint production reduces total input costs.

The ONS estimated that in 2015, 76% of adults bought goods or services on-line, up from 53% in 2008. Light goods vehicles, many delivering items ordered on-line, have seen a 20% increase in miles covered in 10 years (DoT). IBISWorld estimate the same-day courier service sector is worth £7bn a year in the UK and the global courier and parcels delivery market is $246bn. Global annual revenue from taxi operations of all types is estimated to be 10% of that at $22bn.

Take Uber. The Licensed Taxi Drivers Association reported that at least 500 taxis have disappeared from London's 25,000-strong fleet alone due to Uber. In October 2015, it unveiled its same-day delivery service, UberRush. ParcelHero predicted UberRush would capture 10% of the global market, disrupting the FedEx /DHL market. By March 2017, UberRush was still only in New York, Chicago, and San Francisco, the three US cities it initially launched it in. By 8th May 2017, Uber switched UberRush, from deliver-me-anything platform, to UberEats, a delivery service with restaurants in mind. The company collects a delivery fee ($5 in most cities), a cut of around 30% from the restaurant, and a cut of 25% to 30% from the courier on each order, rather than the flat mileage-based fees on Rush.

THE MARKET AND THE ALLOCATION OF RESOURCES

Economists study the allocation, distribution and utilisation of resources to meet human needs (well, wants). Over the years, the question *what role profit might have in the allocation of resources in a perfectly competitive world* has been set for assignments and exams. In part, this is a tool for assessing how well students can tie ideas together from weeks of study. Degrees such as Economics build a knowledge base. Advance micro and macroeconomics builds on Intermediate, and Intermediate is founded on Principles. At level one, we offer the tool kit you need. We also construct the lens through which we view social and economic problems. We begin by outlining what we regard as the resources and their factor returns:
  Land (rent) Labour (wages) Capital (interest) Entrepreneurship (profit)
The *Economic Problem* and the questions of:
  1. what and how much is produced?;

    2.   how it is produced?;

    3.   whom should consume it?

Through history and possibly general consent various countries adopt a variety of means of addressing this problem. Here, we discuss the notion of Economic Systems outlining three archetypes: Command, Market and Mixed Economies. Although it is recognised that the market is a poor master, a course in Principles of Economics outlines how the market mechanism is a solution to the Economic Problem.

The market both signals and rations. Large numbers of individuals signal to producers what they want: through price and profit in a perfectly competitive world, resources are allocated and reallocated to achieve that end. People have limited income. Those that think a good is 'too expensive' either seek a substitute or buy less. In other words, it is presumed that people make the best use of their limited income to maximise their utility in the light of a set of goods and their prices. Here, we are assuming that:

- ❏   the individual is well informed - there is perfect knowledge;
- ❏   no spillovers exist that affect third parties – no externalities;
- ❏   clear property rights - no public goods;
- ❏   perfect competition – not imperfect competition;
- ❏   people are the best judges of their own well-being – no merit or demerit goods/ consumers are rational.

Costs of the Firm

Total Cost = FC+VC   Total Revenue = P×Q   Average Total Cost = AFC+AVC;

Average Revenue = TR÷Q   ATC = TC÷Q

AVC

=VC÷Q; AFC=FC÷Q

Marginal Cost = ΔTC÷ΔQ Total Profit = TR–TC   Marginal Revenue = ΔTR÷ΔQ

In order are the TC (left-hand scale), MC, AC, AVC, AFC (from the top and on the right-hand scale).

At zero output, VC = 0 so TC = FC. The AFC declines with volume. When drawing, the AVC and AC are at a minimum when cut by the MC (at $q = 66$ and 71).

In order are the TC (left hand scale), MC, AC, AVC, AFC (from the top and on the right-hand scale). At zero output, VC = 0 so TC = FC. The AFC declines with volume. When drawing, the AVC and AC are at a minimum when cut by the MC (at $q = 66$ and 71).

Q	TR	AR	MR	TC	MC	AC	Profit
10	220	22	20	318	14.4	31.8	-98
11	240	21.8	19.6	332.1	13.8	30.19	-92.293

Profit Maximisation

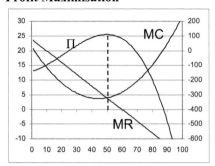

In expanding output from $q = 10$ to $q = 11$, $\Delta TR > \Delta TC$. At $q = 11$ MR was greater than MC, so there was a marginal profit but overall (Total) profit was negative. The figure right shows three lines: Total profit Π, MC and MR. The peak of the total profit curve Π occurs where $q = 50$. In the table above when $q = 49$ MR > MC, expanding output increases profit and when $q = 51$, MC>MR so profit is lower than when $q = 50$. We conclude that profit is maximised when MC=MR.

The construction of these diagrams follows two simple rules.

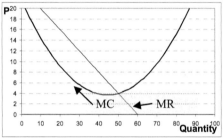

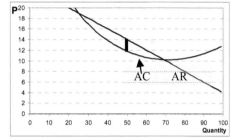

1) Find the quantity where MC=MR, the level of output where profits are maximised or losses

minimised. We have discussed this already above. In this case the quantity to operate at, regardless of the profit or less situation is at $q = 50$.

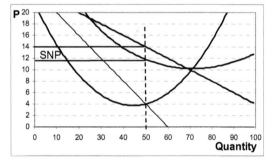

2) AT THAT QUANTITY ($q = 50$)
find the difference between the AR curve and the AC curve.
If AR > AC, the firm is making Supernormal Profit (SNP).
If AR = AC, the firm is making Normal Profit.
If AR < AC, the firm is making a Loss.

Note: SNP = (AR − AC)×q. SNP = (14 − 11.8)×50 = 110. The price will always be taken from the demand curve (which is the AR curve) given the profit maximising quantity q. Price = 14. These rules can be followed for all market structures. In effect, the cost curves remain the same and the shape of the demand curve alters. Above is a diagram showing price (14) quantity (50) and the cost associated with that quantity (11.8). Unless the firm is in perfect competition making only normal profit, the lower cost line *does not* go through the lowest point of the AC curve.

So, how are economic decisions taken through the workings of the market? Our idealised model for this analysis is Perfect Competition. Necessary conditions for the perfectly competitive model:-

❑   A large number of relatively small buyers and sellers all of no economic power.

If there are large numbers of sellers, then any one seller's supply will be so small in relation to total market supply that increasing or decreasing his/her output will not have any effect on the price. This implies that the firm is a PRICE TAKER. We use the small ≡ price taker in trade diagrams. Similarly, buyers are so small in relation to total market demand that again no one buyer can influence the price. This forms the basis of the perfectly elastic demand curve of the firm.

❑   Buyers and sellers are perfectly mobile and perfectly informed.

❑   There are no barriers to firms entering or leaving the market.

❑   The product is homogenous.

We assume these to ensure uniformity of the market. Given that all the products are the same and everyone is aware of where the good is sold and at what price, any increase in price will encourage buyers to look elsewhere.

❑   Profit Maximisation.

Profit and the profit motive are central to the allocation of resources. It is the financial incentive given to the entrepreneur that drives them to innovate, minimise costs and prices, and be efficient.

Advantages of the perfectly competitive environment

❑   Price = marginal cost i.e. this is the optimum position and suggests that resources are being *allocated efficiently*. The marginal benefit from consumption = the cost to society of its production.

❑   Competition acts as a spur to efficiency. If a firm becomes less efficient than other firms, it will make less than normal profits and go out of business. If it is more efficient, it will make super normal profits until firms copy its more efficient methods. All firms have access to the same knowledge. Any firm not incorporating the most effective technology will collapse. Customers will pay only the lowest price.

❑   Competitive situation will encourage new technology as firms try to make super normal profits.

❑   Because the product is homogeneous there is no point in advertising, which can be seen as a waste of resources.

❑   The firm in the long-run will produce at the lowest point on the AC curve – is cost efficient – *productive efficiency.*

❑   The consumer gains from low prices, since not only are costs kept low but also there are no super normal profits to add to prices.

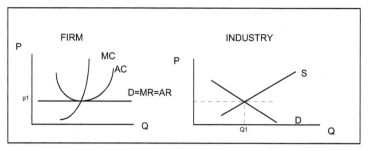

The price observed by the consumer is determined by the interaction of TOTAL INDUSTRY or MARKET SUPPLY and DEMAND. The [representative] firm takes the market price so the demand curve of the firm is perfectly elastic. Observe that the market price determines the position of the firms' [horizontal] demand curve.

Our initial position entails the PC firm making only normal profit. This is an equilibrium position: there is no tendency for firms to enter or leave the industry.

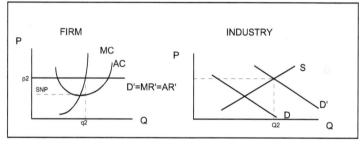

Equilibrium is disturbed by some news - a change in demand conditions. Assume the good becomes more fashionable. If the market demand curve shifts from D to D', the market price rises to p_2 and market quantity to Q_2. Remembering that MR=AR and AR=D and the firm's demand curve is linked to the market price, the demand curve of the firm shifts upwards (D to D'). The firms currently in the industry work their way up their MC curves. At the new MR, the firms produce more output, at q_2 where MR' = MC (hence the supply of produce) and this output is sold at the higher market price, p_2. The firms now make supernormal profit (SNP).

Note that the firm diagram should display the right information – do not guess – know what you are doing. When going through the diagram, it should look like the one right. If the market price is p_1 – the firm operates at q_1 and makes normal profit. If the price is p_2, it makes SNP and the output is q_2 – to the right of q_1. Moreover,

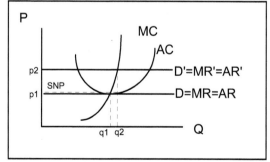

there should be three horizontal parallel lines: the original demand curve D, the new demand curve D' and the third line associated with the costs when operating at q_2. If the first line is not distinguished from the third, you have *not* completed the diagram correctly.

SNP is the signal to other entrepreneurs that are currently outside the industry to enter the industry by gathering together the factors of production and setting up a firm in competition. As there are NO barriers to entry, there is market access. Firms can break in. This increases the number of firms in the industry. The industry's scope for production is enhanced so the industry supply curve shifts to the right (S to S'), leading to a fall in market price. Whilst SNP is being made in the industry, firms will continue to enter the industry. So this process will continue until all SNP is eroded. The representative firm is back at square one (well p_1, q_1 long-run equilibrium) but the industry has moved from Q_1 to Q_3.

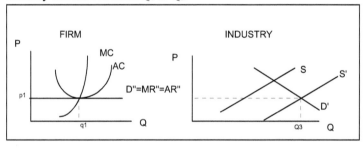

So what has occurred here? Why is this process important? Perfect competition leads to CONSUMER SOVEREIGNTY. Consumers, through the market, determine what and how much is to be produced. Firms have no power to manipulate the market - the only thing they can do is to increase their efficiency for short-term super normal profits but in the long-run the consumer will benefit from lower prices. There was a change in tastes. Consumers collectively wanted to consume more of the good. This information was signalled through price to producers. Those in the market place responded by expanding output but they also made SNP. This profit was the signal to entrepreneurs to shift resources from one use to another. Because there is an absence of barriers to market entry, these itinerant profit seekers acted as a counterweight, driving price down. What the consumer wanted – the consumer got. Through price and profit resources were drawn into the industry.

In one sense, this is unlikely to be entirely true. Unless the industry is small, the price of materials and labour could have gone up.

Note that the entrepreneurs are acting in their own self-interest, pursuing profit. Indeed, it is this drive to maximise profit that benefits consumers. Profits come from making things that consumers wish to buy. Thus, profit motive (inadvertently) drives firms to facilitate the maximisation of well-being. Friedman (1970) and Hayek (1967) argue that:- so long as it plays by the rules *a business has one social responsibility: increasing profits and, hence, enhancing shareholder value.*

However, there are two main problems with perfect competition that can be overcome by other forms of market structure.

❑ Because firms in the long-run do not make super normal profits they may not be able to afford large research and development (R&D) budgets to make themselves more efficient and create new products.

❑ Also, there is no consumer choice in that the product is not branded or differentiated in any way, therefore other models may be seen as more relevant to real world conditions.

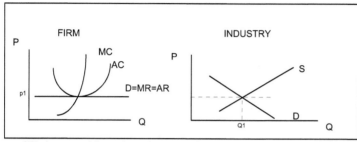

Let us examine the obverse. Again, our initial position entails the PC firm making only normal profit. This is an equilibrium position: there is no tendency for firms to enter or leave the industry.

Equilibrium is disturbed by some news, a change in demand conditions. Assume the good becomes less fashionable. If the market demand curve shifts from D to D', the market price falls to p_2 and market quantity to Q_2. Remembering that MR=AR and AR=D and the firm's demand curve is linked to the market price, the demand curve of the firm shifts downwards (D to D'). The firms currently in the industry work their way down their MC curves (above the AVC). At the new MR the firms produce less output, at q_2 where MR' = MC (hence the supply of produce) and this output is sold at the lower market price p_2. The firms now make a loss.

A loss cannot be made for ever so this is the signal to entrepreneurs that are currently inside the industry to leave, releasing resources to be used elsewhere. As there are NO barriers to exit, there is market egress.

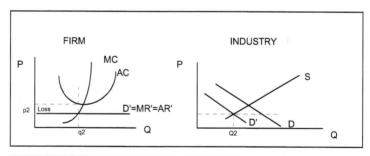

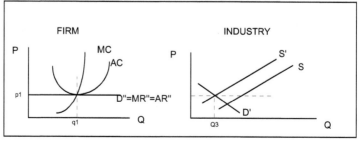

This decreases the number of firms in the industry. The industry's scope for production is diminished so the industry supply curve shifts to the left (S to S'), leading to a rise in market price. Whilst losses are being made in the industry, firms will continue to leave the industry. So this process will continue until all loss is eroded. The representative firm is back at square one (well p_1, q_1 long-run equilibrium) but the industry has moved from Q_1 to Q_3. This time, a loss of interest in the product, through price and profit, leads to resources being released for better uses.

The efficient market hypothesis uses this vehicle to explain why an asset's price should reflect all information.

The Small Trucker
Perfect Competition is often criticised by the new economist as an irrelevance as there are no real world examples. This may not be the point... however, the trucking industry does come quite close. Obviously, one barrier to entry is the capital needed to buy a truck, but after this the industry has favourable characteristics. Most of the market is dominated by small providers (Eddie Stobart has only 10% of the market). The 33,000 UK truckers make around 1.5-2% profit – more or less breaking even. Fuel makes up 50% of the running costs.

Ethics Inherent in the Demand Curve
Edelman's Earned Brand survey suggests something akin to Friedman's defence of corporates social responsibility. Of the 14,000 respondents in 14 countries, 57% buy or boycott products because of a brand's stance on political or social issues; 27% more than three years ago. Almost a quarter of consumers are willing to pay more for those products where brands share their values. Indeed, 67% will try a brand for the first time because of its position on a controversial issue. By contrast, WGSN the trend forecaster, suggests increasingly, people are looking to companies to fill the void around social problems as a tribal mentality and public mistrust in governmental institutions grow.

COMPETITION AND CONTESTABILITY

Competition is viewed as desirable. Through rivalry among competing firms, technologies and processes, members of society are free to choose from a set of options that, whilst maximising consumers' well-being, results in making the best use of a set of resources. Beneficial outcomes include low price, low cost and the incentive to be efficient. In the real world, (i.e. not restricted to Perfect Competition) competition also drives firms to be innovative and provide the consumer with a variation of product as well as provider. By operating at a larger scale and investing in innovative products and processes, large firms can lower unit cost.

In neoclassical theory of the firm, the Monopoly is the *sole* supplier in the industry.

Monopoly power may not be in the public's interest because:
- There could be a higher price and lower output than under perfect competition;
- Of a lack of competition that may lead to higher cost curves, X-inefficiency;
- There is a lack of a drive to be innovative;
- Monopoly profits are an exploitation of the consumer;
- It may exert undesirable political pressure on governments.

In practice the monopoly is replaced by the oligopoly. Thus, market imperfections associated with a small number of providers include the exploitation of the consumer, slack financial control, consumer insensitivity, relatively poor innovation, collusion and predatory behaviour. We consider three perspectives or theories of competition:-.
- Structure Conduct Performance
- The Austrian School of competition
- Contestable Market Theory

Two of these suggest the monopoly/oligopoly can still serve the public interest.

Structure-Conduct-Performance
The Structure-Conduct-Performance (SCP) is defined as the relationship between market structure, firm conduct and firm performance. SCP was based on the following causation:
1. that structure of the industry influences managerial conduct. Lower concentration leads to more rivalrous competitive behaviour;
2. that conduct influences performance. Less market power leads to more competitive behaviour, which produces greater social well-being.

Structure
Structure: refers to market structure defined mainly by the concentration of market shares in the market. This will include:
- Size and number of firms:- From PC vs Monopoly analysis (see Monopoly Power), the monopoly extracts 'monopoly profits' by charging too much for the product. The market share of the largest businesses (measured by the concentration ratio) is a measure of the market power (see Herfindahl Index).
- Barriers to market entry:- This element can be tied to the above point, so that with an open market the number of firms and the extent of overseas competition is a constraint on price. However, this also relates to how firms from outside the industry can break in. In practice, major firms can inject competition by switching focus from one market to another. Despite low running costs, one major barrier could be the short-run high set-up costs. The degree to which an industry is vertically integrated, either forward or backward integration, can also act as a barrier. Buyers or suppliers are already tied in to formal arrangements that are difficult to breach.
- Independence:- In theory of the firm a separate entity competes with another with an identical set of resources. In reality, firms are not identical. Some may achieve competitive advantage, not through their own devices but through their relationships with other firms. Thus, network economies are a difficult area to

assess. A variation of this was the Keiretsu. Informal relations between families of Japanese companies would appear like a restrictive practice to the Americans.

❑ Barriers to market exit:- Switching costs from one provider to another could act as a disincentive to change and so an exit barrier. This may include finding an alternative provider or source, or breaking a contract. A sunk cost is an incurred, irretrievable cost. It can be a past or future cost, either fixed or variable. For example, a factory could be 'sunk' fixed cost because it was a one-time expense and cannot be recovered, or a regular payment on a contract to lease this building. A variable sunk cost could be the power usage for this factory. Once incurred the sunk costs do affect future decisions but would be a disincentive to enter into arrangements where they can occur.

❑ Homogeneous product:- One of the problems for the consumer is choice; are they equipped to make a good, informed choice? Asymmetric information and bounded rationality limit the buyer's ability to identify the best price from several million, in the case of mobile phones. So that the consumer has but one decision to make, and that is on the basis of price alone - perfect competition assumes away alternatives. In reality, there is price discrimination and a hierarchy of variations that serve differentiated markets. A branded good can act as a barrier to entry.

❑ From a Porter-like perspective, the relative power of the buyers or suppliers is important. If industry is dominated by a small number of firms but their buyer or supplier industries exerted sufficient power to maintain pressure to keep price low, the structure may not be deemed problematic.

❑ Porter also identifies the threat of substitutes as price/profit limiters. Here, we are looking at the scope for the consumer to switch to alternative products. For example, cable linked *or* mobile devices can provide telecommunications.

Conduct / Behaviour of Firms
How does market structure affect pricing, output and other decisions of businesses within the market?

❑ There may be anti-competitive behaviour. For example, with large firms there might be predatory pricing, which acts as a barrier to entry.

❑ How might independence manifest itself?
  o Long-term arrangements that could make sense for planning purposes could also appear as restrictive practices.
  o Are the firms agreeing price and output levels collectively to boost profits? Collusion among oligopoly firms is not that rare and generally not in the interests of the consumer.

❑ How important is non-price competition in the market? Heavy advertising can act as a barrier to entry and, in a Baumol model sense, is characteristic of an oligopoly market.

❑ Merger activity, particularly horizontal mergers, makes a poor structure worse. Mergers are not always problematic. With the *Market Power Hypotheses* a horizontal merger can be justified for the social good or for the national interest. If profits are negative collectively and the industry has high costs, a merger and a managed reduction of capacity make more sense than a protracted price war. Post-Corona virus mergers are inevitable.

❑ A key measure of monopoly power relates to the scope for raising price above marginal cost. So pricing and, hence, **monopoly profit** are key measures of nefarious activities.

❑ Innovation, and the measure, R&D, are indicative of activities good for society. One would expect that, more economic progress would result from a more innovative industry, which is facilitated by R&D. There would be a better allocation of the resources than the economy can command. In general, the larger R&D budgets are commonly found with larger firms.

❑ With asymmetric information, the seller can baffle the buyer with excess information or choice. Utility companies, for example, would offer two systems; one with and one without a standing charge. However, the second was more or less the same as the first for all but the most frugal users. This choice could lead to the consumer choosing the wrong product or service – the adverse selection. Government sought to address this with utility tariffs by limiting the number of tariffs.

❑ A variant of this is misselling. Banks in particular have been fined heavily for selling inappropriate products to unsophisticated, ill-informed customers.

❑ Without having the opportunity to choose between providers, consumers cannot impose any pressure on firms. Having a selection is not sufficient. Poor conduct from firms has entailed bombarding the consumer with choices so that they are disinclined to switch or if they do, they switch to a worse contract. Overall, a key measure of a competitive environment is customers *switching providers*. Switching could be a sign of dissatisfaction so a lack of switching may point to the reverse. The banking sector has been reviewed several times. In 2002, the Competition Commission investigated the supply of banking services to small businesses by clearing bank. In 2008, the Office of Fair Trading investigated the provision of personal current accounts. In 2011, the Independent Commission on Banking recommend promoting financial stability and competition. However, they have always stopped short of restructuring the industry. It was the European Competition Commissioner that forced Lloyds to sell off TSB. In October 2015, the Competition and Markets Authority (CMA) reported that switching could save £70/year. Those who regularly utilise an overdraft facility could save as much as £260/year.

❑ Just 57,779 used the 7-day switching service to move accounts in September 2017, was less than half of the 120,774 of March 2016 and the lowest number since the scheme was launched in 2013. Banks were offering account holders financial incentives to stay (HSBC) or shift (Halifax, Clydesdale and Yorkshire), so something had changed.

❑ Despite Repo rates being at historically low levels, in September, Moneyfacts reported that credit card interest rates were on average 24.7%, above the 23.4% last seen in 2006. Price way above costs is exploitative.

❑ Santander showed its hand in January by announcing that, from 5th May, the interest paid on balances up to £20,000 in its 123 account would be cut from 1.5%

to 1% and its overdraft rate is set at 39.9% interest. Nationwide, HSBC and RBS set their rate at just above 39%, with Barclays setting its rate at 35%. Around 19m use overdrafts from which firms earned £2.4bn in 2017. Around 7.3m use an arranged and unarranged overdraft and 14m use an unarranged. 30% of overdraft revenues come from unauthorised overdraft fees and interest rates. The Financial Conduct Authority planned to shake up the 'dysfunctional' overdraft market, by stopping banks and building societies from charging higher prices for unarranged overdrafts than for arranged overdrafts. This is an illogicality. The new rules came into force in April 2020 requiring providers to charge a simple annual interest rate on all overdrafts with no fixed fees. The Corona virus heightened the fears over banks exploiting the market. The Financial Conduct Authority (FCA) weighed in with proposals for banks to offer:-

- A three-month repayment freeze on loans
- A temporary freeze on credit card and store card debt up to three months
- Zero interest for three months on up to £500 for customers affected by Corona virus using an arranged overdraft for up to three months

The FCA also said that consumers using any of these measures should not see their credit rating affected. In a timeframe reserved for emergency measures, the FCA wanted the proposed measures to be considered by Monday 6 April, and implemented 9th April.

❑ The 4 big Australian banks, treated as arms of the state are worse, prioritising profit over customer welfare. In May 2018, a report found that they lied to the regulator on a regular basis. AMP, a financial advisor, lied 20 times. CBA was investigated for 50,000 breaches of money laundering (See CSR in virus times).

❑ In April 2014, Ofgem found that between 2007 and 2012, 5.6% of objections made by British Gas to business-to-business customers who wished to switch suppliers were invalid, so incorrectly blocking them from going elsewhere. British Gas also failed to give some businesses notice that their contract was due to end. Fining it £1.3m for the affected businesses, a further £3.45m into an energy efficiency fund; and a £800,000 penalty, the total came to £5.6m. This covers two issues of competition. Blocking a switch would lower the competitive pressure. Also, with a limited time to make an informed choice, customers will be deterred from switching.

❑ In December 2017, Apple admitted that it deliberately made changes to iOS to slow down some models of the iPhone. The practice was confirmed after a customer shared performance tests on Reddit, suggesting their iPhone 6S had slowed down considerably as it had aged but had suddenly sped up again after the battery had been replaced. Apple charged £79 to replace iPhone batteries, and also covers the work under its AppleCare policies. Some believe that Apple slows down older iPhones to encourage people to upgrade. Apple pointed out that as the lithium-ion battery ages, devices unexpectedly shut down. When in cold conditions, batteries become less capable of supplying peak current demands when they have a low battery charge. In February, French prosecutors imposed a fine of €25m after its software updates were found slow down older iPhones. In effect, it engaged in quasi-planned obsolescence, which is illegal in France.

❑ In August, Casio was fined £3.7m by the Competition and Markets Authority (CMA) for pressurising retailers to sell its keyboard and digital pianos at recommended prices. Between 2013 and 2018, it monitored compliance with its price policies through the internet.

❑ The CMA also found that Apsen Pharmacare colluded with two rivals to keep them out of the UK market and then raised the price of fludrocortisone. It was fined £2.1m, plus a £8m NHS refund.

❑ In May 2019, the CMA alleged that, between 2013 and 2018, the price of Prochlorperazine rose from £6.49/ pack to £51.68, increasing the cost to the NHS from £2.7m to £7.5m, even though it dispensed fewer packs. Four suppliers colluded. Alliance supplied exclusively to Focus, which paid Lexon, which shared payments with Medreich.

❑ In August 2016, four of the 6 largest European truck makers were fined collectively €2.93bn for jointly manipulating price and delaying emissions reductions measures in diesel trucks. This would include MAN and Scania, both Volkswagen marques. They had been collaborating from 1997 to 2011. MAN was exempt as it whistle-blew. The Road Haulage Association began preparing legal action seeking damages of £6,000×650,000 trucks = £3.9bn. Scania denied any wrongdoing, but, in the end, was fined €880m in September 2018. Commissioner Vestager pointed out that the EC had uncovered nine cartels in the automotive sector and fined companies more than €6bn for their illegal behaviour in the past decade.

❑ Following the emissions scandal, it emerged in July 2018 that Volkswagen and Daimler being investigated for collusion in fixing the price of diesel emissions treatment systems. Bosch agreed to pay $327.5m in colluding with VW, installing the software, which itself was fined €1bn. In January, Ford was being sued for using similar software in trucks. Daimler car engines in June 2018 were found to have five "illegal switch-off devices" possibly used by the bulk of Daimler's new Euro 6 diesel car fleet (1m vehicles).

❑ In March, France's Autorité de la Concurrence fined Apple (€1.1bn), Tech Data (€76m) and Ingram Micro (€63m) for colluding. Apple and its two wholesalers agreed not to compete with each other and to prevent other distributors from competing with each other. About half the French retail market for iPhone, iPads and personal computers between 2005 and 2017 was stifled. Around 2,000 independent resellers competed with Apple, whilst buying stock from it. When new products were launched, Apple favoured certain wholesalers by giving them more stock, while others found themselves without enough to satisfy customer demand.

Predatory or limit pricing is a problem for both CMT and SCP. Here, the price is set by the large firm to prevent market entry or drive out a competitor – much like the aim in a price war.

❑ EU Competition Commissioner imposed a €242m fine in July on Qualcomm, for abusing its market dominance. Controlling 60% of the world market for chipset market, it engaged in predatory pricing. It sold its chipset over 2009-2011 to two large customers below cost with the aim of excluding rivals, such as Icera.

❑ In November, Ofcom upheld a find of £50m on the Royal Mail. It engaged in predatory pricing against Whistl. Although never imposed, Royal Mail upon which it relied outside of Manchester Liverpool and London, threatened to penalise clients whose regional split of addresses was different to the Royal Mail's.

❑ A letter to the Telegraph in 2014 from the CEO of First Utility claimed two issues of interest. First, Ian McCaig asserted that the big six energy companies were engaged in **limit pricing**. They were setting tariffs so low as to attract customers from new rivals to quash competition. Second, the costs of this policy were being borne by those on standard tariffs. This is at odds with the claim that tariffs in 2018 were 'rip-offs.' Legislation was proposed to allow Ofgem to limit how much companies can charge their 11m standard variable tariffs (SVT) customers. Ofgem estimated the price difference between the average SVT default deal and the cheapest rate in the market was £308 (December 2017). One way around this is to scrap SVT – the regulated bit. Of course customers are still likely to be better off by searching and switching themselves (see Competition Thoughts). Between April 2016 and May 2017, the large and medium-sized suppliers charged consumers on SVTs a similar amount (£1,074 and £1,082 respectively). Over the same period, on average, consumers on fixed tariffs were charged £116 less by the six large suppliers, and £165 less by medium-sized.

Citizens Advice estimated in July 2018 that there was £7.5bn of *excess profits*[2]. The average company rate of profit was running at 10% and none earn less than 7%. The big six made £54 of profit per dual fuel customer in 2016.

Facebook members outside the US and Canada, are governed by terms of service agreed with the company's international HQ in Ireland. In May 2018, the EU's General Data Protection Regulation permitted regulators to fine companies of up to 4% of global annual revenue for infractions for collecting or using personal data without users' consent. Of the 1.9bn Facebook users potentially protected, 1.5bn were in Africa, Asia, Australia and Latin America. Facebook shifted this latter group to fall under the corresponding, but more lenient US legal framework.

Performance

Performance: social efficiency - mainly defined by extent of market power. The notions are that the monopoly is sloth-like and inefficient, whilst exploiting the consumer. Indicators:

❑ Size of business profits. In SCP, evidence of excess profits rates is indicative of exploiting the consumer. Trends in real price levels over time can indicate whether prices and hence profits are suitably modest, e.g. BG and wholesale gas prices.

---

[2] https://www.citizensadvice.org.uk/Global/CitizensAdvice/Energy/EnergyConsumersMissingBillions.pdf

❑ Efficiency is a major outcome of the competitive process. Allocative efficiency concerns allocating resources to maximise well-being. Productive efficiency relates to achieve the maximum feasible output from a given set of inputs.

❑ Technical progress is an outcome of investment decisions; possibly in R&D; possibly on human capital. A more technically advanced society has a higher standard of living. Investment in these areas is key indicators of future growth.

❑ Growth in output and productivity are the sources of rising incomes. Does it lead to rising labour productivity in the industry?

❑ Quality of the output or service can rise or fall depending on the state of the economy. Better quality goods would last longer, leading hopefully to less waste.

Unfortunately, SCP tells us that socially desirable corporate performance can only be achieved by a 'good' market structure comprising many equally-sized, small firms. In the neo-classical world, this would involve rivalrous rather than collusive price setting, little rather than a great deal of advertising and a great deal of innovation, although small firms may find this difficult to fund. If you like, competition is the spur that keeps the firm running just to stand still. The threat is always there that without the drive to be competitive rivals will steal market share. Largely, it posits that the greater cost of market entry makes it easier for existing firms to maintain SNP. Market concentration decreases the cost of collusion between firms and results in SNP. The theoretical predictions of SCP appear to be difficult to reconcile with the reality of the evolution of some market structures. It could be that conduct affects structure, through merger activity. Indeed, with the most efficient firms taking market share from rivals, performance can affect structure also. This gives them more market power. The fine line between market dominance and economic efficiency comes with the 'abuse of dominant position.' The EC focuses on evidence of abuse rather than market dominance.

Google –FANGS and Regulation

Concern for innovation or non-price effects rarely animates or drives investigations or enforcement actions, especially outside of the merger context. Economic factors that are easier to measure, such as impacts on price, output, or productive efficiency in narrowly defined markets, have become disproportionately important. One of the problems with SCP in pegging competition to short-term price and profit outcomes is these are not consistent with the architecture of market power in the modern IT economy. Static competition under-appreciates the risk of predatory pricing and how integration across distinct business lines may prove anti-competitive. The economics of platform markets create incentives for a company to pursue growth over profits. Under these conditions, predatory pricing becomes highly likely and which down plays profit as an indicator of monopoly practice. Because on-line platforms serve as both market-maker and supplier they to control the essential infrastructure on which their rivals depend - information. This dual role also enables a platform to exploit information collected on companies using its services to undermine them as competitors. Take the EC antitrust investigation into Amazon to establish whether it maintained barriers to market entry into the ebooks market through clauses in contracts with publishers. There are two types:

1. it requires to be informed of more favourable or alternative terms offered to competitors;
2. it seeks the right to terms and conditions at least as good as those of its competitors.

It has 90% market share of the UK market, one of the two largest markets in Europe. In September 2018, without a complaint, it launched an investigation into this dual role over Marketplace. Like Tesco et al, it has its own-brand products, worth possibly $7.5bn in 2018.

The European Commission in April 2013 found Google results were favouring its in-house services to the detriment of consumers in areas such as maps, finance or weather. In February 2018, Google was fined 1.36bn Rupees (£15.2m; $21.2m = 5% of Google's average annual revenues in India) by India's competition regulator CCI for abusing its dominance in the country. Users searching flight details were directed to Google's own flight search page, disadvantaging rival businesses. The complainants, Bharat Matrimony and a consumer protection group, filed in 2012. In June 2017, Google was fined €2.42bn by the European Commission after it ruled the company had abused its power by promoting its own shopping comparison service at the top of search results. In July 2018, Google's fine was €4.34bn (2 weeks of revenues, below the 5 weeks max). It was ordered it to stop using its Android mobile operating system to block rivals. With the free Android system running on 80% of the world's smartphones, it is a virtual monopoly. As they cost more and require users to exert significant effort to adopt, Vestager argued that competition from Apple iPhones was not a sufficient check on Google's dominance. Moreover, although phone owners could download alternative web browsers or using other search engines, only 1% used an alternative search app, and 10% a different browser. In March 2019, another record €1.49bn fine for abuse of dominant position stopping publishers from placing any search ads from competitors on their search results pages, forcing them to reserve the most profitable space on these pages for Google's ads, and a requirement to seek written approval from Google before making changes to how rival ads were displayed. Google put its own shopping links at the top of the list of results, with rivals' elsewhere. The smaller mobile phone screen accentuated the advantage denying other companies the chance to compete on their merits and to innovate. It denied European consumers the benefits of competition, genuine choice and innovation. The EC has been investigating Google Shopping since late 2010, based on complainants such as Microsoft and Foundem. TripAdvisor, Expedia, eDream, HomeToGo and 30 other firms complained to the EU Competition Commissioner in July that Google's search engine favoured its own hotel rental search platform, OneBox.

Amazon launched an Australian site in December 2017, and its Prime service for faster delivery, in June 2018. In response to a sales tax on internet purchases, in July Amazon excluded Australians from their overseas sites. The Australian government extended its 10% percent goods and services tax (GST) to all goods bought on-line from overseas, effective July 1st, requiring on-line retailers to collect the tax. This could constitute third degree (geographical) price discrimination. The alternative explanation is in the tax collection system. Ebay's decision to build the new tax collection and payment system had paid off with early figures suggesting Australian shoppers were not swayed by the new tax.

The Importance of the Click Monopoly
The Australian Competition and Consumer Commission launched an investigation into Google and Facebook in December 2018 over the bundling of Chrome, creating a near monopoly position on internet search. The top three in any search get 35%+17%+11% of the clicks. The top 10 on page 1 get 95% of clicks; the top of page 2 gets 1%, so controlling page 1 matters. The ACCC believes that for every A$100 spent on digital advertising in Australia, A$47 goes to Google and A$21 to Facebook. Procter & Gamble's chief brand officer told the Association of National Advertisers' media conference in March 2018 that the average view time for an ad on a mobile news feed is 1.7 seconds. Consumer data company, Dunnhumby, find that the average time that an ad is viewable on retailer sites is about 16 seconds, where 'viewable' is when at least half of the ad is on the screen. Dunnhumby estimated that almost £100,000 of sales of a leading brand of dishwasher tablets came from customers exposed to a banner advert on Tesco website, with 6% of the sales occurring in a store, and 2,200 new customers had added the brand to their on-line favourites list as a result of the campaign. This translated into a return on advertising spending of £11.34 for every £1 invested, far more than an average return on ad spend of £2.62 for every £1 invested across all media types (Nielsen, 2016).

Retailers like Tesco and Walmart are aggressively attracting big advertisers like Kraft Heinz and Procter & Gamble to their websites. Specifically, they are selling more ad space, pop-up banners and search-bar keywords to consumer goods companies. What they are offering is guided buying. The target consumer has a revealed preference to buy; using their individual shopping habits, they are guided to specific products. This on-line ad revenue offers significantly higher margins for retailers than selling goods in stores. Retailers are offering pop-ups, banner ads, and money-off deals which, in return earn the advertiser anything from 25¢ to $2 each time a shopper clicks on a sponsored search item, depending on the product being sold.

Advertising Revenues
The German advert blocker, Eyeo, developer of Adblocks Plus, was paid by Amazon, Google, Microsoft and Taboola to 'white-list' their adverts. As a free addition to Firefox and Chrome, an advert blocker would undermine the business model of these internet-based companies. The unknown fee was estimated at 30% of the ad revenue that would be unblocked. On-line advertising revenue is estimated at $120bn, $69bn on mobiles. From June 2015, iOS 9, the Apple operating system included ad-blocker. This can be seen as part of a privacy and security theme that differentiates iOS from Android.

Digital advertising, a rising market is under threat. In May 2015, Facebook signed a content and an ad revenue sharing agreement with nine organisations including BBC

News, the Guardian and NYT. Social media now controls access to news. This agreement reflects its power in the market over the ad revenues upon which news outlets would rely. It also gives Facebook editorial control over what has prominence – a Google problem.

In April 2016, this was made more evident when its CEO, David Pemsel, threatened to ban readers that used adblockers. This followed a warning from CityAM and Incisive Media in the UK. In Germany, Bild's owner Axel Springer in 2015 forced readers to choose between a subscription and advertising, which shifted at least 14% to switch off their ad-blocker. A further battle is being fought over web revenues. From June 2016, Tesco Mobile was offering customers a discount of £3/month on their bills if they use the app, Unlockd, which displays adverts and offers from companies including BA, McDonald's and the Sun.

In effect targeting Google and other advert revenue dependent, data-heavy users, network providers were offering ad-blockers. This would provide some leverage to get Google *et al* to share some of the pain of the network providers. From September 2015, Digicel became the first mobile operator to block adverts. The most exposed are those that rely on the open web. The costs to the industry range from $1bn (UPS) to $22bn (PageFair and Adobe). Interestingly, it is Google that is the most exposed of all. It is likely that without adverts the free rider generation will lose services.

Google - Another Microsoft SCP view
The list of innovative products that Microsoft is associated with, but, in fact copied, is noteworthy. The icon-based operating system was an innovation on the Apple Mac but copied by Windows. Wordperfect and Lotus 123 were market leaders in word processing and spreadsheets until Word and Excel swept them away. Pegasus email was trounced by Outlook and Netscape fell to Internet Explorer. However, this was not necessarily because their products were better. Microsoft's facilities are bundled. Why buy a package when MS provides it free with the bundle. In 2009, the EC required Microsoft to offer customers choice. The operating system would be required to present a list of browsers, such as Firefox, Opera with IE. In response, Microsoft stripped out Internet Explorer from the Windows bundle.

Margrethe Vestager, the EU Competition Commissioner, in April 2016, accused Google of bundling. By June 2018, she was to instigate formal proceedings. That is restricting users of Android in a similar way that Microsoft had constrained users to utilising Explorer and media player. Android accounts for 80% of mobile devices, but it is given away. Earnings come from complementary sales and advertising. In February 2014, it was shown that Google's contracts suppressed competition. A contract with HTC to distribute Google products, such as Gmail or search, was contingent on all Google applications being pre-installed onto the smartphone with Google search as the default. At its peak in 2000, Windows controlled 97% of the world market. However, by 2016, on all computing devices it was down to 26% of the operating system market.

In April 2016, Getty Images, in effect, claimed that Google was doing to it what Microsoft did to Pegasus email – giving a rival service away free. Getty claimed that, from January 2013 when high resolution, large images were presented during searches on Google.com and Google.co.uk, Getty's revenues dropped propitiously. They did not see a revenue drop on French and German versions of Google where these images were not available.

Post 2000 Performance
Robert Gordon finds that American companies are looking weak when it comes to technological innovation. The fifth long wave is waning. There is a decrease in the productivity of research spending. Comparing US spending on research and development with increases in reported labour productivity, the system needs a lot more R&D spending to keep improving at the same pace. More precisely, it would take a doubling of research effort every 13 years just to avoid a productivity slowdown. McKinsey Global Institute in 2017 reported that average annual US productivity growth was 2.1% between 1987 and 2004 but only 1.2% in the subsequent decade.

If the stream of innovation is thinner, fewer companies should be able to enjoy entrepreneurial profits and durable competitive advantages, so lead to a narrowing of profit margins. However, Gutierrez and Philippon measured the contribution to annual national productivity growth of the four largest US companies by market capitalisation in 62 industries (= 248). The companies at the top shifted over the years, so the list always included the winners of the period. From 1960 to 2000, the annual average contribution to productivity growth of companies was 72bps. From 2001 to 2016, the average was 43bps. The pattern is similar for market shares. In 1980 domestic sales of the 248 = 29% of GDP, but by 2016 = 25%.

Corporate profit/GDP between 1991 and 2000 was 5% but for the following decade it was 10%. Profit did not feed capital spending. Private investment declined in the same periods (17.6% to 16.2% of GDP). The IMF found the same but across 27 countries two-thirds of them in developed economies. Examining detailed financial statements for 900,000 firms from 2000 to 2015, 'mark-ups' increase by 6% overall, but by 30% in the firms which already had the highest 10% of mark-ups. Once corporates have significant market power, they slow down their pace of technical improvement, particularly digital technology industries. In sophisticated and highly specialised industries, the market leaders benefit from network effects and economies of scale, which squeeze smaller rivals. With few constraints on pricing, market winners are also profit winners. This trend to higher profitability and market dominance can cause problems.

Despite what claims are made at the outset, *mergers* increase size which often brings higher mark-ups. However, more rapid increases in market share also accelerate the arrival of the technological tipping point, when companies have more to lose from disrupting their own technology than they can gain from adding new customers.

Hirchman-Herfindahl Index

As discussed numerous times in various *Updates*, Structure-Conduct-Performance emphasizes structure as a means of assessing the likely conduct and hence performance of companies. An assessment of changing structure, where barriers are high (and the market is not that contestable) is necessary. One measure of market concentration is the Hirchman-Herfindahl index. The formula $\sum_{i=1}^{n} S_i^2$ is based on market share (S) of the n firms in the industry. The US Dept. of Justice posts the following:

- ❑ HHI of 1,500 to 2,500 points is considered moderately concentrated;
- ❑ HHI in excess of 2,500 points is highly concentrated;
- ❑ Mergers that increase the HHI by more than 200 points in highly concentrated markets are presumed likely to enhance market power.

If there were 6 firms having equal market share, the HHI would be 1,667. If two of them merged, the index would rise to 2,222, clearly over a 200-point change. Notice that with similar market shares, the HHI is lower. If one of the 6 collapsed and the remaining 5 attained shares so that each controlled 20% of the market, the HHI would rise to 2,000. Thus, a measure of market dominance is captured here.

UK mergers are exempt from scrutiny if the turnover of the firm being taken over is £70m or less and the combined firms will have no more than 25% market share. In

	MS	MS²	MS²
Aldi	7.50%	56.25	56.25
Asda	15.30%	234.09	
Co-Op	5.90%	34.81	34.81
Iceland	2.30%	5.29	5.29
Lidl	5.30%	28.09	28.09
Morrisons	10.60%	112.36	112.36
Ocado	1.10%	1.21	1.21
Other Outlets	1.60%	2.56	2.56
Sainsbury's	15.90%	252.81	973.44
Symbols & Independent	1.70%	2.89	2.89
Tesco	27.70%	767.29	767.29
Waitrose	5.10%	26.01	26.01
Total	100.00%	1523.66	2010.20

April 2018, Sainsbury's announced a £7.3bn takeover of Asda. The combined revenues were £51bn. Despite the claim that none of its 2,800 stores would close, it was estimated that there were synergies of at least £500m, and interestingly, enabling prices to be lowered by about 10% on many products. It was blocked by the CMA a year later on the basis of price rises in local markets. HHI would have jumped from 1,524 to 2010 and market share would be 31.2%. That said, over that period market Sainsbury's and Asda's share dropped by 0.3% each.

Tesco's March 2018 purchase of the wholesale group Booker supplying 5,000 outlets, was cleared unconditionally, when the regulator accepted that the presence of Aldi and Lidl deterred the merging parties from raising prices. Discounters account for 22% market share in Europe, up from 17% a decade ago. Moreover, September 2018 saw joint venture between Carrefour and Tesco on global purchasing and expanding their own-label ranges, tightening a squeeze on major brand producers, such as Nestlé and Kraft Heinz.

In May, Liberty Global and Telefonica agreed a £31bn merger of UK businesses. This brings together Virgin and O_2. The entity could save £6.2bn/yr by the fifth full year. O_2 is the UK's largest phone company with about 34m users. Virgin has 3m mobile users and a further 6m broadband and cable TV customers. By bringing together different platforms, the tie-up will create a major rival to BT. However, there are obvious competition problems.

Oligopoly (the focus of SCP)
Either explicitly or implicitly, if they act as one (so like a monopoly), oligopolists may find long-run profit are maximised jointly. Acting as one when either coordinated or uncoordinated, implies less rivalry. Cartels comprise coordinated oligopolists that agree price or output quotas among themselves. Based on oil, perhaps OPEC is the most famous inter-State cartel. Colombo, Sri Lanka, India, Kenya, Indonesia, Malawi and Rwanda formed the International Tea Producer's Forum. Collectively, they control more than 50% of global production. Note, there is an incentive to renege on the agreement, which could undermine the cartel. Russia in March was a case in point.

In practice, the monopoly is far less common than its close companion, the oligopoly. Oligopoly market is defined as small number of firms sharing a large proportion of an industry or market, such as firms producing an almost identical product, e.g. metals, chemicals, sugar, petrol. Alternatively, oligopoly firms produce differentiated products, e.g. cars, soap powder, cigarettes, electrical appliances, that are quite similar. Because there are only a few firms in the industry, each firm's decisions will depend on the perceptions of the potential behaviour of rivals. Therefore, firms are mutually dependant – they price interdependently.

You become weary of the lame competition debate. Take energy. Firstly, the government claimed that domestic customers of the big six energy companies were paying on average £1.4bn a year more than they would in a truly competitive market. The government knows that this claim is costless to make to them – anyway it regulates it. Secondly, Lawrence Slade, CEO of the industry body, argued a cap would damage investment and competition. The industry knows that can still make large profits. Centrica raised its electricity charges by 12.5% in August 2017, claiming it made a loss on electricity supply. E.On in March 2018, in effect, raised SVT rate by £22/year. It removed various discounts for paperless billing and using both electricity and gas, making it 'easier for customers to understand its tariffs and to compare them with competitors.' Paperless and double tariffs are standard! Moreover, blaming the cap, Centrica added an extra 4,000 jobs to be shed by 2020, saving £500m/yr. This takes the total to be made redundant to 9,500, and a saving of £1.25m/yr.

The industry and the government know that competition is skewed. In 2011, there were 14 energy providers. By June 2018 it reached 70. In 2018Q4, small and medium suppliers grew to a market share of 26% and 27% in electricity and gas. Moreover, those with less than 250,000 customers do not pay certain environmental charges. Government policies add £165 to a bill, up from £81 in 2014. This threshold could drop to 100,000. But these can fail. By March 2019, 10 new entrants into the energy market had failed, Brilliant Energy - which supplied energy to 17,000 households failed. This followed National Gas and Power, Iresa, Gen4u, Usio Energy, Extra Energy, Spark Energy Supply Limited, OneSelect, Economy Energy and Our Power. Customers are commonly shifted to another small provider. Economy Energy and Our Power customers have been automatically switched to Ovo and Utilita, both of which were under investigation. Many of the customers of failed firms have faced difficulties owing to poor customer service. This puts into sharp relief whether this is a good thing. From a CMT basis, these firms act as a threat, forcing the incumbents to behave well. But this might be stressful for subscribers.

Ofgem calculated the HHI for various sections of the electricity and gas wholesale markets for small and large energy buyers. Here, the market dominance of the largest suppliers is not so great and getting smaller. The wholesale market is becoming volatile. PwC estimate that 17% of industrial companies are looking to generate some electricity, particularly on site. Carriage for domestic suppliers makes up 26% of the bill. Northumbrian Water saved £12,500 using the Bran Sands solar scheme. The cost/unit is half that off the grid. Lightsource Renewable Energy suggests that even

HHI	2016	2017
E small	1,276	1,200
E large	1,112	1,017
G<73,200 kWh	1,544	1,320
G>73,200 kWh	1,115	1,270

without subsidies businesses could save 15-25% of their electricity bill using solar. Hanson built a £13m 12MW solar farm in its abandoned Ketton Cement works, saving £7-8m over 22 years = 5% of its total energy bill.

Ofgem recognises that the grid charges will have to be reviewed with this trend. Indeed, Citizens Advice highlight that National Grid, across gas and electricity in 2016/17 made an operating profit of £2.1bn in their UK network business.

Airline Income Issues
Periodically an airline admits where its real profit strategy is aimed. 60% of United Airlines' $5.8bn revenue in 2017 were additional charges or optional extras. Half of Sprint Airlines' $657bn revenue was not ticket and 28% ($2bn) of Ryanair's was not ticket. Indeed, over 10 years the top 10 airlines saw a rise in revenue from $2.1bn to $29.7bn. Ryanair take a stepped approach to customers so that they can sell more to their existing group. The lowest level involves the ticket, then car hire, booking a hotel room and buying tickets for activities such as tour guide. The top level is the opportunity in the airline's one-stop shop.

In the 10 years from 2007 the number of people flying internationally from Britain grew 43% to 229m/yr. By contrast internal, domestic flights fell by 10% to 22.8m. The fall has seen the number of routes with more the 1,000 passengers/yr from by 40 to

188. A key driver is tax. As £13/passenger. For a small airline, such as Flybe, it is 20% of the average fair, possibly 50% with promotional fares. Long haul rail transport grew by 40% over a similar period to 145m suggesting that the closure of routes benefits alternative transports. Budget airline continue to collapse as the European airline sector grapples with over-capacity and high fuel costs. Recent failures include Britain's Flybmi, Iceland's Wow, Germany's Germania, Nordic budget airline Primera Air and Cypriot counterpart Cobalt.

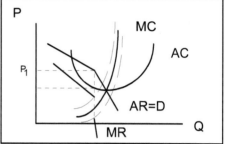

A non-collusive oligopoly is associated with the kinked demand curve. The kink can be explained in terms of its inelastic and elastic portions. Revenue increases if price rises on the inelastic portion but falls on the elastic. As a result, in the figure right, the oligopolists choose to operate at the kink at P_1; any movement away from that point will lead to a reduction in revenue. Alternatively, the kinked demand curve of Sweezy carries the presumption that if an oligopolist cuts its price, to avoid losing customers/market share, its rivals will be forced to follow suit, whereas if an oligopolist raises its price, because they can gain extra custom from not doing so, its rivals will not follow suit.

A Price War in Mortgages
One of the regulations that emerged for the financial crisis was separating and investment banking operations. This led to HSBC starting a mortgage price war in 2015. The price of the average two-year fixed rate 95% LTV mortgage fell from 4.79% in 2009Q1 to 2.49% in 2019Q1, while the number of such products has doubled to 146.

	Dec-17	May-19
Lloyds	1.96	1.43
RBS	1.71	1.67
Tesco	1.52	1.43
Nwide	1.38	1.37
HSBC	1.32	1.16
Sector	1.6	1.43

As an oligopoly of a £1.4tn, the market comprises six lenders holding 70% for over a decade, and an additional 43 Building Societies accounting for around 23%. HSBC increased its UK mortgage book by 10% in 2019 to £94.2bn, holding 6.6% of the market. The margins on two year mortgage rate over two year swap rates (bps) show why Tesco decided to leave. Dropping from 0.0152% in 2017, it saw no future profits. Tesco and Sainsbury's left the mortgage market in 2019. Participating from 2012 to May 2019, Tesco sold its £3.8bn mortgage book to Halifax in September. Sainsbury's £1.9bn was being purchased by NWide in 2020. NWide profits fell from £516m to £309m in the 6month to November.

A Price War Foregone
In March, the World Travel and Tourism Council (WTTC) estimated that up to 50m jobs could be lost because of the Corona pandemic, with the travel sector shrinking by up to 25% in 2020. Travel bans stop tourists. On 11th Trump banned US-Mainland European flights. The free market made things difficult. Aviva stopped selling

insurance for travel disruption and LV= suspended selling travel insurance all together. A more market approach was to raise the price to cover the heightened risk. When travel bans emerged, the Association of British Insurers claimed that standard policies did not include forced closure by the authorities.

One group particularly exposed to the virus is the cruise ship industry. The Diamond Princess cruise ship was quarantined in Japan in February. In March, the Grand Princess suffered an outbreak of the virus off the coast of California. On 23rd Western Australia prevented the Swiss-owned MSC Magnifica cruise ship from disembarking. Of 1,700 passengers on board the ship, more than 250 complained of respiratory illnesses. On 8th April, the Ruby Princess had its "black box" removed. The liner, owned by Carnival Corp, was given permission to disembark its passengers in March without health checks. The then 15 of the 51 Australian Corona virus deaths were associated with that action.

These floating villages face the same problem as other population centres – social interaction leads to contagion. But they are used to this e.g. food poisoning and the norovirus. Normally, cruisers go to the nearest port, disembark passengers and sanitise the ship. The loss of revenue is not that great if the ship is ready to start cruising again within a matter of weeks. The cases above combined with not allowing the ship to be cleaned and so returning to active duty with kettling infectious with non-infectious passengers, was calamitous.

Nearly one-third of Carnival's sales are derived from extras like premium dining or shore excursions. To encourage excursions and to maximise throughput many modern cruise liners have relatively small cabins. Also, most cruise ships are registered offshore in places like Panama and the Bahamas. This allows them to avoid labour laws so that the companies to recruit cheap workers from developing countries, pay them less, and work them harder. It also saves tax. Asking for a bail-out when avoiding social responsibilities is problematic. The holiday destinations may be less than happy to help as well. Cruise ships deposit thousands of tourists in crowded cities clog-up some boutiques for five or six hours and then go back on board for dinner.

In a month, Carnival lost some $15bn in equity value from the Diamond Princess outbreak (= 5× net income in 2019). Royal Caribbean Cruises saw its market value drop by almost 60%. The industry had 26m passengers/yr and revenues of $46bn/yr. Given an oligopoly with high fixed costs, one would expect a price war and cut-price fares. Rather than a price war, Princess Cruises suspended all operations for 18 months. The issue will be whether the mature punter be put off by the health risk? As elderly passengers suffered in quarantine on board ships within sight of the shore, what price would have to be offered for the industry to survive? Fortunately, fuel costs, rather than rising with use of low sulphur oil have collapsed, so oil future could be purchased.

Because the oligopolist will lose revenue if they change price in either direction, rising costs may not alter price. The MC curve moves anywhere in the gap (indicated by the dashed MC curves) in the MR and the firm will not change its price. Practically, what we see is an alteration of the product. Possibly as a result of the falling value of Sterling, Toblerone, choosing to change the shape of the bar, and *not* raising the price, elected to put bigger spaces between the segments. The move resulted in the weight of the 400g bars being reduced to 360g and the 170g bars to 150g, while the size of the packaging remained the same. Perhaps a fine example of this backfiring was the 2015 decision by Mondelez to change the recipe for Cadbury's Creme Eggs using cheaper chocolate. The product was the same for 45 years. Research by IRI for The Grocer found that it lost more than £6m in sales revenue in 2016. A recent examination of chocky activities can be seen below left. Comparing 2014 with 2018, Hobnobs appear cheaper, reduced from £1.90 to £1.83, a 3.68% reduction. However, less well observed, due to the reduction is size, the unit cost rose by 17%.

	Weight Grms		Price £		Unit cost £/g	
	2014	2018	2014	2018	2014	2018
Hobnobs	250	205	1.9	1.83	0.76	0.89
Jaffa Cakes 2p	150	122	0.84	0.87	0.56	0.71
Jaffa Cakes 3p	450	467	2.35	1.55	0.52	0.33
Snickers 4p	136	119	1.58	1.33	1.16	1.12
Snickers 7p	232	167	2.38	1.9	1.03	1.14
Toblerone	400	360	3.5	4	0.88	1.11
Twix	58	50	0.45	0.6	0.78	1.20
Twix 4p	200	160	1.2	1.38	0.60	0.86
Yorkie	55	46	0.59	0.62	1.07	1.35
Yorkie 3p	160	132	1.57	1.25	0.98	0.95

The Jaffa cakes two pack was not much worse value than the 3 pack at 52p/g in 2014. However, the three pack saw a reduction in price and increase in weight, whilst the two pack saw the reverse. This could in part be linked to second degree price discrimination. However, that does not work with Snickers, which despite the extra volume, unit cost for the 7 pack is greater than the four pack.

Although we are discussing Oligopoly, the monopoly is the standard unit for discussing whether the market is efficient or not. Or whether there is a market failure where a suboptimal level of output is produced. From this, the profit maximising firm with market power and the **cartel** draw a criticism.

The diagram below shows the standard comparisons. Under Perfect Competition, the market price is determined by the interplay of Supply and Demand. Market price would be P_1 and market quantity Q_1. The industry supply is based on the Marginal Cost curves of the firms in the industry.

The formation of a cartel or a monopoly from these providers changes the analysis. The supply curve is now the MC curve of the cartel. As the cartel is large relative to the market, to sell more it must lower price. The marginal revenue from selling the additional unit should be no less than the MC. It is in the cartel's interest to restrict supply to Q_2 and charge the monopoly price P_2. As a result of this action: price rises from P_1 to P_2, reducing consumer surplus; output is lowered from Q_1 to Q_2, reducing producer surplus; but the cartel's marginal cost per unit C is less than the price P_2 (The gap is not total SNP).

At price P_1 a competitive market can be analysed as:

Consumer surplus	A+B+F
Producer surplus	C+D+G

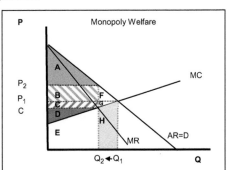

At price P_2 a monopoly produces less - Q_1 to Q_2 and can be analysed as:

Consumer surplus	A;
Deadweight loss	F+G;
Input cost	E;
Reallocated resources	H.

Hence, there could be a higher price and lower output than under perfect competition.

But Monopoly can benefit the community due to:
- Economies of scale - larger plant, centralised administration. These benefits may be passed on to consumers in lower prices;
- More large scale investment, such as the HS2 project can only be delivered by a large firm;
- More R&D - innovation and new products – the promise of entrepreneurial profits may encourage new (monopoly) industries producing new products;
- Natural monopolies - where it only makes sense to have one firm (only one provider of pipes to your door);
- Greater stability – Monopolist can provide steady employment.

In neo-classical economics, we assume monopoly profits are protected by insuperable barriers to market entry. Barriers to entry may take the form of:
- Natural monopolies - only one provider of pipes to your door so you cannot switch providers;
- Advertising and branding - where a market is dominated by one seller it would be difficult for a new firm to break into the market i.e. to attract customers away from a familiar brand;
- Lower costs for an established firm - will have specialist production and marketing skills, likely to have cheaper suppliers and access to cheaper finance;
- Monopolists could use limit-pricing to reduce access to the market. Price is set so low to deter entrants (is this bad?);
- Aggressive tactics - can sustain losses for longer than a new entrant e.g. engage in a price war (retaliatory price cutting);
- Legal protection, such as copyright, patents;
- Control over key factors of production;
- Control over wholesale or retail outlets.

Austrian Perspective

The Austrian School of thought, inspired by Schumpeter, proposes that profit of itself is not evidence of nefarious practices, nor is a monopoly necessarily a source of market failure. Rather than the static view of competition whereby a stable economic environment is populated by established firms producing a well-known product using techniques that are known by all, competition is dynamic and subject to imperfect information.

Relaxing the assumptions of a homogeneous product and perfect knowledge, competition, according to Schumpeter, is driven by innovation. The firm exploiting new products processes and markets serves the consumer. The entrepreneur utilises new technologies, driving forward technical progress. Profit is the incentive for this innovation and the reward for taking risk.

Assume all parties have only impacted (asymmetric) knowledge. That is, the customers, suppliers of resources and entrepreneurs are aware partly of each other's capabilities and needs. The actor that responds most quickly to new information is the entrepreneur. Others may copy but the entrepreneur leads the way. This information may be freely available to everyone or, possibly in world of constantly changing taste, only revealed when the consumer can see what is on offer. To acquire information about consumer tastes the entrepreneur presents something new to the market. If this product is not to the consumer's taste, sales will be modest and losses may lead to the product being dropped. However, considerable profits may follow the launch of a product that consumers find highly desirable. This new product is distinct, produced by a single firm and generates significant profits, not directly related to the marginal cost. From a SCP perceptive, this is problematic.

Depending on whom you read, one can suggest that entrepreneur has two roles: opportunity spotter and a risk bearer. For Schumpeter, only a small number of people can be entrepreneurs who can bear the risk of losing their shirt on an investment of sizeable proportions. They are risk-neutral whereas most are risk-averse – that's what makes them different. The scope to spot opportunities though could be in all of us. The basis for profit could be the reward for identifying gaps in the market and getting a product there before others. Alternatively, realising that a process can be improved, someone being entrepreneurial but not risking their own money could initiate this.

In this world, there are three type of profit: *Monopoly, Windfall,* and *Entrepreneurial.* The monopoly profits are those that are generated by the restrictive or collusive activates that SCP focuses on. The windfall profits are those that are not related to barriers or investment. The entrepreneur just has good fortune. It is more like gambling than investing. The entrepreneurial profit is the reward for spotting the *opportunity* and taking the *risk.* In a sense, the fruits of investment follow after years of research in the area. Without the reward, the risk may not have been taken and hence, the innovation would not have occurred.

The process that the Austrians envisage is that once the entrepreneur succeeds their monopoly position is only temporary. As with perfect competition, once the creator is rewarded with high profits, others see these profits. In perfect competition, using the freely available information, they break into the market. With this Austrian school this could include mimicking, so driving price downward. However, the pioneering work may drive others to innovate in the same area to improve existing products and so they then become temporary monopolists. The process entails a succession of temporary monopolists developing better, more powerful products for the consumer. How long this process might take is open to question.

Monopoly Patent
Holding a patent acts as a barrier to entry and yet the income stream from this patent is what drove the entrepreneur to innovate in the first place. Today, technology companies squabble over patents. Patent laws may be a help in certain industries but be a hindrance in others. From an Austrian perspective, a patent restricts a potential monopolist from emerging from that pack of innovators desperate to improve on the existing model. From the pharmaceuticals industry's perspective, copycats steal some profits but are not innovating. Mainly because of the need for large clinical trials, bringing a new drug to market is inordinately expensive. To amortise these costs, monopoly rights over what has been produced are spur to future invention: without them the risk-reward ratio will deter the exploitation of new drugs. However, recently patents in pharmaceutical industry permit legal exploitative pricing strategies. The FT noted that the pharmaceutical industry:

- Raise price annually – the new normal from 2017. Some, under pressure, have promised to keep them to single figures but this turns out to be 9%, or 7% above the cost of living rise. Humira rose from $792.14 in 2007 to $2923.22 for 40mgs. The best example is an Aids medicine that was increased in price by 5,000%.
- Raise price twice a year – the old normal. Pfizer's Viagra rose from $12.03 in 2007 to $88.45 in July 2018.
- Being the sole producer (even without a current patent) – the classic example of finding a medicine without rival producers and bump the price. Cerecor, the only maker of 5mg pills of Millipred, off-patent for years, rose from ¢40 in 2008 to $16.87 in 2017.
- Stymie the competition – formularies drugs are lists of drugs that insurers and employers are willing to allow doctors to prescribe. In effect, they exclude very expensive ones. However, access to these lists can be purchased, keeping cheaper alternatives off the list. This purchase is through the rebates given to pharmacies benefit managers.

Eli Lily Pfizer and the like extracted over $1bn in 2016H1 selling branded drugs to consumers rather than generics. Prozac was on the market at $11.39/pill when the generic costs 3¢. Lipitor costs $10.59 when the generic costs 13¢. The EpiPen was increased in price by 500% in 6 years. When under pressure during the presidential election the EpiPen price was reduced. Casper Pharma raised the price of a bladder infection antibiotic to $2800. Later Nostrum Labs raised the price of their version from $474.75 to $2,392. This treatment has been around since 1953. The CEO, Nirmal

Mulye, implied it was a moral imperative to maximise profits. These were the liquid forms, which were more difficult to produce. In the UK, the price was £446.95.

In 2019Q1, almost 3000 drug prices were increased in the US. Greed trumps social responsibility. But in May 2019, 44 US states filed a lawsuit accusing 20 drug companies of a sweeping scheme to inflate drug prices and stifle competition for more than 100 generic drugs.

Perhaps the worst of capitalism, on January 23rd Rising Pharmaceuticals, a New Jersey based company, which produced the antimalarial, Chloroquine, increase price from $7.66/ 250mg pill to $19.88/ 500mg pill. It was one of the drugs being tested against Covid-19 and the outbreak in China was becoming alarming.

Should mobile phones and the like be granted the same protection as a drugs company? Drugs companies may need 20 years' worth of protection. It is suggested that, with the Hi-Tec electrical products, the patent protection inhibits innovation and should be removed. The iPhone and the iPad sold many millions of units within their first years. With the latter, Apple has been rewarded by the first-mover advantage. Perhaps we could view these two cases by examining monopoly vs. entrepreneurial profit. Buying a patent just to extract rent is a case of monopoly profit. Holding a patent to amortise the costs of development is entrepreneurial profiting.

There is a new form of behaviour where an 'entrepreneur' holds patents with no intention of using them to fabricate products. They wait for a major corporation to use them so that the entrepreneur can then sue. This is much like companies buying up ip-addresses, parts of the broadcast spectrum or telephone numbers they suspect will be useful in the near future. Moreover, control of intellectual property is becoming the driver behind mergers. Google, in May 2015, was accused by the EC of 'abusive enforcement' of its intellectual property rights over a technology vital to the smartphone, acquired from Motorola. The action was to thwart Google from preventing innovation by Apple. The technology, which should become an industry standard, should be licensed on a non-discriminatory basis.

Contestable Market Theory
Where it is unlikely that the firms in the industry can be anything other than large, the consumer can still be served if the market is 'contestable.' Contestable Market Theory (CMT) has similarities with SCP. As with any perspective of competition, the threat of greater rivalry requires low barriers to market entry. Indeed, implicitly, the market should be mature and the product well understood so that the consumer is not subject to exploitation of an asymmetry of information. The key difference between SCP and CMT is in the number of competitors. A contestable market only requires a threat of competition, not actual competition. The threat of market entry should force the incumbent [possibly a monopoly provider] to keep the customer happy by maintaining a good service, and prices and profits are modest. This means that the large firm can

be limited to a range of activities that are socially desirable: there is an incentive to be innovative and to exploit economies of scale.

Contestable Market Theory focuses on exit costs. A deterrent to market entry is the assets that the firm is left with if it is squeezed out of the market. If the assets are market specific and the costs of such investment are irretrievable, these are called sunk costs. Crucially, the definition of a 'market' is rather specific. If we were analysing bus deregulation, a market could be a specific bus route. Is a bus limited to that route? As it can be transferred almost costlessly to another route, it is not a sunk cost.

Other pre-conditions for a contestable market are that new entrants face no additional costs or retaliatory price-cutting from the incumbents. By assumption, new small players not squeezed out by monopoly practices or by significant cost disadvantages. Like Perfect Competition, this is a standard. The model predicts that a monopoly will behave in a socially desirable way if it could be subject to hit-and-run competition. Thus, for there to be potential rivalry, the new entrant needs to have access to the market relatively costlessly, with low set-up costs.

By developing a second hand market for the assets necessary for market entry, contestability can be fostered by the State. Where the market is regulated, market access can be promoted by partial deregulation. Controls on retaliatory activities are needed and subsidies for set-up cost.

If a firm is protected from competition due to the ownership of a resource or patent needed to enter the industry, the same outcome could result – a monopolist player. However, this monopoly can be overcome by innovation. This is not a feature of CMT.

Landing Slot Monopoly
De facto the landing slot is a barrier to entry. A plane needs access to the airport. Slots can be very valuable in normal times and can be sold much like a fishing quota. To retain a slot under a scheme at airports they must be used at least 80% of the time. Airlines, such as Virgin, were running nearly empty planes to avoid slots being reallocated. One UK carrier would have to operate 32 flights over two weeks in March @40% occupancy (5,000 seats empty) without rule changes. So fuel is expended to maintain an oligopoly.

Interestingly, with airline mergers, because they are indicators of market power these slots are bargaining chips and regulators can force their disposal. When BA took over BMI in 2012 BA gained 54 BMI slots. The 'remedy' for too much market power at Heathrow was to dispose of some slots. Flybe used the 12 flight remedy slots to compete with BA on Scottish routes to Edinburgh and Aberdeen links with Heathrow, so making those 'markets' contestable. Following the collapse of Flybe, BA reacquired them. They now do not have to be used for UK flights, and there is no competition. BA then abandoned Gatwick.

The Networked Industry
We have stated the consumer can still be served if the market is 'contestable.' A contestable market requires only a threat of competition, not actual competition. A market without any competitors could still serve the public. One would have thought that a natural monopoly, such as a utility, would pose major problems. The theory of natural monopoly is an extreme case where the economies of scale are such that an industry may only be in equilibrium when there is one producer. With utilities, such as gas and electricity, it only makes sense to have one pipe or cable running to the house. The LRAC would be such that a second player in the market, taking some (equal) market share, could result in both firms making a loss.

A close examination reveals the natural monopoly element is the grid. Separating the grid or network from the service provider can make the market contestable. The customer selects from a number of competing service providers, each of whom can send the same product along the grid. Thus, a consumer can select from a list of 20+ electricity or gas providers, each of whom can use the same cable or pipe to the consumer's accommodation. If a rival is willing to offer electricity or gas at a lower cost, the consumer can switch. This threat of switching keeps the current provider on their toes.

In an effort to improve contestability Ofcom forced Openreach to extend access to rivals to BT. Before, rival accessed telegraph poles and underground ducts to lay their own fibre networks to reach residential and small-business customers. In May 2019, this was extended to rivals serving large businesses as well. This also encouraged a faster roll-out of high-speed fibre cables.

Watering Down
In April 2017, the water market in England and Wales for 1.2m businesses, charities and public sector bodies was made contestable in that they were able to choose their supplier. Ofwat estimated that a net benefit of £200m. The next stage is deregulating the market for domestic customers. The benefit for this is up to £2.3bn. In June 2017, the lack of competition was estimated by Greenwich University to cost each HH £100/yr (£2.3bn). This is based on comparing the situation at privatisation in 1989 with the following era. Over 10 years to 2016 dividends of £18.1bn were paid out of £18.8bn post tax profit – almost all. Investment, funded by borrowing, resulted in £500m in interest payments. Water bills grew 40% faster than inflation over the 28 years. Investment declined by 10% to £4.56bn/yr in the decade to March 2018. Companies might prefer being fined to investing in waste disposal.

Open Access
Both sides of the Atlantic are tackling the issue of broadband and access. A concern regularly raised is the increasing demand placed on network providers by bandwidth hungry services like Facebook. With postal services, some customers pay for a faster service (1st class). If one looked at email being delivered by the web, 'net neutrality'

would imply all post would be treated equally and there would be no discrimination based on speed. However, internet service providers (ISPs) want to charge on the basis of the user's willingness to pay for speed, particularly with data-heavy applications. If there is pay for content, there will be a two-speed approach: some providers will pay for favourable treatment.

Network neutrality is, to some extent, based on a sharing of pain. The proprietary network (dumb-tube) provider is unwilling to bear the heavy cost of investment alone. Since 2008, YouTube video traffic from Google is flooding networks, leading to an imbalance in cost and benefits. Until they can amortize their investment costs, charging will be high on their agendas. It wants to shift from charging access to the internet to charging for heavy use: move from delivery to weight. This must be resolved otherwise the EU's hope of a significant investment in network infrastructure of possibly €300bn will not result. The House of Lords reported in February 2014 that to drive the economy forward, broadband and the digital revolution would be front and centre: broadband should be treated as a utility. This was mirrored in February 2015 by the US Federal Communications Commission, which decided to treat broadband as a public utility. In June 2016, the US Court of Appeals for the District of Columbia Circuit ruled that broadband providers must act as "neutral, indiscriminate platforms for transmission of speech". The Federal Communication Commission switched US policy in December 2017. Although this may prevent start-ups from succeeding, the big winners from the neutrality were the FANGs, so their profits/power may be changing the policy landscape.

The current system in the US allows local cable companies to act as local monopolies, which is credited with generating the highest cable charges in any developed country bar Mexico, Chile and Turkey, combined with speeds only one tenth as fast as those in Singapore. The implication was that users would have received a bill that reflects their usage. Now that's not the case. There remains a problem of investment. The claim is that this would reduce the rate at which the infrastructure would improve.

Regulatory Capture
Regulation is an alternative means of addressing monopoly. Regulation entails a quasi-government body imposing on the industry the incentives and disincentives that competition should provide. This commonly involves setting price (for UK utilities) or rate of return (for US utilities) targets. 'Effective' regulation, though, is based on full information. The regulator is reliant on the information that the firms whom they regulate provide to them. The firm has an incentive to provide the regulator with a view of the business that best suits the corporation, not society. Thus, it has an incentive to boost its cost base or play down any likely benefits from innovations. For example, Severn Trent was accused of manipulating its accounts to underestimate its profits to the water industry regulator, OfWat, in 2004. Perhaps a worse accusation is that the Chief Regulator and the minister to whom they reported might have had an eye on the future. When they retire, these people may find that the firms that they were regulating are interested in hiring them. The likelihood of this may be inversely related

to the harshness of the imposed regulatory regime. In October, the House of Commons criticised the OfWat for favouring the investor.

A variant of this is the advising minister. The Liberal Democrat, Steve Webb, who was a pensions minister, joined the board of Royal London. He was in post during the largest pension reform of recent decades. Gregg McClymont, Webb's Labour shadow, joined Aberdeen Asset Management. Both lost their seats in the 2015 election. One could argue that this is the usual reward for regulatory leniency. However, the reforms were opposed by the industry. These appointments could be about contacts and influence as the policy is implemented, and how future changes can be moulded.

In January, Federal Aviation Administration (FAA) was seeking to fine Boeing $5.4m for 'knowingly' installing faulty parts on 737 Max planes. This followed that claim in one internal communication in April 2017 that the plane was "designed by clowns who in turn are supervised by monkeys." Boeing was planning at that time to push back against requirements that 737 Max pilots should receive training on simulators, which would have led to higher costs for its customers, making its aircraft less attractive. The FAA had made a habit of delegating parts of the regulation process to Boeing due to cuts in funding. For the 737 Max, FAA managers reportedly pressured the agency's safety engineers to pass over safety assessments to Boeing itself.

Competition Policy Thoughts
In a sense, the large firm cannot be *expected* to behave in a socially desirable way. The profit motive only produces favourable outcomes if its less desirable behavioural traits are limited. One approach, if you like, the backstop approach, entails legal constraints. To maximise their profit, businesses may drive hard bargains and even mislead or bluff their customers /suppliers so that they pay over-the-odds. As such, the market place is not necessarily fair and businesses are morally ambiguous. The law may require a given set of information be made available to buyers or a good last a minimum period of time. But this does not limit the price to be 'fair.'

One of the tests of competitive pressure is the ease with which one can switch providers. If switching costs (barriers to exit) are high, this would lower the pressure to keep the customer happy. Also, if there are no real alternatives, because of the limited number of competitors or that the industry has a common rather undesirable way of treating customers, what can you switch to? Having a variety of providers with distinctive products is OK if they are simple. Complex products, such as pensions, require considerable time and some guidance in selling to avoid an adverse selection. Here, a skilled technician that is not a tied agent should advise. Pension advisors that are paid commission are incentivised, perhaps inappropriately. In May 2017, the Conservative party announced it would put a cap on energy prices. As noted above, legislation was introduced in February 2018. This is a sign that reliance on switching to force good behaviour DOES NOT WORK. Lethargy was estimated in January to cost 12.4m HH £709m in excess fees for home insurance. The Citizens Advice Bureau suggested that those that do not shop around paid more than they should. Overall, insurance, mobile phone and other broadband services added £4bn/yr in excess charges. Hitting a 6-year high, 15.8% of customers switched energy provider in 2016. The CMA reported in 2016 that over a 3-year period, 35% of HHs with earnings over £36,000 switched but for those with under £18,000 the rate was 20%. Ofgem finds that ⅔ of the 17m HH are on the SVR. Which? argued that customers were confused by the choice of tariff.

CSR and Enlightened Self Interest
The US coal industry may have thought that Donald Trump would save it. However, it might be the CSR of another industry, insurance, will kill it off. 25 of the world's largest insurers are refusing to cover miners and power generators that use coal. Global warming would directly affect their profitability. Examples include Axa and Zurich. That said, 54% of coal-fired power stations in Europe are loss making. This will rise to 97% by 2030 if climate change targets are to be met. The costs of exit (shutting) though are high. Redundancies and clean-up are expensive... so investment may be driven by profit rather than CSR.

In March 2018, BlackRock, the largest shareholder in Sturm, Ruger & Co and American Outdoor Brands (formerly Smith & Wesson) was considering offering investors the chance not to invest in gun firms. It also called for those firms to explain how they monitor safe use of weapons. On-line lender Kabbage withdrew funding for the manufacturing of assault rifles and for the purchase of guns for under 21s. United and Delta airlines and rental giants Hertz and Enterprise, stopped offering discounts to NRA members. First National Bank of Omaha did not renew NRA-branded credit cards. Chubb stopped underwriting an NRA-branded insurance policy. Insurer MetLife Inc also cut ties. Dick's Sporting Goods, no longer sells assault-style rifles. Walmart raised the minimum age for anyone buying guns or ammunition to 21.

In 2005, legislation was passed to shield gun makers from responsibility from misuses of their product. In November, families of the victims of the Sandy Hook School mass shooting in 2012 (26 killed) won a landmark ruling at the Supreme Court whereby it refused leave to appeal against the finding that they can seek compensation from the arms manufacturer Remington Arms. Within two days, American Outdoor Brands split their company into two, separating the firearms from the rest of their portfolio. They were finding insurance more difficult to secure.

The Bank of England concluded that financial scandals can be categorised in to seven groups: price manipulation; inside information; reference price influence; circular trading; collusion and information sharing; improper order handling; and misleading the customer. Compared with 200 years ago price manipulation techniques have changed but one can see the similarities. For example, fabricated twitter accounts were set up to spread fake negative news about Audience, a tech company and Sarepta Therapeutics, a biotech company. Misleading the customer was evident in The British Steel pension scandal. Members of the £15bn pension fund were given the option to shift their assured benefits to a new fund linked to Tata or to the Pension Protection

Fund in August 2017. Of the 130,000 members, 11,000 asked for quotes on the value of their pension by December 2017 1,700 had left. Funds worth between £300,000 and £500,000 were being transferred in to vehicles that were unsuitable or with unhealthy charges. There is an accusation of misselling. Advisors were offering little advice other than to transfer, prompting a description of a feeding frenzy, particularly at the Port Talbot plant. This could be an ethical stance or possibly a commercial one. There could be major claims following this misselling.

Follows the FCA investigation of the role of financial advisors and the Tata Steel pension arrangements agreed with the pension fund and the regulator, Personal Financial Society for financial advisors highlighted that, when specialising in pension transfer advice, its 37,000 members were increasingly finding it difficult to get insurance.

In February 2018, Unilever added to the pressure on Google and Facebook to exercise greater responsibility on postings or they would refocus some of the €7.7bn marketing budget. This could be about something else. P&G spent $100m on digital marketing in one quarter in 2017 but saw no impact on sales. Are ads being viewed by people?

In March, 2020 General Motors reached a $120m with owners who claimed that their vehicles lost value because of defective ignition switches, which have been linked to 124 deaths. GM recalled over 2.6m vehicles since 2014 and paid more than $2.6bn in penalties and settlements, including $900m million to settle a Dept. of Justice case. The case is about reputation and resale values. Owners suffered economic losses from buying vehicles based on GM's reputation for safe cars, which resulted in lower resell values.

QUASI MARKETS

A merit good is one that, if left to the market, would be under-consumed. In other words, government believes that individuals are not able to make good judgements about its consumption: consumers are not rational in that they cannot make good, long term decisions. Education is one such merit good; health is another. However, health also has another dimension. Under-consumption of health can have a negative externality: one person's under-consumption can lead to another falling ill. Individual investment in health has positive a social benefit in that one person keeping healthy reduces the likelihood of someone else falling ill. Also, investment in education should increase the likelihood of innovations that reward that education. As the social is greater than the private marginal benefits, the market failure suggests an under consumption of these services. To address the failure the State could subsidies them or make then free at the point of consumption. The post-war UK welfare-state provided education and health as a universal 'right' with fee-charging providers for the wealthy queue-jumpers.

Conservative governments introduced reforms to Education in 1988 and Health Care in 1991 that were designed to allocate resources in a more 'efficient' way. It was believed that markets allocate resources efficiently and so operating the public sector in a more business-oriented fashion, where competition is allowed to flourish, would improve the provision in these sectors. This is the new style of public management.

Market and Government Failure
Although markets allocate resources relatively efficiently, they are not without imperfections. For example, one area of inefficiency, [or *market failure*] monopoly, is associated with exploitation of the consumer, slack financial control, consumer insensitivity, and relatively poor innovation. Under these circumstances, the State could regulate the provider or nationalise it for the good of the nation. But this latter point led to, in many areas of the public sector, the State being a monopoly supplier. The equivalent to market failure inside the State sector is *government (State) failure*, where the allocation of resources by the State favours privileged groups, or resources are wasted due to general misallocation. This is said to arise because the absence of market pressure to reform and become more efficient.

Through choice, variety and rivalry, private sector providers facilitate the maximisation of well-being of consumers. In the neoclassical world, competition results in resources moving to where they produce the highest value. To inject competition into the State's provision and address government failure, internal or 'quasi' markets are introduced. Although the consumer's choice is at the heart of the allocation model, it is not clear that their utility is. Where decisions are too complex for consumers to make, choice is tempered by some guidance from the State. However, *at a basic level, to signal preferences to providers, consumers must have choice of provider that is separated (not vertically integrated) from the purchaser of the service.*

Quasi Market Assumptions
Quasi markets are modelled using a series of assumptions. Akin to perfect competition, an efficient quasi market requires:
- many providers and purchasers. As in perfect competition rivalry is important. However, from contestable market theory, merely that threat may induce desired outcomes;
- all market participants should be perfectly informed. If consumers are to make rational choices, they need reliable information [and be perfectly mobile];
- providers and purchasers must respond to financial incentives. Without the profit motive, the drive for efficiencies may not be there;
- no cream skimming:- only picking the low hanging fruit.

Propper (1993) appeals to Contestable Market theory to suggest that the threat of competition is sufficient to force incumbents to behave as if actual competitors exist in their environment. However, Contestable Market theory requires that entry and exit are costless, linking the two, placing emphasis on sunk or irredeemable costs. Glennerster (1991) notes that in the schools' sector, entry, exit and sunk costs are high and can be incurred over a prolonged period, suggesting that many providers are necessary for contestability.

In practical terms, providers, such as schools and hospitals, are expected to behave like businesses, so we describe them as Small and Medium-sized public enterprises (SMPEs). From this basis, a number of freedoms must be granted to the SMPE so that desired outcomes can be achieved. As with customers, the SMPE must be given freedoms to make choices about who to employ, what to produce, supply to whom and to buy from whomever. The State devolves powers to the SMPE so that it can make its own decisions and could generate its own funds. In this system, services are 'sold' to 'customers' and the provider is remunerated accordingly. For example, each school child has a package of resources earmarked for their education. A school is allocated these funds on the basis of 'selling' its 'educational services' to the school child. The school can increase its revenues by registering a greater number of pupils. Thus, the centre-piece of these reforms involved SMPEs *competing* for customers (pupils and patients). Rivalry, as competition theories suggest, provides the incentive to be 'better', more efficient and innovative. Parents would prefer to send their child to a 'good' provider. Good providers attract more custom and, hence, more income, whilst poor ones lose 'market share' and revenue. In a business environment, success is rewarded and the threat of failure should act a spur to improve the provision. This should be translated into a public sector environment. Good providers should be allowed to expand and poor ones contract – with the possibility of closure as a last resort.

Complications exist in the public sector that create additional behavioural problems:-
- As providers may not be profit-oriented or owned privately, it is necessary to incentivise providers and purchasers financially;
- In the market place, consumers pay directly for services but they do not 'buy' services from their NHS GP, or pay the full price at the dentist, rather a form of earmarking funds is employed. One could view this as a non-tradable 'voucher' system;
- Services are 'purchased' by GPs from hospitals on behalf of their patients, so it is not necessarily the customer exercising the right to choose;
- No cream skimming is assumed. Customers (patients and pupils) must be attracted to the provider on a level playing field. The providers must be unable to filter the high maintenance from the low, or the able from the less able. Each provider must take their fair share of the high-cost, low-reward customers.

Asymmetric Information
Choice requires information. There is an adverse selection problem. Both the State and consumers are subject to 'asymmetric information' in that they may not be aware of the relative merits of the local schools and hospitals in the same way the providers are. Information that reveals the relative merits of the providers needs to be made available to the public. This implies that measures of service and success must be identified. For schools, a natural measure could be 'A' level-point averages; for hospitals, waiting

[list] times; and most recently KIS data for Universities. Compiling the information into a ranked hierarchy produces the 'easy to understand' league table. 'Yard Stick' competition suggests that, through the provider's league position, the tables reveal 'successful' and 'less-successful' SMPEs. Targets are also applied, such discharging or transferring 95% of Accident and Emergency (A&E) cases within four hours.

With this information focus one could point to three areas of concern. Firstly, a natural consequence of focusing on a target is that this may be traded-off against aspects, particularly those that are difficult to measure e.g. quality. To address the ignored elements, government introduce new targets. Secondly, the provider can manipulate much of the information that customers need to make an informed choice. Providers have an incentive to engage in 'gaming', or manipulate the data government uses provide a false picture of the service provided, either to earn more resources or to boost a league table placing. Third, the data selected may have little bearing on quality. Keeping students happy is not necessarily congruent with making them employable. Performance data on vascular surgeons was published. There is heterogeneity within what is measured. Those surgeons that take on the most difficult and complex cases may appear to be performing badly, when in fact they could be the leading specialists in their field. So, any yardstick competition is flawed by incomplete and complex data, and could lead to risk aversion. The measure may become useless. Grades in GCSE were replaced with numbers in 2017 to reflect grade inflation. The emphasis on grades lead to a 'rise in standards' but the grading did not provide sufficient differentiation. Again, measurement can produce unintended outcomes.

One of the most obvious outcomes of the quasi market system revolves around the requirement that what is measured should be relatively simple to understand and, importantly, measurable directly. Take the example of schools and 'A' levels. Converting a grade into a point is simple enough, perhaps too simple. If all 'A' levels test the same skills and operate at the same standard this is not unreasonable. However, in June 2008 researchers at Durham University provided a hierarchy of 'A' levels placing media and sociology at the weaker end and science, maths and languages at the harder end. Knowing that easier 'A' levels are available but that each grade merits the same point regardless of course, schools may guide pupils to 'easier' 'A' levels. Casualties of quasi markets include the subject of chemistry, where university departments have closed due to too few quality undergraduates being enrolled, and economics, where only 3 teacher training graduates completed their programmes in 2008. STEM was a reaction to this. Pupils at private schools are being guided towards 'tougher' GCSEs. Despite comprising only 7% of the total of pupil entries, they make up 28% of those that study physics, chemistry and biology separately. The majority take the less demanding double science award. This difference in emphasis affects 'A' level and then degree choice. Universities are criticised for not taking enough from the State sector when there might have been guided away from taking harder qualifications by instruments of the very system they are keen to promote. A variant of this entails the filtering out weaker candidates by schools. This entails not permitting weaker candidates to take exams, possibly expulsion, or enter the 6th-Form so that the grade point average is maximised. Clearly, not all schools are doing this. The NSS is a key measure of success. However, the Augar report into HE analyses employability and programmes with 'good earnings', so LEO data is now a focus.

Cream–Skimming
The 'earmarking' of funds regardless of the ability to pay suggests a more equitable system than one based on endowments. Providers may seek to avoid high maintenance/more expensive consumers where there is a block payment system or seek them out in a payment-for work-done system. To overcome the former problem, the high maintenance customer could merit a larger package of resources. However, the purchaser may seek to buy services for less expensive clients on their behalf. That is, rather than an NHS hospital, encourage patients to go to a private sector clinic. So hospitals may make a 'loss' because they deal with complex and the private sector, more simple but profitable work.

Business Choices
As with a small business, a SMPE is forced to make choices about their provision. In a perfectly competitive environment, the product is homogeneous, costs are identical and price is determined externally. With SMPEs this is not the case. Perhaps monopolistic competition, where there is some idiosyncrasy is permitted, is more applicable. The school must determine its employment strategy; increasingly its marketing strategy; how it raises additional funds; its specialty and non-core curriculum; and out-of-hours provision etc.. The government offers a reward to well-run SMPEs by granting them greater autonomy (such as Trust status). Of particular focus are the finances of the business. The government demands efficiencies to be achieved. Indeed, it builds them in to their financing model, in effect under funding the SMPEs based on the expectation that, given the provider is a better judge of the provision than them, the shortfall should be left to the SMPE to address. The managing of funds is a key theme of the reforms. One might argue that the system obfuscates a process of resource rationing in a clever manner. The State expects schools and hospitals to raise additional fund from their own activities, so shifting some of the funding burden to the providers themselves and, hence, to users and benefactors.

Efficiency
Efficiency could be defined in terms of maximising output from a given set of resources or a Pareto efficient state where a reallocation of resources to improve the well-being of one person results in the deterioration of another's. However, one assumption in the standard analysis of welfare is that the goods are homogeneous. Within a quasi-market the notion and, hence, the comparisons of costs cannot be divorced from the quality of the product or service. A low cost could be related to inferior quality so that, as a result of the proffering of poor quality services, the welfare of the users may not be optimised. Where monitoring is weak, agents may not adhere to contract. Quality is difficult to assess and costly to monitor suggesting that

the organisation will not focus much attention on it. Government sets more and more targets to ensure that the public service addresses a broad range of activities. These targets will be the focus of the organisations – at the expense of other goals e.g. a hip surgeon told to perform other operations to meet targets that might be missed. If funders do not believe that unmonitored work will be undertaken, the logic is that *it will not fund it*. This implies only those things that are measured will merit a reward. For the hospitals, funders will support what the electorate can see, e.g. nurses and doctors in the hospital, but be unhappy about the training costs.

What Constitutes Failure?

The presumption that those towards bottom of league tables are inefficient could be unfair. Being placed at the bottom of a table of a hierarchy of things that are measured does not necessarily mean that what is provided is less than satisfactory. A ranking does not reveal quality *per se*. One provider must find itself at the bottom so perhaps additional information is required. This could include the composite figure that is used to develop the ranking or a threshold measure of success. Adjustments to the data are needed. The assumptions inherent in operationalising perfect competition squeeze out all but one dimension to the decision, which provider offers the cheapest product/service. Thus, a sound footing for decision-making is necessary. Schools, for example, could be adversely located, having a deprived catchment area. Adjustments are made for this. Nevertheless, schools are free to opt for more difficult 'A' levels to stretch their pupils, which would lead to weaker results and a lower ranking, *ceteris paribus*, which is not taken into account, directly.

If fair comparisons can be made and a school achieved a low ranking consistently, or fell below a threshold of success, what does the quasi market business model demand? If a commercial business is unpopular, it loses trade. This will happen with the 'poor' SMPE, as it should experience declining pupil intakes. However, if the providers are making the 'wrong' decision, the SMPE could be punished financially by, say, withholding some funds, providing them with an incentive to improve their provision, but from a contracting financial base. Sadly, this is one area where the model works imperfectly. A weak provider is not in a strong position to weather a cut in its funding whilst increasing the quality of its provision. Reducing its income will possibly plunge the SMPE into a vicious circle of morale-sapping cost cutting, worsening quality and declines in pupil enrolment, possibly threatening lives.

Payment System

The disbursal of funds from the purchaser to the provider is far from costless. There will be a contract between the parties. If the reward system entails a block payment for providing services to a given number of clients, there has to be an arrangement for over or under-expected usage. This is particularly complex where there is a multitude of services bundled up in the block payment. The logic of the system is that the provider is the best judge of what and how they meet their obligations.

An alternative approach is payment for work done. This is far more information-intensive. Each procedure merits a payment, which implies each must have a price. Once undertaken, if a reward is sought, an invoice must be presented to the purchaser. This implies that, to ensure resources are allocated based on the work done, a significant number of personnel from both the providers' and purchasers' sides of the billing process is needed.

Dentists Cream-Skim

Shifting from payments by results, from April 2006 a fee structure with over 400 separate charges for different procedures was replaced by three bands of fees. Simple tasks merited £16.20. More complex procedures, such as fillings, extractions, or root canal work earned £44.60 and £198 for bridges, dentures or crowns. Under the previous system, dentists had a financial incentive for carrying out complex dental procedures. Subsequently, the dentist was paid for those on their books. This pushes them to cream skim. Dentists have avoided 'high maintenance' patients with bad teeth by requiring new patients to demonstrate a track record of visiting dentists in the previous three years. Indeed, dentist's leaders report that preference is being given to those who are deregistered when a dental practice leaves the NHS. Family members were also given preference on the belief that they too would have been regular dentist visitors. Perhaps more concerning is the dropping of children from NHS dental registers.

Management

As providers may not be profit oriented or privately owned, it is necessary to incentivise providers and purchasers, financially. This can prove a major problem, when, for example, the government wishes to open up the provision of healthcare services to the 'third sector' to achieve efficiencies and inject the atmosphere of competition.

Professionals, who are a key source of government failure, are not entirely trusted. Traditionally, the professionals ran the schools and hospitals, but like a business that could not fail, decisions were not necessarily made with the customers' approval in mind. If you listen closely, government ministers will state with some earnestness that, without targets, these professionals lack the incentive to be diligent. They should not be left to make the decisions, the market should. Professions need to be 'managed'. The system requires a shift of resources to reflect a more devolved, data rise environment. Schools require a business manager, known as a bursar, and hospitals need more accountants.

Inevitably, more non-frontline staff will be employed to ensure that targets are not missed and league table sensitive activities receive attention. There will be trade-offs between quality and cost. Strangely, despite mistrusting the professional over certain areas of the provision, public sector professionals are relied on as experts to make complex ethical decisions about resource allocations, particularly improving efficiency without compromising quality. Notice how the Corona virus pushed the expert ahead of the manager. Under quasi-markets this is not appropriate – any yet it feels right.

Avoiding Penalties

GPs were given the target of scheduling a consultation within 48-hours of a patient making an appointment. This has led to scheduling of consultations to fall entirely within the 48-hour limit. In other words, the target results in patients sometimes losing the scope to make an appointment three or more days in advance.

NATIONAL INCOME ACCOUNTING

National Income (NY) is defined as an estimate of the value of the goods and services made available as a result of a country's economic activity over a given period of time (usually one year) and reduced to a common basis by being measured in monetary terms. In attempting to measure the national income of a country for a particular year we are assessing the *flow* of goods or wealth produced in that particular year: we are *not* concerned with the *stock* of goods or wealth produced in the past.

We can learn about the measurement of National Income by looking at a Primitive Economy. The first settlers come to Lincolnshire and during the course of the first year produce 3 types of goods.

i.   wheat   - to stand for consumer goods
ii.   huts   - to stand for consumer durable goods
iii.   tools   - to stand for capital goods

If we assume the primitive economy has no money and all goods produced must be handed in to a central authority for distribution, then we can measure the total amount produced in that economy in its final year in three ways:-

i.   At the OUTPUT stage: we could add up the total amount produced and handed to the Central Authority.
ii.   At the INCOME stage: we could add up the shares of the product handed to each family
iii.   At the CONSUMPTION and SAVING stage: we could add up the total amount of these goods that the families had in the course of the year either consumed or saved i.e. how they disposed of their income. We can conclude that
TOTAL OUTPUT = TOTAL INCOME = TOTAL CONSUMPTION and SAVING

In a modern economy the measurement is done through the medium of money and over 1 year. Thus, in the same way using money as our measure the total value of the output that is produced (TOTAL PRODUCT) will be equal to the total amount that is available to share out in wages, salaries, rent and profit (TOTAL INCOME) which again must be equal to the total amount which consumers can spend (TOTAL EXPENDITURE). In the following example, a bushel of wheat is sold for £1000. This production might involve the payment of £600 wages and salaries, £200 rent, £100 interest charges, £100 profit. The recipients of these incomes will have £1000 to spend or save. If this is carried out for the economy as a whole, the same principle can be represented in a diagram illustrating the circular flow of income.

Firms produce that output

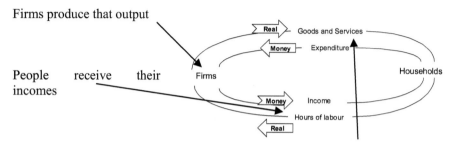

People receive their incomes

These incomes are spent on goods and services produced. The households that provide the factors of production for firms do so in exchange for money. Firms use these factors to produce goods and services upon which the public spend their incomes. These incomes will be spent on those goods that households have thus helped to produce. We can measure national income at three points in the circular flow of income.

Thus, total or *national output* will *equal* total or *national income* will *equal* total or *national expenditure*. All three totals are usually referred to as NATIONAL INCOME of the country for a year. Each method of income accounting faces certain problems:

The **output** or **product method** attempts to measure the total value of goods and services produced by all sectors of the economy (public and private) during the course of a year. Essentially, we are seeking to measure *work done*. A good guide to work done is work paid for.

There should be an inclusion of goods and services that do not change hands against money. Examples include:
- ❑ Goods consumed by those that produce them, e.g. farm produce consumed on a farm. In less developed countries this problem has to be allowed for otherwise figures for output and income can appear unrealistically small.
- ❑ Unpaid services, such as household duties. A value for the work done should be imputed and included.
- ❑ Government services must be valued at cost of providing them. If £1bn is spent on education, then this is regarded as the total income generated.
- ❑ Rented houses provide an income in the form of rent. An amount must be included for living in owner-occupied house according to their current rental value.
- ❑ Double Counting - care must be taken to include only the value added at each stage of production process e.g. value of flour must not be included in value of bread.

The **total domestic product at factor cost** is essentially the sum of value of all goods and services produced in a year. The following adjustments must then be made:

❑ Deduct Stock appreciation. Allowance has to be made for the fact that this value of output may rise because of a rise in price of work in progress and goods held in stock.

❑ Residual error. This allows for statistical discrepancies in collection of data usually added by different means and from different sources for income, output and expenditure.

After these adjustments, the total becomes **gross domestic product at factor cost**. The following adjustments must then be made:

Net property income from abroad is where UK property owned abroad such as subsidiaries yield incomes in the form of interest, rent, profits etc. is included as part of output. Foreign property held in UK will cause income to flow abroad. Add this.

After these adjustments the total becomes **gross national product at factor cost**. Capital consumption or depreciation entails replacing worn out obsolete capital equipment. This output does not represent an addition to the capital stock.

Gross Capital Formation – Depreciation = Net Capital Formation

After these adjustments, the total becomes **net national product at factor cost (NNP) or national income**.

The **income method** is calculated as the total value of all incomes received by individuals and enterprises in the economy during the year. Incomes are in the form of wages, salaries, rent, and profits. The criterion is 'is the income the payment rendered by a person or his/her property?' Or is the income the result of output? The sort of difficulties one might face include:

❑ Transfer incomes and payments are incomes received unrelated to any economic activity. They represent a redistribution of income e.g. student grants, pensions etc.. They must be removed unless they are provided by the private sector.

❑ Taxation: include gross incomes as these are generated from output. They must be added in.

❑ Profits of companies: whether distributed or undistributed, must be included as they are incomes generate from output. Also, include trading surpluses of public corporations, nationalised industries and Local Authorities.

After these adjustments, the total becomes **total domestic income at factor cost**. Stock appreciation (revaluation of stock) must be removed, as should residual error. The total becomes **gross domestic income at factor** cost. Removing net property income, the total becomes **gross national income at factor cost**. Adjusting for capital consumption or depreciation, the total becomes **net national income at factor cost**.

The **expenditure method** measures total amount spent on consumer goods and services and net additions to capital good and stocks in the course of the year. These include:

☐   Current personal spending by private individuals on goods and services.
☐   All government-spending central and local government spending except transfer payments.
☐   All investment spending (Gross domestic capital formation).
☐   Saving provides funds for investment, spent on capital good and for private consumers, such as their investment in house purchase.

Also included are stocks of goods not sold and goods but still on assembly line as these are outputs that have yielded an income. It must be included in expenditure and may be regarded as involuntary investment.

After these adjustments, the total becomes **total domestic expenditures at market prices**. Adjusting for foreign transactions (add export spending subtract import spending), the total becomes **gross domestic expenditures at market prices**. Subtracting taxes and adding subsidies produces **gross domestic expenditures at factor cost**. Then, adding net property income results in **gross national expenditures at factor cost**. Subtract capital consumption to produce **net national expenditures at factor cost**. O=E=Y.

Gross measures (GDP, GDI, GNP and GNI) reflect work done or wealth generated. Net measures (NDP, NDI, NNP and NNI) subtract capital consumption from the gross measures. The consumption of fixed capital or depreciation relates to an allowance for replacing the buildings and equipment that is gradually wearing out. As it shows output accounting for the state of the productive capacity, in a sense, the net figure is the more useful.

As part of a quinquennial revision of the national accounts, the US Bureau of Economic Analysis, in the summer of 2013, changed the composition of NDP. One notable variation in the composition of capital in recent years is the increased importance of information and communications technology. This is a fast depreciating asset sector. This would increase total capital consumption, *ceteris paribus*. Moreover, GDP will be 3% larger because corporate expenditures for intellectual property will be classified as 'capital investment.' Previously, they were an 'input cost.' All costs of buying a house are now seen as an investment. Before, just estate agents' commission was included. R&D is now part of capital investment. A taxi firm's purchase of a vehicle is viewed as a 'capital investment.' As this wears out, there is consumption of fixed capital, but this is disregarded entirely in the GDP number. The value above the labour time and the fuel is summed to form value-added in GVA, which ignores input costs. Thus, reclassifying corporate purchases as 'investment' rather than 'input' inflates value added or GDP but not NDP.

As measures of well-being, NDP and GDP/head are imperfect. Kenyan real GDP/head grew by 10% over 1993-2009 but the number with electricity doubled, the proportion with a phone went from almost zero to 60% and the proportion with a flushing toilet tripled. These changes in well-being are not captured by the GDP values.

Using UN standards for compiling national income, Japan's 2015 GDP was reevaluated from ¥499tn to ¥531tn. This was, in part, boosted by R&D spending, patents and copyrights. Potential growth is estimated at 0.5%. Given discussions elsewhere about full employment in Japan and upward revisions of growth and GDP, Japan appears to growth at full employment without inflationary or wage pressures.

Happiness
The French government, in 2009, appeared to be leading the way in incorporating unfashionable but logical economic policy ideas into their armoury. Stiglitz and his International Commission on the Measurement of Economic Performance and Social Progress considered how to assess well-being and the use of GDP as a proxy for this. At a basic level, GDP measures output – what is produced. For this to be a measure of well-being, income would have to be closely associated with utility – the homo economicus' acquisitiveness predominates. However, in this era of greater social and environmental concerns, is more consumption enhancing utility? The human costs of production are not measured. Working longer hours may boost income but it comes at the cost of leisure, perhaps more stress, and a less fulfilling family life. Investment requires a temporal shift of resources: less consumption now for more in the future.

The Commission proposed adjustments to the way GDP is calculated; new measures of well-being and happiness; and new metrics for environmental and financial sustainability. By taking into account its high-quality health service, expensive welfare system and long holidays, one consequence of these changes, is to improve France's measured economic performance.

The founder of Enlightenment Economics, Diane Coyle, suggested that happiness is not a 'policy useful' measure; policy levers cannot affect it easily. Rather, good health and type of employment, which are strongly linked to well-being, can be affected by government nudging.

The ONS reported[3] that the likelihood of reporting very high life satisfaction as a result of doubling of the share of spending on a particular category, April 2016 to March 2017, showed people do not like paying for communications. Take two people with the same level of household spending for example: the one who spends double the share of their spending on communication is 38 % points less likely to report very high life satisfaction than the other spending less in this way.

---

[3] ONS 15 May 2019 Personal and economic well-being: what matters most to our life satisfaction?

	Likelihood of very high	Income	Odds ratio	Age	Odds ratio
Miscellaneous*	-14.5	£18k <	1	70+	1.74
Household furnishings	9.3	£18k up to £24k	1.0	60-69	1.79
Recreation	8.0	£24k up to £32k*	1.3	50-59	1.13
Hotels and restaurants*	18.2	£32k up to £44k*	1.1	40-49	1
Food*	-18.2	> £44k	1.0	30-39	1.25
Communication*	-38.4			16-29	1.36

There is a schism between income and expenditure. There is evidence that respondents were more likely to report higher life satisfaction if they have higher household expenditure but *not* income. However, breaking down income into quintiles, those whose household income was between £24,000 and £44,000 are significantly more likely to report higher life satisfaction with increasing income. The odds ratios of higher life satisfaction associated with 10% higher household disposable income is 1.3. Age is another key variable. Happiness is *U* shaped. Using 40-49 as a benchmark, all other age groups are happier.

GNP or GDP – Does it Matter?

GDP covers wealth generated within the borders of the country or region concerned. GNP measures wealth generated by the citizens/ corporates of the country or region. GNP = GDP + incomes (remittances), dividends and profits earned outside the country or region – incomes, dividends and profits earned inside the country or region but not by its citizens.

Ireland is an example of a country where the distinction matters. The cornerstone of Irish industrial policy is low corporate taxes (12.5% of profits). In effect, it is a tax haven. It has attracted FDI especially regional HQs from the US and Europe, such as Google, Yahoo and Forest Labs. 20% of Irish GDP being profit must be both taxed lightly and remitted overseas. Any attempt to boost the tax-take from this quarter would be self-defeating. The footloose investment would relocate. In 2009, a deficit ratio based on GDP of 12% would become 17.9% based on GNP. Ireland, a county that requested regional assistance, has a higher GDP/head than the UK.

PPP

We use GDP/head as a measure of the relative standard of living. In an important sense, the measure is based on relative income per head. If priced in different currencies, the data needs to be converted. Exchange rates, if allowed to move freely and with perfect capital movements (freely convertible), should reflect relative costs. So, a basket of goods should cost the same in both

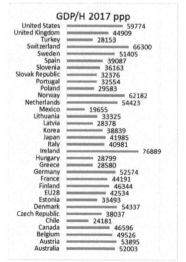

GDP/H 2017 ppp

United States	59774
United Kingdom	44909
Turkey	28153
Switzerland	66300
Sweden	51405
Spain	39087
Slovenia	36163
Slovak Republic	32376
Portugal	32554
Poland	29583
Norway	62182
Netherlands	54423
Mexico	19655
Lithuania	33325
Latvia	28378
Korea	38839
Japan	41985
Italy	40981
Ireland	76889
Hungary	28799
Greece	28580
Germany	52574
France	44191
Finland	46344
EU28	42534
Estonia	33493
Denmark	54337
Czech Republic	38037
Chile	24181
Canada	46596
Belgium	49526
Austria	53895
Australia	52003

countries. However, this should be adjusted for purchasing power in the local currency. In the chart right, Ireland had the highest income per head at $76,889.

PPP theory states that the relative exchange rates between two countries should equal the relative price levels in the two countries concerned. In the chart right, OECD estimated GDP per head in dollars for 2017 for a variety of countries. The UK value $44,909 at current prices. China was at $16,762 in 2016.

The Economist's Big Mac is a variant on PPP. The notion that one could find a collection of goods common to both countries is central to PPP. The Big Mac is a standard product found in a range of countries. The relative costs of a Big Mac in both countries could be a proxy for relative general costs of living.

Problems
GDP is a product of the mass production era, measuring quantity rather than quality. Having four memory sticks is better than three. Having four spoons is better than three but is it better than a knife, fork and spoon?: in output terms, no, but in terms of eating a meal, yes. Products, like computers and, latterly, mobile phones, are problematic for national income accounting. Normally, a higher price not associated with inflationary pressures, implies the product is of a higher quality. But the price of computers tends to fall whilst their power rises. In particular, Moore's law saw the price of computer power fall 70%/yr for 3 years, now that decline is 3-4%. The consumer is better off, whilst the assessment using GDP by the expenditure method would have them as worse off. Interestingly, the reverse is not true. There is no downgrading of GDP because of goods becoming shoddier. As reported above, shrinkflation is not uncommon. Goods can be priced the same but fall in unit size. Thus, there is an upward bias in its estimate. Given that the definition of a recession rests on GDP estimates, this can provide a politician with an incentive to time the introduction of changes to estimates.

The number of hours worked to generate that GDP is also important. If two countries generate the same GDP from the same population, but one does it using fewer worker-hours, does this mean they are equally well-off? In GDP terms yes, but in leisure time, not.

GDP/capita is an average and may not reflect the well-being of the median income group or those at the bottom of the income hierarchy. Adjustments need to be made for the distribution of income.

Excessive consumption in one era, which would boost GDP, could compromise the productive capacity in a later one. Depreciation of productive capacity is accounted for with NNP but does that include a degradation of the environment? No account is taken of depleted resources. With finite resources an over-consumption, which lowers current cost would add to well-being today whilst worsening it tomorrow. With open access, 'tipping points' may be passed, leading to a sudden collapse of fishing stocks, or worse, irreversible global warming.

Externalities, such as pollution, are not included in GDP unless expenditure is allocated to cleaning up the mess. The consumption of bads is treated in the same way as goods. Heroin and cigarette consumption are just as good as green vegetables. They hold a value in GDP terms based on the expenditure made on them.

If there is a catastrophe, capacity loss is a NDP issue but not for GDP. However, the reconstruction effort is a GDP issue. This, through a multiplier effect, can stimulate further growth. Energy Saving Trust reported in July 2013, from a survey of 86,000 British households, that the average shower lasts 7½ minutes. If this was reduced to 6½ minutes, £215m would be saved on utility bills. 95% of people boiled the kettle every day with 40% using one over four times a day. ¾ of households overfill their kettles, wasting £68m/ year. Although these are unproductive uses of water, they count towards GDP.

When calculating GDP how does one account for home ownership? If I pay for work to be done on my house, money changes hands and that work is included in the GDP estimate. Although increasing the value of my property, DIY work does not enter the GDP estimates, but it should (as work is done), hence a value needs to be imputed. The third party criterion states that if an activity were both productive and could (under usual circumstances) be contracted out to a third party, then it would be included in an extended boundary of production.

Similarly, rented houses provide an income in the form of rent, but a home that is occupied by its owner, does not. GDP would be higher if two neighbouring owners that swapped houses and paid rent to each other compared with them living in their own houses. Again, a value needs to be imputed.

Yet another problem area is the consumption of something below the price the consumer is willing to pay. Consumer surplus provides utility/happiness that is not priced. This is made all the worse with internet services provided free of charge. These services are very valuable to many. To value this is difficult. If forced to pay for news, people avoid it so the Independent and Guardian say are vulnerable and the New Day failed. Maps and Images are offered free destroying companies that sell those services. Again, time using the service multiplied by a utility value may be a way forward. US GDP between 2007 and 2011 could have been 3% higher because of the free service consumption. Measuring internet traffic might present a more rapid growth rate.

In the ONS' *Household satellite accounts: 2005 to 2014*, it attempts to measure non-market work done.

Total Output = CoE + IC + GoS + Imputed Rentals

CoE = Compensation of Employees is the equivalent labour costs that would normally have been paid to maintain the housing services using market sources

IC = Intermediate Consumption are goods and services (resources) used up by housing such as utilities as electricity or water

Intermediate Consumption	£222,692m
Input of household production of housing services	£116,639m
Input of household production of transport services	£21,658m
Input of Housing services produced by owner occupiers	£166,386m
Total	£527,375m

GoS = Gross Operating Surplus is the market equivalent profit which a third party contracted in to provide some of the household upkeep activities could reasonably expect to generate in any given year.

$$GVA = CoE + GoS$$

GVA excludes imputed rentals for housing as this is already accounted for elsewhere.

Home Services in Hours/Yr

Year	Cleaning	Gardening	DIY
2005	180	54	42
2006	178	55	41
2007	179	54	39
2008	180	52	38
2009	179	52	37
2010	178	51	36
2011	175	51	35
2012	172	51	35
2013	171	50	34
2014	169	49	33

Left are examples of hours of labour used for imputing GDP. Here, average annual hours carrying out household upkeep tasks per person, 2005 to 2014. There was a general decline in the time spent cleaning, doing DIY, and gardening/person but the imputed value of the work increased, resulting in the growth of GVA of household housing services at an average of 1.4%/yr.

GVA of informal childcare was £320.6bn in 2014 making it the largest component of home production (31% of the total). Private household transport (£235.8bn = 23%). This value is approximately 6.5 × total household expenditure on publicly provided transport.

Nutrition services of households is a term that covers home catering. This includes all activities related to the provision of food and drink, such as cooking, shopping, setting the table, and washing up.

Output = total number of calories consumed in the home × cost per calorie eaten out.

The value of home nutrition services was £144.3bn or £2234/h, up from £1632 (37%). The number of calories eaten per person declined by 8.1%. The price of food and drink eaten out (in restaurants, cafes, and pubs) is used as the monetary value.

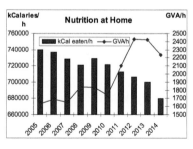

The number of adults receiving informal adult care remained largely static between 2005 and 2014. However, there has been an increase in the number of hours per cared-for person, leading to 4.2% average annual growth in the GVA of informal adult care.

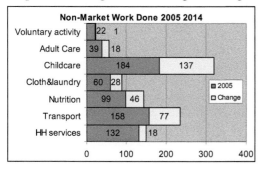

Gross value added of volunteering activities = total number of hours by type of voluntary activity × an appropriate wage rate to estimate output of frequent formal volunteering.

There has been a general downwards trend in the total number of volunteered hrs (2.28bn to 1.97bn) when the population grew 6.9%, implying the average number fell by 19.3%.

GVA of clothing and laundry services was £88.4bn in 2014, growing by an average of 4.3% per year.

The GVA of home production includes adult and child care; household housing services; nutrition; private transport; clothing and laundry; and volunteering in 2014 was £1,018.9bn. Extended GDP (EGDP) which includes home produced services was £2,836.2bn in 2014, in current prices. The proportion of total home production to GDP grew from 52.2% to 56.1%. ONS provides current prices. Prices rose by 38% between 2005 and 2014. The largest component by value, childcare, increase from £184bn to £321bn. There was a 2.9% increase in the total number of hours of formal childcare, when the average hourly cost of a child minder increased by 61.1% from £2.52 per hour in 2005 to £4.06 in 2014.

OUTPUT GAP

The standard theory of the inflation, used by all the major central banks, assumes that the rate of inflation is driven by the size of the output gap in the economy (i.e. the extent of spare capacity) and by expected inflation. As such, the notion and the assessment of the gap are important to economic policy. The output gap is a measure of lost production. It is based on two notions, both of which are complex and difficult to assess. Potential output provides a view of what could be produced; what could be the level of income at a time. Actual output is what is produced. The gap is forgone production/wealth generation.

The time path of the actual level of production is commonly characterised as a business cycle. A cycle has a sequence of four phases: trough, expansion, peak and contraction. Underlying that cycle is a trend. The trend could be measured by assessing the gradient from peak-to-peak or trough-to-trough. It is common to find that quarterly change data is assessed either by comparing the period's value with an earlier one, i.e $\Delta x_t = x_t - x_{t-p}$. If $p = 1$, it could provide a 'lumpy' picture of a quarterly change. If $p = 4$, the comparison is an annual one, which should provide a smoother time-profile. For monthly data, $p = 1$ or 12.

One way of viewing potential and actual output over time is illustrated in the diagram below. The trend's slope represents potential growth rate. The actual growth rate is captured by the business cycle. Various authors interpret the trend slightly differently. In Sloman, the trend is positioned above the cycle and represents potential output. The gap between John Sloman's trend line and output, as measured by gross domestic product (GDP), represents the output gap (A). If GDP growth is above trend, the output gap closes. However, actual output is never greater than potential. Robert Gordon draws the trend line through the cycle and it represents natural real output. The natural real GDP is a level of output consistent with zero change in inflation. If GDP is above trend, actual unemployment rate is below the natural rate in an Expectations Augmented Phillips Curve (EAPC) model, and greater inflation ensues. Gordon also defined the output gap as the percentage difference between actual and natural real GDP (B). He also defined the output ratio as the ratio of natural to actual GDP. A figure over 100% implies inflation would be accelerating.

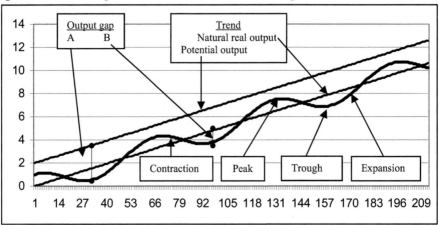

Okun's Law

There are two versions of Okun's law: the static and dynamic. The static or gap version: is $Q = Q_n - \delta(u_n - u)$, where Q is actual and Q_n potential or natural output. Krugman restructures the gap expression as $u = u_n - \lambda(Q - Q_n)$. As these natural rates are difficult to assess, we use the dynamic. $\dot{Q} = \dot{Q}_n - \gamma(\Delta u_n - \Delta u)$ (dot indicates growth rate of). Here, the actual growth rate is related to the gap between the change in the natural and actual rates of unemployment. Assuming the change in the natural rate of unemployment is approximately equal to 0 and that potential growth is α, the expression becomes $\dot{Q} = \alpha - \gamma(\Delta u)$. With potential growth of ($\alpha =$) 3%, and $\gamma =$

2, a 2% fall in unemployment leads to a rise in actual output by 7%, 4% higher than the potential rate.

If the trend in Q_n falls, output growth will so do. This is a secular as opposed to a cyclical recession. Credit cycles have been with us for as long as there has been credit. However, some prove remarkably damaging. In a sense, one has to distinguish between a trend and a cycle. There are three types:
1. Output is permanently lost but the trend remains. The example is Sweden in the 1990s;
2. The trend is lower. An example is Japan since the 1990s where there is a productivity puzzle and a secular recession;
3. Output is lost permanently and the trend is lower trend (see PLOG and secular stagnation).

The third being the most damaging and encompassing the two others is worthy of comment. Over indebtedness, when the crunch comes, leads to mass defaults. As firms fail and make workers redundant this causes a loss of output. Moreover, if banks are more cautious, this could stifle growth further down the line.

Larry Summers proposed four reasons for believing in a secular stagnation thesis:-
1. Even though financial repair had largely taken place several years ago, recovery has only kept up with population growth and normal productivity growth in the US, and has been worse elsewhere in the industrial world;
2. Despite ultra-loose credit in the run up to the crash, only moderate economic growth emerged;
3. Short-term interest rates were severely constrained by the zero lower bound: real rates may not be able to fall far enough to spur enough investment to lead to full employment. Of course, now governments utilise negative interest rates, this implies there is no longer a clear lower bound.
4. Deflation and falling wages nominal wages are likely to worsen performance by encouraging consumers and investors to delay spending. More interestingly, deleveraging and the lack of borrowing redistributes spending to high income and wealthy but low spending creditors from high-spending debtors.

In November 2013, some awful realisations were arrived at. The PLOG acronym emerged; the *p*ersistent *l*arge *o*utput *g*ap. It will be presumed by the OBR that output will be below capacity for possibly 7 years, suggesting that monetary policy, QE and low interest rates, will not move [equilibrium] economic output to full employment. Across the Atlantic, Summers and Krugman suggested that the RR* in the global economy had been around –2 to –3% since at least the mid-2000s, but that the actual real rate (at least on bonds) had been positive. The level of spending at any given set of interest rates is likely to have declined (the demand for money has shifted left).

The definition of RR* *equilibrium real rate of interest or* the neutral rate is that rate consistent with full employment and stable inflation (or zero output gap or full employment). In March 2015, Yellen was saying that the US RR* was close to zero but rising, with a long-term rate of 1.75%. The *Taylor rule* is $R_t = RR^* + \pi_t + 0.5(\pi_t -$

2) + 0.5Y_t, where R denotes the federal funds rate, π is the current inflation rate, and Y is the output gap $Q - Q_n$. If RR* is assumed to equal 2% (roughly the average historical value of the real federal funds rate) and the natural rate of unemployment is assumed = 5½%, given that core inflation in April 2015 was running close to 1¼% and the unemployment rate was 5.5%, then the Taylor rule would call for the nominal funds rate to be set a bit below 3%. But if RR* is instead assumed to equal 0% and u_n = 5%, the rate should be less than ½%. In April 2016, core inflation was up to 2.1% suggesting a rate of 2.3%. In June 2018, RR* was 0 < 1.5% with a 0.9% median. HSBC, JP Morgan and Heteronomics in July were more pessimistic putting it at -0.5 to 0% so that R of 1.5-2% ultimately would be needed to keep inflation steady at around 2%.

With actual > equilibrium output there has been a prolonged period of under-investment in the developed economies, with GDP falling further and further behind its underlying long-run potential, leading to a PLOG or secular stagnation. The actual output does not wrap around the old trend, but a lower path reflecting the damage done to the capital stock and the effective supply of labour by the recession. Investment demand may have been reduced due to slower growth of the labour force and slower productivity growth. Risk aversion following the crisis and has led deleveraging by both States and consumers and more precautionary holdings. The costs of financial intermediation (banking) have risen.

Adjustments rely on cuts in interest rates and wages, but although nominal interest rates can fall below zero, can they fall sufficiently to find equilibrium? Also, monetary policy will not encourage current against future consumption. Due to a redistribution of wealth to the very wealthy, this lowers MPCs and APCs so that consumption may be lower. Declines in the cost of durable goods, especially those associated with information technology, mean that the same level of saving purchases more capital every year. Therefore, none of the normal forces for restoring equilibrium apply.

Extrapolating IMF/OECD estimates of potential GDP output from before the 2008 crash, Lawrence Ball from Johns Hopkins University estimated the loss of potential output in 2013 across 7 developed countries was 7.18% plus a 2.56% output gap. Potential growth had dropped from 2.39% to 1.68%. The corresponding figures for the UK are 10.98, 2.14, 2.66 and 1.85.

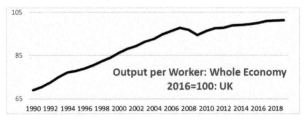

Output per Worker: Whole Economy 2016=100: UK

Productivity
Productivity quantifies how an economy uses its resources, by relating the quantity of output to inputs. In the graphic left, using index numbers with

2016=100, GDP Output/hour is displayed. We see uninterrupted growth in productivity until 2007; then it stagnates.

It was estimated by the ONS that, of the 4.3% UK productivity drop, oil and financial services explained 1.3% each and utilities a further 0.65%. In other words, three industries accounted for ¾ of the decline in long-term productivity growth. In April 2015, poor growth was ascribed to lawyers, accountants and management consultants, whose output had grown by 2% after, when before 2008 they had grown at 3.8%/yr. Telecommunications, banking and finance had a similar tale. Recruitment grew at the same rate as before when output growth did not. The new steady state growth of output per worker is 1.75%. By February 2018, the BoE was suggesting that workers had shifted from high to low productivity sectors. From 2002Q2 to 2007Q3 output per man-hour increase by 9.6%. From then to 2017Q3 it increased by 2.5%, a 7.1 point decline. Of this, 5 points are explained by shifts from sectors such as aviation and mining to health and hospitality. The collapse of finance is still in evidence. Over 2002-07 it contributed 1.6 percentage points. Over 2012-17, it contributed 0.2 percentage points to productivity growth.

In December 2018, Britain's productivity gap with France was reduced when adjustments were made for hours of work. As Brits work fewer hours than thought, they have more leisure time and greater productivity per hour; both boosting well-being.

A recession, as defined as two consecutive quarters of negative growth is problematic with differing potential growth rates. The US trend of 2% would fall into a recession less often than Japan with a trend of 0.5%. It is proposed that rather than zero, use a fixed number, such as two consecutive quarters of growth 200bps below trend. So the US it would be below zero but for Japan, it would require shrinking by 1.5%.

This sluggish productivity growth rate can lead to:
- Lower real wages: Businesses cannot afford to maintain wages in line with prices when their workers' efficiency levels are sluggish;
- Higher unit costs: If running at about the same level, pay increases can be afforded. However, rising raw material costs might be passed onto consumers in higher prices;
- Balance of payment problems: Thirlwall's Balance of Payments Constraint Hypothesis is predicated on the core having a faster productivity growth rate than the periphery. Its enhanced competitiveness leads to a favourable trade performance. Thus, export growth is related to relative productivity growth and lower unit costs;
- Lower profits: The periphery is trapped in a cycle of lower productivity leading to lower profits for companies, which affects re-investment to support the long-term growth of local businesses;

- Lower economic growth: A sluggish potential growth rate will constrain the growth of actual output. For any given level of output growth, the output gap will be narrower, implying demand pull inflation will be higher.

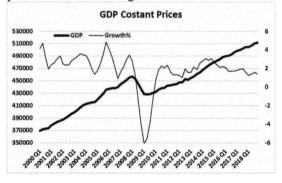

The issue of a secular recession is interesting. In the graph right, we can see GDP/quarter at factor cost (ABMI). The annual growth rate from 2000 to 2008 was 2.50%. The trend following the crash from 2009 to 2018 the annual growth rate was 1.3%. However, from 2000 to 2018 the annual rate stands at 1.86%. Since 2011, the rate has sat at a steady rate of around 1.93%. Of course this reversion does not have to be related to productivity.

Social-Uselessness

Adair Turner has, over some years, discussed the restructuring of the economy. The productivity paradox is in large part due to a shift in employment from high productivity sectors to slow with the corresponding wage divide. Of the 10 sectors forecast to provide 29% of all new jobs in the US over the 10 years from 2014, 8 have below median wages. Some jobs generates are socially-useless, zero-sum, rentiers. Including arbitragers, tax lawyers, marketers, lobbyists, these contribute little to actual output/ social well-being. Worryingly, even higher education can be zero-sum (just reshuffling the rank order for jobs). The new economy extracts monopoly rent through the patents on the technology we all use. Previously, he criticised socially-useless lending. A key example is housing – more lending for the same dwelling. This is compounded by the rise in land values, the classic area of economic rent. Over the medium term, this rent needs to be taxed more to offset the lower level of employment and wage. Indeed, corporates are just not willing to pay tax. The IMF reported in September that 38% of DFI was involved in no real business activities (socially-useless). Around £15tn of this capital was most likely seeking to avoid tax. Apple neither makes or has a substantial design element in Ireland yet that is a major DFI for it. Although this is a well-established trend, the UK's share has jumped from 3% in 2009 to 18% in 2017. The leaders are Luxemburg and the Netherlands. In 2015, it also estimated that $450bn (1% of GDP) of OECD and $200bn of non-OECD (1.3%) of capital is profit shifting.

Corona – Beyond Numbers

The numbers coming from the various august institutions in March, April and May were beyond anything seen before. The International Monetary Fund and the Economist Intelligence Unit heralded the world economy would shrink at its fastest since the Great Depression. The ILO estimated nearly 200m could end up out of work. In early April, the United Nations reported that 81% of the world's workforce of 3.3bn had their place of work fully or partly closed. In just 2020Q2, 6.7% of working hours across the world were lost. Oxfam estimated more than half a billion people will fall into poverty.

Whilst they estimated the global economy will contract by 3% in 2020, the IMF forecast the UK economy to shrink by 6.5%. Office for Budget Responsibility (OBR) were more pessimistic @ 12.8% with 35.1% collapse between April and June. Unemployment could rise by 2.1m to 3.4m by the summer, rising from 3.9% to 10%. Policies for dealing with this scale of a problem would be experimental.

HISTORY AND INDUSTRIAL STRUCTURE

Different theories, ideas and paradigms about the capitalist system abound. One group, Marxists, discuss 'organized' and 'disorganized' capitalism. Dunning talks about 'liberal', 'hierarchical' and 'alliance'. Porter discusses 'factor-driven', 'investment driven', 'innovation driven' and 'wealth driven'. The main point is that over the life-cycle of capitalism as a whole, different forms of social organisation and political structuring emerge as dominant for a period; and capitalism as a whole has, in consequence, to be understood as moving inexorably from one model to another over time. Different eras can be associated with qualitatively distinct mixes of technologies, forms of business organization, characters of labour forces and State functions that come to predominate within it. Allen and Massey (1989) discuss three models: Long Waves; Regulation; World Systems. These have disappeared directly but have emerged in various forms, such as Industry4.0.

Long Waves theory suggests economic activity has been characterised by many authors in terms of cycles. Van Duijn identified (1983) four periodicies.
- These are the 40-60 month inventory or Kitchin cycle;
- 6-10 year so called Juglar, business or trade cycle based on investment;
- the 15-25 year building or Kuznets cycle;
- the Kondratieff 48-60 year cycle.

Technology destroys old jobs and creates new ones. It is a key source of productivity growth. There are several relevant notions about technological progress. Schumpeter (1939) identified clusters of innovations that he argued have generated these long waves. Firstly, the Industrial Revolution of 1780-1842 was based on cotton textiles, iron and steam power. The second wave, called Bourgeois Kondratieff, was due to railroadisation. This wave lasted until 1897. The Neo-mercantilist Kondratieff of 1898 to 1940/45 was based on steam ships, gas and electricity. The Post War cycle was based on petrochemicals, electronics and the automobile. Massey (1979) described a process by which a regional-industrial character could evolve through innovation and rounds of investment.
- ➤ Long waves do not fit within broad macroeconomics as macro is essentially industry-neutral and makes no value-judgement about investment appraisal.

Building on the work of Perez (1983), Tylecote (1991) distinguishes three types of innovation:-

1. First, enabling technologies present new factors of production that are clearly cheap by existing standards, and are likely to become pervasive. These enabling technologies or *styles* are water, steam transport, steel and electricity, the Fordist style, and microelectronics and biotechnology. When the potential for further productivity growth is exhausted, each is superseded by the next, which Tylecote argued, took around 50 years. The innovation in enabling technologies provides the basis for developments in the other two.

2. The industries, such as electricity generation, that *make* the new factor should be distinguished from the second type of innovation. These industries *use* the new key factors. Chlorine and aluminium production are examples of industries that could ably exploit electricity generation. This second type of innovation precipitates a third type related to 'new' goods and services. The home computer can be seen as an innovation that exploits one of the technological drivers of the fifth long wave, microelectronics. This, in turn, formed the basis for a third type of innovation, the computer software industry. Products of the third type should have a high-income elasticity in the first instance, but become commodities as their life cycles mature.

3. The diffusion of a new style is characterised by new labour skills; new products; substantial expenditures on infrastructure projects and, importantly, new patterns of spatial exploitation and hence, competitive advantage. By implication, the competitive advantage of a company or region may be undermined by a change in *technological style* that could lead to the obsolescence of key products and processes.

The Small-Big Beast: Apple
As with the computer, the mobile phone is embedded in the fifth long wave. Although it began life literally as a phone that was portable as opposed to fixed wire, today, with innovation, the mobile smartphone is a minicomputer. It is a second type of innovation, whilst the enabling technology, microelectronics, drove companies to put down fibre-optic cable or mobile phone masts and substations.

In July 2009, the number of mobile phone connections reached 5bn: there were 3.3bn connections (½ the world) in November 2007. This astonishing growth has change the world's capacity connects to each other and to the internet. In 2009, there were 1.73bn with access to the internet. By December 2019, 4.57bn (59% of the world) were linked. There are places in Africa where you cannot get running water but you can stream a video. With its computers, by licence agreement, Apple software is only permitted to run on its hardware. The smartphone market, though, was dominated by Nokia (39%) but was destroyed by the Apple iPhone.

- The iPhone spawned the Apps industry. Apple alone has 9m software developers. A further industry followed, based on location. The driverless car will be dependent on the technology the mobile phone generated.

- The climax of the computer age, the peak of the dotcom bubble in the 1990s (March 2000) saw Tech companies worth 33% of all publicly traded companies. In 2018 we were back to 25%.

3D printing is thought to offer a major reduction is design and development costs. Take the example of a Ford engineer designing an intake manifold engine part. Using software, they could take 4 months at a cost of $500,000. 3D printing technology could reduce that to 4 days and $3,000. GKN is developing a metal printer that can reduce machining time for a titanium bracket from 4 hours to 40 minutes and cut material usage by 30%. Siemens predict that spare parts industry will change. Rather than storing parts, they can be made to order, close to the customer. Using conventional technology, a GM stainless steel seat bracket would require eight components and several suppliers. With 3D, it is 40% lighter and 20% stronger.

A Stitch in Time

Little has changed in the manufacture of T-shirts since the invention of the sewing machine. Mechanisation of the process can be seen in four stages: picking up the cloth; aligning it; sewing it; and disposing of the garment. Three of the four are not yet automated because of the flexible fabric with numerous tiny processes in their implementation.

The motivation for pushing for a sewbot - a robot sewing machine - relates to politics, logistics and just-in-time. Fashions are ephemeral; reducing lead times can provide a competitive advantage. Producing in the US, not only placates Donald Trump, but shortens delivery distances and time.

Levi Strauss is accelerating its use of lasers to automate the way its jeans are made. Lasers will finish a pair of jeans every 90 seconds, rather than two to three pairs an hour, currently. Levi uses overseas contractors to make the vast majority of its products. Reshoring is related, in part, to the faster fashion cycle utilised by low-cost, fast-fashion brands such as Zara and H&M. Akin to the lean/JIT seen in the car industry the combination of flexible machines and software the time-to-market will drop from six months from the start of the design cycle to weeks - even days in some cases. The number of steps involved in the finishing process - which used to involve hand sponging and sand papering wear patterns and other details onto the denim - will drop from 18 to 20 steps to around three.

Drones and Crawlers

Poland and South Africa to have fully developed regulations and laws permitting both unfettered commercial drone flights and flights that go beyond a visual line of sight. Non-military drones have enormous potential to both enhance and replace labour. A key area is height. Ladder climbing or dangling from ropes has risk implications. Also hard-to-reach locations, such as oil rigs, offshore wind farms or gas pipelines, involves time getting to the problem. The cost of a drone inspection of a wind turbine is roughly half the $1,500 cost of a human doing the same job. In 2017, BP, the largest operator in the US Gulf of Mexico, piloted Maggie, a magnetic crawler, which can move across rigs, platforms, and pipelines above and below water using ultrasonic test devices and high-definition cameras. A crawler can cost $60,000 or $600 to $1,000/ day, plus the operating technician to rent. Drones and crawlers can do inspections in about half the time of rope access technicians, while placing fewer workers in harm's way. The 2010 Deepwater Horizon rig explosion killed 11 people. Warehousing is further area of innovation. They are now the workhorses on-line that retailers rely on. Today's inventory management requires workers to scan items manually. A key area of improvement is in the misplaced items or faulty inventory records. Pinc, one of the firms offering aerial robots, claims almost 100% accuracy. For a warehouse that is 95% accurate, it means that 5% is ambiguous. So if the warehouse is storing $100m worth of inventory, $5m is uncertain.

A further factor is productivity. Argon Consulting argues that two drones can do the work of 100 humans over the same time period. Of course, they don't need the tea breaks and can work a 3 shift day. Whilst creating 10% more jobs in the field, automation technologies, including artificial intelligence, will replace 17% of US jobs by 2027 – a net loss of 7%. Automation reduces the demand for lesser qualified jobs whilst boosting the need for specialised skills within the logistics sector. Between October and April 2017, 89,000 shop workers were laid off.

The Internet and Disintermediation
Technology is leading to disintermediation that is the merchant traders that buy from farmers and sell to retailers. Archer Daniels Midland, Bunge, Cargill, and Louise Dreyfus (ABCD) had an information advantage which is waning. Market traders have access to satellites that can see crops. Farmers can observe market prices from the cabs of the self-driving tractors.

Estate agents are also information conduits that will be subject to disintermediation. To find a new markets agents in the UK (Gerald Eve) and (Cushman and Wakeman) the US are looking to long term advisory roles, moving from one-off fees. Large landlords such as British Land, do what agents used to do. For example, marketing campaigns, attend meetings with lawyers, and agree terms with tenants are now undertaken by in-house leasing teams. Agents must deliver complex transactions that are difficult to duplicate, including financial advice.

Nike in June 2017 announced a 1400 (2%) cut in jobs as part of a refocused strategy away from physical outlets to direct on-line sales. In part, this reflects a just-in-time approach, chasing fashions particularly in 12 global cities where 80% of sales growth is expected to come. Then again, it also will reduce its range by 25%. Ikea, like Nike, also announced that sales will shift more to on-line and away from out-of-town outlets.

Fisher/Clark
The Fisher/Clark thesis posits that manufactures can grow independently of agriculture, and services can grow independently of manufactures. Hence, the decline of manufacturing (deindustrialisation) may not be that significant. Historically,

deindustrialisation or at least the movement of resources from one sector to another is linked to rising prosperity rather than mass unemployment. The story of technological change is usually short-term pain for long-term gain at least for the economy overall. Take farming. Over the past 150 years the UK has lost 1.5m farming jobs while agricultural output has grown by

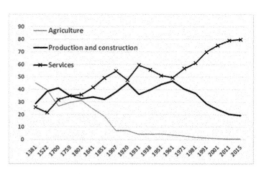

about 400%. From the figure above you can see the decline in the proportion of those that worked in farming from the 1841 Census in GB (22.35%) to 0.9% in England and Wales in 2011.

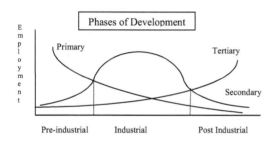

The Fisher/Clark is becoming problematic. Peak industry is occurring at lower per capital incomes and lower shares of total employment. Peak years are: Mexico, 1980; Brazil, 1986; India, 2002; UK, 1961; and US, 1953. The IMF noted that productivity growth linked to manufacturing, could be duplicated by the service sector. Globally, the share of manufacturing employment and output was stable for 50 years implying productivity improvements are not automatic. Performance in advanced economies was not improved by a shift from the secondary to tertiary sectors. Industrialisation was the route out of poverty for the developing nations, absorbing the great unskilled. This forms the basis for the creation of a middle class that values education. There needs to be a sector for these to join otherwise there will be very many well-educated disappointed young people. For example, with industrialisation, the first sector normally a country develops is textiles. Bangladesh's exports are made up of 82% clothes: this is generated by 2.5% of the population. Indeed 27m in the Indian subcontinent make textiles. Chinese factory wages in 2017 stood at $3.60/hr, similar to Portugal and South Africa. It was 5 × Indian wages. Although jobs are to be lost in the developed, it is the developing world that will be the big loser. Recently, 400 robots have replaced car workers in Chennai, in a labour abundant country. This could mean that the peak in manufacturing employment is much lower than ever before.

Bank of American Merrill Lynch estimated that 45% of all manufacturing jobs over the next 10 years would be replaced. UK employees on £30,000 or less are five times more likely to be replaced by artificial intelligence in the next 20 years than those paid in excess of £100,000. Take the IKEA flat pack chair. Nanyang Technological

University showed in 2018 that robots could assembled the frame of a dining chair in around 20 minutes. You could say it took three years designing and programming the robot (made of arms, grippers, sensors and 3D cameras). However, soon robots will fully assemble a piece of furniture from a manual, verbal instruction or by just looking at an image of the finished item.

Deindustrialisation also hits the service sector. In June 2016, Bank of America announced that up to 8,000 jobs out of 68,400 were to go from its back-office staff. In the previous 7 years 1,400 retail branch staff had gone. As this represented a quarter of the establishment, this was a significant shift.

The call centre can add to the productivity of the service sector. The standardisation of service sector jobs could reduce the costs of provision. This though does not resonate with all customers, who like the human touch. Another productivity increase in banking is the total mechanisation of a branch. As around 95% of branch activities could be mechanised, banks would become rather spartan affairs. Since 2010, transactions at branches have fallen by 30%. Both changes were a result of technological advances. Back-office processes can be digitised. Branches become less populated as banking goes mobile. Financial advice could be automated, with sophisticated decision-trees giving the customer relevant information about financial products. Indeed, this overcomes misselling incentives. That said BoA planned to increase sales and advisory staff to increase revenues. Citigroup CEO in February suggested possibly 10,000 jobs in its call centres could be replaced by AI. 30 of the most common customer journeys could be easily automated. That represents half of the jobs in that realm. Indeed, Citi suggested that route was better than joining with SunTrust-BB&T in a merger. In October 2017, the National Australia Bank announced 6,000 jobs were to go by 2020. This represented 18% of its full-time equivalent workforce. As with manufacturing the services sector is subject to productivity enhancing developments that costs jobs. In the eighties the ATM was introduced. This was followed by mass branch closures over the next three decades. Offshoring some functions led to more job losses as well as the rise of the apps and mobile banking. At the same time as these jobs are to go, NAB is to hire 2000 new people with digital skills: AI; robotics; and automation technologies.

Software robots will replace 4m back office jobs in the US by 2021. Forrester Research argued that routine work done by humans in front of computer screens, filling the gaps between fragmented systems, is more cost effectively done by computers themselves. Licence agreements costing $8-9,000/yr are cheaper than the equivalent 3-4 full time staff.

The Estimated Effect
In March 2017, PwC reported that around 10.4m jobs in the UK could be replaced by robots over the next 15 years. This is equivalent to 30% of those currently employed. With the advent of driverless vehicles Transportation and Storage is one of the most vulnerable sector where 56.4% of current jobs are soon to be replaced. This makes up

4.9% of all the jobs to go. Manufacturing will lose a further 1.22m jobs, comprising 7.6% of all jobs to be lost. 2.25m jobs will disappear in retail and wholesale as shops could become more like 'showrooms', where customers look at goods before buying them on-line. This would lead to more giant warehouses, such as Amazon's. The skill factor, as ever, is important. 12% of graduate degrees or higher are at risk whereas those with only GCSEs face a 46% chance of losing their jobs.

Frey and Osborne (2013) suggest the *safest jobs*: Recreational therapist; Healthcare social workers; Surgeons; Athletic trainers; Clergy; Foresters; Audiologists; Choreographers; Dentists; Farmers. *Most vulnerable*: Library technicians; Accounts clerks; Insurance underwriters; Maths technicians; Sewer workers; Telemarketers; Title examiners; Tax preparers; Cargo handlers; Watch repairers.

In Australia, a 2015 study from the Office of the Chief Economist found that 44% of Australian jobs were highly susceptible to automation, with telemarketers and bank workers at the top of the list. By contrast, the Asian Development Bank estimated that across 12 developing countries over 10 years to 2015, technology had destroyed 101m jobs whilst creating 134m.

		% of Industry Jobs	Jobs
Domestic personnel and self-subsistence	0.3%	8.1%	0.01m
Education	8.7%	8.5%	0.26
Human health and social work	12.4%	17.0%	0.73
Other services	2.7%	18.6%	0.17
Agriculture, forestry and fishing	1.1%	18.7%	0.07
Arts and entertainment	2.9%	22.3%	0.22
Mining and quarrying	0.2%	23.1%	0.01
Construction	6.4%	23.7%	0.52
Accommodation and food service	6.7%	25.5%	0.59
Professional, scientific and technical	8.8%	25.6%	0.78
Information and communication	4.1%	27.3%	0.39
Real estate	1.7%	28.2%	0.16
Electricity and gas supply	0.4%	31.8%	0.05
Public administration and defence	4.3%	32.1%	0.47
Financial and insurance	3.2%	32.2%	0.35
Administrative and support services	8.4%	37.4%	1.09
Retail and Wholesale	14.8%	44.0%	2.25
Manufacturing	7.6%	46.4%	1.22
Transportation and storage	4.9%	56.4%	0.95
Water, sewage and waste management	0.6%	62.6%	0.13
Total for all sectors	100%	30%	10.4m

In 2015, 38% of robots are found in the car industry (103,000 in 2016); 20% were in electronics (91,300); with chemicals plastics and metals making up a further 19%. Small firms are not well placed to use robots. Currently, it takes a lot of man-hours and money to service robots: the engineering can cost 3 to 8 times the hardware. Boston Consulting Group estimates that a human welder costs $25/hr. A robot has operating cost/hr $8. The extra cost of maintaining a robotics system be amortised over a five-year period.

In January 2019, Walmart announced that it would raise its starting wage to $11/hr, up by $2. As a result someone would be earning $22,000/yr. There will also be 10 weeks of maternity paid leave. The expected additional costs amounted to $700m/yr. As with the raising of minimum wage in the UK much of the benefit is likely to be lost as it would increase the incentive to automate.

Flexible Accumulation Abandoned?

The introduction of lean production in the US 1980s and much of the 1990s, caused major ructions in the car industry because they simply could not compete with low-cost, efficient, well-built Japanese cars. The approach is now standard in Strategic Management and Operations Management texts. However, for Honda, Toyota and Nissan, there have been a slew of recalls 2014 for problems with components such as airbags, sliding doors and engines. In 2018, for example, Honda recalled about 600,000 cars in China because when driven in cold weather sludge was collecting in the engines of six models while the sliding doors on its US. Odyssey minivans started opening while the vehicles were moving. In J.D. Power's study of vehicle dependability in the US, one of Honda's two main auto markets along with China, it dropped from 4th in 2002 to 5th in 2015 and 18th in 2019. Five quality blunders have helped squeeze the operating margin at its global automotive business to 2%-3% - hitting profits. Its motorcycle business had a margin of 13.9%.

At a two-day gathering in March 2019, Honda's CEO, Takahiro Hachigo, told their suppliers that it string of costly recalls and other quality blunders meant it needed to plot a new course, centralising decision-making at Honda's Tokyo headquarters. Its standalone R&D division was brought in-house and cutting some senior management roles. This should be followed by a simplification of the way Honda designs cars and put its engineering resources to more effective use at a time when it needs to develop cars for an electric age.

The localisation model, which accounts for 40% of sales meant that Honda created too many regional models, in addition to an array of types, options and derivatives for its global models creating a complexity of its vehicle range and all the associated engineering processes. The Accord sedan comes in 13 versions, including three hybrids. GM's Malibu has five.

Before, localization was central and the R&D unit was a key driver for innovation. In future, R&D will work closely with key departments, such as purchasing, manufacturing, quality assurance, and sales and marketing. The aim is to reduce engineers' workloads by about a third to free up time and resources for Honda's technical divisions to research technologies for the cars of the future. Besides the quality issues and engineering workload linked to the proliferation of regional models, the advent of new technologies requires Honda's big-spending technical division to act less independently. Suppliers were asked to help Honda slash its range of cars and dumb-down model-types and options including using more common parts, from engines and transmissions to door handles, rear view mirrors and knobs.

Deindustrialisation: The Adjustment Cost

IPPR suggested that the closure of a steel works will be similar to the collapse of employment in the pits. Tata employed 15,000 directly and a further 25,000 elsewhere. IPPR estimated that the cost to the exchequer in lost VAT, income tax and a rise in benefit payments would be £4.6bn. In October 2015, 2,200 Sahsviriya Steel Industry

UK employees and 1,000 contractors at the Redcar blast furnace and its steel slab-making plants lost their jobs. These were supported by a £80m government package: £30m for redundancy payments and £50m for retraining, business start-up grants, wage subsidies for employers taking on former steelworkers and support for Teesside businesses.

The decline in steel in Teesside is rapid. From 33,000 employed in 1980 what was left after Redcar was around 1,200. The task force managing the support had committed £14.5m to training and support for businesses and jobs. It had agreed 10,855 training courses for nearly 3,000 people and says 1,342 former SSI and supply chain workers have moved off benefits into full-time work or training. Also, 71 businesses started by former steelworkers. The number unemployed locally before the closure was 5,600; the collapse added a further 900. The wage that those employed earn is lower. Manual workers were on £33,000, plus overtime. An electrician could have been on twice the £20,000 a year for a current vacancy.

The Work Foundation and Birmingham Business School found that, following the collapse of MG Rover, 90% of the 200 people surveyed were in some form of employment within three years. Of the 6,300, about ⅓ of the workers had found new roles in manufacturing and were earning roughly the same as they had at MG Rover's Longbridge plant in Birmingham. But ⅔ were earning less, with the falls averaging £5,640 a year. Of the 60% that shifted from manufacturing to the service sector, most had suffered a pay fall, averaging over £6,000 a year. Almost one in four of the 200 interviewees then said they were theny in debt or drawing on their savings.

Fort, Pierce and Schott argued that Trump may be defending the wrong bit of manufacturing. Between 1977 and 2012 the number of US manufacturing jobs halved from 20m to 10m, but non-manufacturing plants that were owned by manufacturing firms increase employment from 13m to 25m. These jobs were IT and design. In other words, deindustrialisation occurred but within manufacturing firms.

The Spatial Dimension Analysed
In the Centre for Cities' Cities Outlook 2018 it suggests that automation and globalisation generate and destroy jobs in different parts of the country. It estimates that 20% of existing jobs in British cities are likely to be displaced by 2030 (3.6m jobs). In conjunction with Nesta, a consultancy, it projects that 53% of all jobs at risk in cities are just in five occupations, with Sales Assistance and Retail Cashiers making up a fifth of the total.

Significantly, however, this risk is not spread evenly across the country, with peripheral cities/regions in the North and Midlands more exposed to job losses than the more affluent cities in the South. Around 18% of jobs are under threat in Southern cities,

Share of jobs at risk in Cities	
Sales Assistance and retail cashiers	19.5%
Other Administrative Occupations	11%
Customer Service Occupations	9%
Administrative Occupations: finance	7%
Elementary Storage Occupations	6.6%

compared to 23% in cities elsewhere in the country. It considered the political dissatisfaction and divisions highlighted by the outcome of the EU referendum in 2016 that automation and globalisation would exacerbate. Top 3 British cities most at risk of job losses resulting from automation and globalisation are Sunderland, Wakefield and Mansfield. The least threatened were Hi-Tec and University cities.

THE LOCATIONAL CONVEYOR BELT

The Centre for Towns added yet more colour to the future of places debate. It reported in November 2017 that from 1981 to 2011 large towns and cities were in receipt of 3m of working age whilst medium towns and smaller settlements attracted 2.75m plus a further 2m over 64s. Only 30 years ago inner city populations that had grown rapidly in the late 19th and early 20th Centuries had dwindled. With a 10% increase on overage and some city centres doubling in size since the start of the 21st Century, the reversal that has taken place especially in the north of England and the Midlands. Centre for Cities reported in November that mapping from a notional city CBD centre Liverpool grew by 181% (9,100 to 25,600 people) between 2002 and 2015; Birmingham 163% (9,800 to 25,800); Leeds 150% (12,900 to 32,300), Bradford 146% (1,300 to 3,200); Manchester 149% (14,300 to 35,600) and London 22% (268,700 to 327,200).

The analysis in McCann (2013: p.125) suggests both denesters and young people should be dominant. The number of 20 to 29-year-olds in the centre of large cities (those with 550,000 people or more) tripled over 2001 to 2011, to comprise half of the population. Some are students, whose numbers grew with the expansion of university education, but the draw is high-skilled professional occupations, reflecting the growing importance of sectors like financial and legal services to the UK economy, supplying half of the cities' work and the short commute: 32% of city centre residents walk to work.

Change 1981-2011	Under 16	16 to 24	25 to 44	45 to 64	65 plus	Total	OAP/100	Dependency
Village	-172855	-145953	-123044	804394	566301	928843	61.0	73.5%
Community	-71209	-43335	63789	512481	389797	851523	45.8	59.8%
Small town	-171743	-90720	177206	763196	566096	1244035	45.5	46.4%
Medium town	-166440	-133746	333016	658194	445432	1136442	39.2	32.5%
Large town	-116690	48731	681024	538985	236534	1388584	17.0	9.4%
Core City	185053	120179	1461593	241939	-183048	1825716	-10.0	0.1%
Overall	513884	244844	2593584	3519175	2021112	7375143	22.7	39.9%

Housing, Communities and Local Government Committee found that as shopping habits change, city centres are in danger of becoming ghost towns. In 2018, the High Street lost 22,000 jobs. A fifth of UK retail sales now occur on-line with that proportion likely to grow. Amazon UK's rates, are about 0.7% of its UK turnover, while most High Street retailers pay 1.5-6.5%. The retail industry, the UK's largest private sector employer, makes up 5% of the economy and pays nearly 25% of the overall business rates bill, over £7bn/yr. To 'level the playing field' for High Street retailers taxes on on-line giants should be increased. This is not so far-fetched. In June 2018, the US Supreme court ruled that on-line retailers could have levies imposed on their sales even if they did not have a store in the jurisdiction of the tax-imposing body. This aligns the bricks and mortar with the virtual retailer reducing the cost advantage of the latter. That said, Core Insight reported 5730 stored closed in the US in 2018; but 5480 in 2019Q1 – perhaps a bit late.

Bill Grimsey in his second report into the future of town centres and High Streets in July 2018 made a different claim. 'Forget retail for town centres, they need to become community hubs based on health, education, entertainment, leisure and arts and crafts.' So much like the growth in cities, together with housing and some independent shops, facilities such as libraries and digital and health hubs should be part of the offering to bring back people to town centres. However, towns do not provide the same amenities or jobs as cities.

In fact there is a spatial conveyor belt. The young move to the cities in search of work, later, seeking a pleasant environment, they move out to commuter land and then retirement, possibly downsizing and extracting capital from their property but move to villages. The Centre for Towns argues that in 1981 the proportion of 65+ was similar at 23-26.3 per 100 of working age and was around that in 1991. From then on Core Cities have seen old age *dependency* ratios drop to below 20 with Large Towns at 22.5. Villages saw an increase to 35.6.

Of the 929,000 population increase in population in Villages, 61% was attributable to OAPs. The dependency on a working population that grew by 535,000 was partially offset by the decline in the number of school children. That said, the *change* in dependence divided by the *change* in the workforce =73.5%. In other words, for every 100 new residents 73 were not of working age. Core Cities gained youngsters as quickly as they lost OAPs.

CONSUMPTION AND DEBT

Resolution Foundation reported in July that UK's collective wealth - the value of our property, pensions and savings – in 2018/19 stood at £12.8tn. Of this 36% is property (£4.6tn) 42% (£5.3tn) are pensions and total value of Net financial wealth - savings, Isas, stocks and shares - was worth £1.6tn. The top decile is £670,000/ adult, the median is £105,000 and the bottom is negative due to debt. Those over 60-69 have wealth of £332,000. Those in their 80s have £186,000, 30s have £55,000 and 20s have £2,000 in wealth. The ONS reported that UK households are more likely to be borrowers than savers. The savings ratio in 2017Q1 at 3.7% was at its lowest annual level since 1963. Explanations include expectations of future interest rate rises; low time preference of money; and HH financial distress. Alternatively, one could suggest consumption smoothing.

Forward-Looking Consumption
The simple Keynesian consumption function links consumption expenditure with current disposable income. Forward-looking expectations models of income posit that

consumers maintain a stable consumption pattern, altering expenditure not with transitory income changes, but if they are viewed as being permanent. Friedman's *permanent income* and Modigliani's *life cycle hypotheses* posit that consumption is smoothed relative to income. Gordon defines permanent income as the average annual income that is expected to be received over a period of years in the future. Consumption is a function of permanent income $C = kY^P$, where C is consumption and Y^P is permanent income. With a permanent income hypothesis there is no explicit horizon to this forward planning: the horizon is beyond the current. Modigliani's life-cycle model posits consumption is based on the present value of total resources that the household accrues over a lifetime, suggesting a life time budget constraint and that the value of assets directly affect consumption behaviour.

A Perfect Capital Market
Means emerge, such as hire-purchase arrangements and mortgages, of facilitating the inter-temporal mismatch between accumulating the necessary funds and purchases. A perfect capital market permits the borrower to borrow against the future value of their income or property, negating the need to forego current consumption to accumulate wealth prior to purchase.

Life Cycle Consumption Smoothing
Adair Turner estimates that only 15% of bank lending is for entrepreneurial projects where wealth is created. The remaining 85% goes towards smoothing lifestyle consumption funding (corporate assets, real estate or unsecured personal finance). This is consistent with the above. Campbell and Mankiw argue that a relaxation of financial constraints allows consumers to behave as the permanent income hypothesis suggests. With the abandoning of the special deposit scheme in 1980 and the Building Society Act 1985 plus banks entering the mortgage market in a major way in mid-1981, there was a massive restructuring of the character of debt. Debt became far more commonplace. Over the past 50 years, private credit/GDP has doubled to 200%. More rapidly, household debt in China, Turkey, Singapore, Thailand and Brazil has increased by more than 40% since 2008. Institute of International Finance estimated that as of September 2008 global debt ratio was 214%; by June 2014 it was 245%; and 325% in 2016). Total debt grew by $70tn in the 10 years to 2016 to $215tn.

Turner, though, makes a fair point with house purchases. The funding of house purchase can be associated with construction, but commonly is not. He concludes that the productivity of money has fallen. Increasing money supply has not led to an increase in total productivity.

Life cycle effects concern such phenomena as expenditure related to family composition, where more is spent on a larger membership and maturing children. An employment career captures the notion of a progression, where seniority, responsibilities and salary rise with time. Thus, as the household [head] ages, income rises. However, income peaks when the head is in their fifties and sixties. Following this there is a decline in income, which, perhaps, coincides with retirement.

Fernández-Villaverde and Krueger plot the lifetime profile of expenditure, which turns out to be an inverted-*U* shape.

Income, consumption and wealth over a life time are modelled below. The wobble represents the business cycle over which consumption can be smoothed. The current arrangement shows someone that earns over a 40-year career and dissaves from the assets when they retire until they die at 80. Income rises and then falls. The sum of all saving equals wealth. Notice:

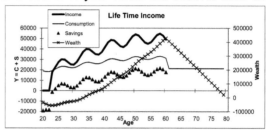

- ❏ so that consumption at aged 70 could be broadly in line with that at 40, the enormous stock of wealth that must be accumulated. The longer people live, the more they MUST save (or pay higher taxes);
- ❏ if there is any smoothing the MPC is possibly tiny, so Keynes' multiplier falls apart;
- ❏ a change in government expenditure could results in changes in savings only;
- ❏ if the income profile is as shown, why not borrow from your future income?

The IFS reported in June 2018 that, contrary to fears and theory, pensioners were too cautious about their wealth. Rather than depleting their wealth to zero (the LCH view), those between 70 and 90 had 69% of their wealth intact. The wealthier half of that group used only 61%. Pension freedoms, like pensions themselves, may only be a stark problem for a minority.

Debt is an emotive subject. Krugman disparages those who claim that, in future we are impoverished by the need to pay back money we've been borrowing. He suggests that using a family finance analogy where the mortgage must be paid in good and bad times otherwise the family home will be repossessed is poor in at least two ways:

1. Families have to pay back their debt. Governments do not. They just need to be able to services the debt ensuring it grows more slowly than the tax base to service it. Taxes are a lot less dramatic than the interest payment analogy;

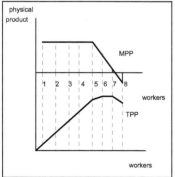

2. An over-borrowed family owes money to someone else, whereas sovereign debt is, to a large extent, money the State owes its citizens. He concedes that foreigners now hold large claims on the US, including sovereign debt. But there are US claims on overseas assets that almost off-set this, with higher yields.

LABOUR DEMAND

A profit maximising firm will, using marginal analysis, employ someone when the marginal benefits are greater than or equal to the marginal costs.

Let us then consider what will determine the amount that increased employment of labour adds to a firm's total revenue. Labour has a derived demand; labour will only be demanded to produce extra output. The marginal product (marginal physical product MPP_L) is the physical additional to total output that results from employment an extra unit of labour. The value of this additional output is the marginal revenue the output sold × the amount produced. In a perfect market, this marginal revenue is the price. The extra revenue generated following the employment of marginal unit of labour is the marginal revenue product of labour (MRP_L). This is the demand for labour.

MRP_L or the value of the marginal product = $MPP_L \times MR\ (P)$

In the case on the below, worker 2 contributes the same amount to output as worker 1. So does 3, 4, and 5. Worker 6 adds less to total output than worker 5. Worker 7 adds less than worker 6 and employing worker 8 leads to a reduction of total output. More formally, if one combines an increasing greater quantity of factors together, with at least one of them being fixed, then after a certain point, diminishing marginal returns will set in.

The firm's short-run marginal cost curve will follow directly from the Law of Diminishing Marginal Returns. Taking the farm example, assume that labour is the only variable input and that each unit receives the same wage. The first unit receives his/her wage in return for his/her unit of output. This wage is the marginal cost of production. We have assumed that so long as each unit of labour has enough room they will be equally productive. Each unit of production will have a marginal cost of one wage. The next unit of labour will not produce the much as the previous one, but s/he will still receive the same wage. Thus, that will mean that whereas previously the entrepreneur paid a wage for a unit of output, now s/he pays a wage and his/her return is less than a unit of output. The full cost of that unit of output will be more than a wage i.e. the marginal cost has increased. The next unit of labour employed will also produce a lower return for his/her wage than the last. The equivalent marginal cost will be even higher. Thus, it is clear that the LDMR directly leads to the firms marginal cost curve.

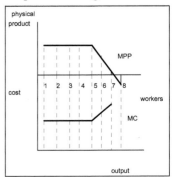

In the diagram right, assume worker 1 produces one unit of output and is paid £1. Therefore the cost of the first unit of output is £1. The return from employing the second worker is also 1 unit, s/he is paid £1 so the MC of the second unit of output is £1. This applies to the 3rd, 4th and 5th unit of output. When DMR set in the farmer pays the 6th worker £1 but in return the total output increases by less than one unit. Thus, to produce the 6th unit of output the farmer has to employ the 6th and part of the 7th worker's time. As both receive £1 the MC of the 6th unit of output is more than £1 i.e. the MC curve is upward sloping.

With $= W = MPP_L \times P$, $MPP_L = W \div P$, the real wage is related to productivity. In the long-run the farmer can vary all inputs. The farmer can then decide the best combination of factors to suit. This decision is determined by the MPP of the factor and its price relative to other factors. Thus, the following holds:-

$$MPP_L \div P_L = MPP_{Cap} \div P_{Cap} = MPP_{Land} \div P_{Land}$$

If factor A's price increased, say the price of labour, the farmer could do two things: 1) Produce less; 2) Substitute more of factors B and C for A. That is, use more land and or capital. As s/he brings in extra units of B and C s/he finds that each will add less to total product or output than before i.e. MPP falls and as the farmer employs less labour s/he moves back up the MPP_L curve of A, i.e. MPP_L increases. This process of substitution continues until equilibrium is achieved. This combining may be limited by the ability of the farmer to vary all inputs. In the long run, all factors are variable, but in the short-run one or more factors may be fixed. Important features of production, such as factory size are fixed over a short period. The scope to fund an expansion of the factors could be limited by the land available.

As $MC = P$, $MC = W \div MPP_L$ The (competitive) firm hires labour up to the point where $MC = MR$ and where $MRP = W$.

The MRP curve is the DEMAND CURVE FOR LABOUR. It describes quantity of labour to employ at every given return to the entrepreneur. It can *shift* when the price of the final product changes; the productivity of labour alters (i.e. the MPP shifts); or there is an increase in demand for the final product and so a need for a greater labour force.

The industry demand for labour curve will be an amalgam of the firms' demand for labour curves but with a slight alteration. As the wage falls the employer will employ more workers and produce more output. Because the firm is small this increase in output will not affect the market price. On the other hand, if all firms increase output, the market price will fall, so

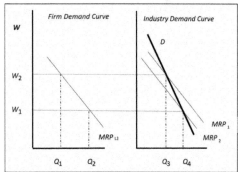

shifting each firms MRP curve to the left (MRP_1 to MRP_2). Thus, the industry's demand curve will be steeper than the individual firms' curves. The industry demand curve is labelled D.

The elasticity of demand for labour will be high if:-

- The price elasticity of the final product is high. If the price falls, there will a shift in the labour demand curve to the left, leading to a lower wage and smaller working labour force. However, a fall in the price of the good will lead to an increase in demand for it, and consequently, an increase in the demand for labour. If the latter effect outweighs the former, employment will rise. If the former outweighs the latter, employment will fall. The magnitude of the latter effect depends on the price elasticity of the product.
- The greater the proportion of total cost that is due to labour, the more sensitive total employment will be to a change in wages. This is key for food retail and care homes.
- The elasticity of demand for factors will depend on the elasticity of supply of complementary and substitute factors. If the wage falls, the increase in total employment will depend on the likely effect on the price of complements and substitutes given this will shift the demand curve for them, the former upwards and the latter downwards. With an increase in demand for complements, if their price rises significantly, this will severely constrain the increase in the size of the work force. With a decrease in demand for substitutes, if their price falls significantly, this will severely strain the increase in the size of the work force.
- The easier it is to substitute other factors for labour, and vice-versa, the greater the elasticity of demand for labour. If it is easy, any increase in wages will lead to the substitution of other factors for labour and a fall in the labour force. The scope for substitution will increase with TIME. The greater the time period you look at, the greater the elasticity of demand for labour.

LABOUR SUPPLY

The supply of labour is generally examined at three levels

- the individual,
- the occupation
- the industry

The Individual Supply Curve

The individual has a set amount of time to divide between earning money and leisure. There is a trade-off. To earn more money s/he must give up, or substitute leisure time. One is the opportunity cost of the other. S/he can choose the length of time s/he works and so selects his/her combination of work and leisure time on the basis of the wage rate offered, how s/he values his/her leisure time, and how arduous the work is.

In the diagram above, *Wr* is the *Reservation Wage*, he wage at which they are enticed into offering themselves on the labour market. Below this wage it is felt to be not worth his/her while working. The reservation wage will be related to the worker's non-working income. For example, if the worker receives £80 on the JSA and £90 working, the compensation of an extra £10 for a week's toil may not be enough. Indeed, the earning of money may lead to a loss of certain incomes from the State that makes the worker worse off. This is known as the poverty trap. The non-working income also relates to interest from capital for the leisured classes.

As the rate rises, the opportunity cost of not working rises. The worker will select a combination such that the opportunity cost of working is opportunity cost of not working. Thus, the worker will give up more leisure time the greater the wage rate, and consequently, s/he has an upward sloping supply curve. This is only true up to a certain point. There are two factors to the workers' earnings. Firstly, there is the wage rate and, secondly, the number of hours worked. As the worker works more hours, the amount of time left to enjoy his/her earnings decreases. After a certain wage rate s/he will find that the cost of offering more work time given an increase above that rate will be greater than the benefit. Why is this? His/her income is such that s/he has an acceptable standard of living this will alter his/her perception of the benefit of working more hours. Also, s/he has a relatively small number of leisure hours and so his/her opportunity cost of leisure will be high. With an increase in the wage rate the perceived costs of working longer hours will exceed the benefits and the worker will substitute leisure for work time. We can say that an *income effect,* or the urge to offer more work time given a higher wage rate is greater than the substitution of leisure for income up to a certain wage rate then the *substitution effect* is greater than the income. Thus, the supply curve of the individual is backward bending after a certain point.

The *Industry Supply Curve* is the horizontal summation of the individual supply curves at every given wage.

The Supply Curve will shift with

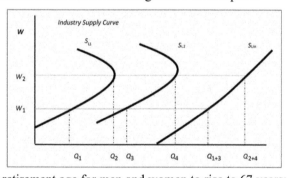

- A change in the size of the working population. This includes raising school leaving age, 16 to 18 years, retirement age for men and women to rise to 67 years; immigration.
- Institutional factors - length of working week, holidays, participation rate (proportion of potential work force working or actively seeking work) which is affected by level of unemployment benefits relative to wage levels and social attitudes e.g. towards women.
- Conditions of service affect the participation rate. Certain jobs may be less palatable than others. This will include working in arduous conditions, anti-social hours, more risky or dangerous, difficult or time consuming travelling to get to. These factors will lead to a smaller labour supply than otherwise, e.g. day vs. night, safe vs. hazardous, pleasant vs. unpleasant working environments.

- Unearned income:- savings, benefits. If Universal Credit is cut, the reservation wages of those not seeking work will be reduced. As a result, some will begin actively looking for work. This has the effect of shifting the industry supply curve to the right, leading to a lower market wage but more labourers in work.
- Market access:- academic, occupational.

Elasticity of supply of labour
The elasticity of the supply of labour is a measure of increase in labour services offered due to a unit increase in the wage paid. It will depend on the factors discussed above. That is labour will be more elastic the cheaper it is to travel to work, relocate home, train for the job, and the better knowledge about the available jobs around. In common with other discussions of supply TIME will affect the elasticity. In the very short-run labour is almost completely immobile. Over a slightly longer period it can move house and job. Over generations a mine worker's offspring can become a doctor.

Total supply of labour is not perfectly inelastic as higher wages will supply e.g. retired, students, married women. The supply of labour to a single industry will be relative elastic as an increase in an industry's wage rate will induce some workers to transfer from other industries. In the short-run, barriers to entry will exist.

The occupational supply curve is based on the notion that there are barriers to entry or labour is immobile between occupations. Occupational immobility can be due to the talents necessary to do the job. These will include high levels of intelligence- to be a mathematics professor, strength- to work in the building trade, and skill- to be a surgeon. This will limit the number of possible workers. Many occupations require long training periods, during which time the trainee may have to be supported by their family. This will deter an individual that wishes to leave one occupation and train for another.

There are a number of occupations that require some financial outlay to enter, such as buying into a solicitors' partnership or funding a small business. Capital requirements will also limit the supply of workers to an industry.

The market supply curve is based on both the occupational supply with the added dimension of geographical mobility. Labour immobility can be analysed under monetary cost and psychic cost. The monetary cost refers to the expenses involved in moving belongings between abodes, and in the case of the home owner, the cost of selling one house and buying another. This in particular can prove to be a major barrier, especially when related to the co-ordination of selling the old one, buying the new one and the start of the new job. There has been a great deal of interest in the difficulty encountered by the low paid or unemployed worker, living in Council accommodation, who wishes to move areas to find acceptable work. The Council accommodation is generally allocated on the basis of a waiting list plus priority for needy cases. Because they moved to find work, finding themselves homeless, a person would not be seen as a needy case. The recent changes in welfare policy have altered this. Social Housing Associations are being encouraged to assist in the process to find work. A standard conclusion is that Council accommodation severely constrains mobility.

The psychic costs of relocating relates to the need to acquire new friends, local shopping knowledge, a new school for the children, a new job for the spouse. Generally, the needs of the children at important times in their educational careers will leave many couples immobile between areas.

The location of the job may be some way from an appropriate workforce. This causes two problems: 1) the compensation needed to encourage workers to commute fair distances; 2) the compensation needed to encourage people to move house to that area. These compensations will be mirrored in their reservation wages.

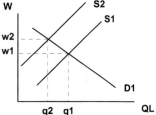

Wage differentials between occupations and regions can be explained under market and non-market headings. The market explanation revolves around market supply and demand conditions with barriers to entry.

Given the same market demand curve, the wage will be higher the further to the left the supply curve is shifted. Let us begin from a state of no barriers. There is a single labour market and all jobs are equally arduous. The wage will be the same for all workers whose reservation wage is covered. If we introduce arduousness or danger, this will raise workers' reservation wage, shifting the supply curve to the left as workers will have to be compensated for the added risk.

If the skill factor required was relatively rare this would limit the numbers who could qualify for the job. The same would be true if the skill factor was attainable by many but the training period was long, hard and expensive.

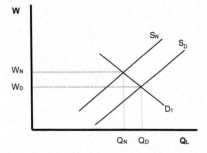

The diagram right shows why there is a market premium for (n)ight work compared with (d)ay shift ($w_n - w_d$). The ONS estimate that 70,000 people now work mainly nights in the UK retail sector, which makes up 3% of the workforce. According to 5 Live Money the number has gone up 50% between 2007 and 2017, women by 77%. Shopping habit changed. Supermarkets, such as Tesco, open 24-seven in some stores, although this is declining. On-line shopping and delivery within 24 hours particularly on-line grocery shopping drives shift-working patterns.

Not everyone will work unsocial hours. However, removing that night premium whilst boosting the basic rate will lead to excessive numbers wanting day shift work; more than there is work, perhaps, as illustrated in the diagram below, lower (QD – QN). Not enough will be happy with night shift, leading to some non-market rewards perhaps.

Hazardous Pay

Walmart on 19th March announced it was to hire 150,000 hourly associates in the US and would pay $550m in cash bonuses to reward workers. Amazon on 21st raised overtime pay for associates working in its US warehouses from March 15 through to May 9. Hourly workers at warehouses would receive $2\times$ pay after 40hrs, up from the $1.5\times$. Two days later it raised minimum hourly rate for associates to $17 from $15 and announced plans to hire 100,000 warehouse and delivery workers in the United States as the

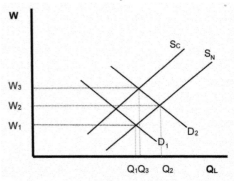

virus outbreak boosts on-line orders. However, the opportunity cost is odd. Amazon offered unlimited unpaid time off to encourage employees to stay home if they do not feel well. Let's consider this Original situation in the diagram above is W_1Q_1. The increase in deliveries shifts the demand curve to the right. However, the supply of workers in a period of the Corona virus (S_C) would be less than otherwise (S_N). Greater incentives need to be offered, so that rather the wage rising to W_2 the rate has to rise to W_3 and that has little impact on numbers.

In Japan, the night shift is difficult to staff whilst not raising wages, so firms don't open at night or operate more family friendly policies. If there are 1.59 jobs for every applicant, but wages will not rise, then vacancies go unfilled. This record occurred in February 2018, the highest value since 1990. Unemployment stood at 2.8%. The value for part time work in April 2017 was 1.77. In contrast to the UK, Japan is keen to invite immigrants in. In 2012, there were 682,000 foreign workers. By 2017, 1,279,000 were in Japan, the increase representing about 20% of the total expansion of the workforce.

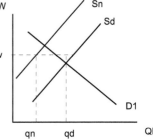

An interesting twist in this wage debate is the outcome for some lower paid workers is that the stagnant wages force them to take a second job. Take home pay may be the same as in 1997, but hours are up by 11%. In 2018, around 7.44m worked at least two jobs (11% of the workforce) up from 5.33m in 2015. Although this is behind the US (around 20%) it is a notable shift in Japan, related to labour reforms. It could be a gig economy thing, yet nearly half of Japanese workers with two jobs are over 50.

Below is analysis of the impact of common wages on different labour markets. Assume there is a market in universities for lecturing staff. The current wage for Marketing and History lecturers is W_1. At this wage there are Q_{D1} Marketing staff (left-hand side) and Q_{S1} History staff. Students switch from History to Marketing leading to an excess demand for Marketing $Q_{D2} - Q_{D1}$ and an excess supply of

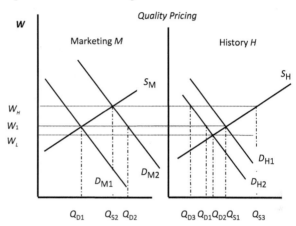

History staff $Q_{S1} - Q_{D1}$. If the wage rate was allowed to fall to W_L in History and rise to W_H in Marketing, this would remove the excess. As work is of comparable worth, both groups could be paid W_H but excess supply of History staff of $Q_{D3} - Q_{S3}$. A solution could be to keep the wage the same but alter quality standards. Allow poorer quality Marketeers in but set greater expectations of Historians. This would undermine the work of equivalent merit argument – the staff are not. We conclude from this that the value of the work done cannot be viewed independently from the market conditions which produced that work. In the long run, lecturers retrain to become Marketing staff.

Gender Pay and the Courts
In 2017, the employment appeal tribunal upheld a ruling that workers in roles across the shop floor can compare their jobs with those done predominantly by men for a higher wage in Asda's warehouses. Typically, the gap was £1-3/hr. With unskilled work, workers should switch from tills to warehouse work, driving wages together. If there is no movement, the markets are separate and so there is a pay differential. From the lecturer discussion above, work is of comparable *worth*. The outcome is equal pay - not market clearing in both markets. For equal pay to correspond to market clearing, $MPP_T \div W_T = MPP_W \div W_W$: the productivity of till work (T) and warehouse work (W) should also be equal. If supply does not drive the wages together, a common cost of capital could. If it is easier to substitute in capital in till work than warehouse work, the wage rates could be different. Otherwise, the number of jobs lost due to automation would be greater for till work.

The Labour of Robots

In labour economics, what we teach is that if the labour market is becoming tight, such that there is pressure on wages, we move along the supply curve and wages are bid up. However, in the long-run an alternative model is used, concerning price. If the price of labour rises relative to capital there is a substitution of capital for labour. In effect, labour is replaced by machines. Depending on the sector, the outcome is to accelerate the use of robots. Take farming. With global satellite positioning, robots can plant, fertilise and now harvest some produce. Importantly, for an aging farming population, it could drive tractors. Japanese farmers, average age 67, are looking to the driverless tractor to extend their working lives. Estimated to cost 50% more than conventional vehicles, like driverless heavy vehicles, the autonomous tractors could work alongside piloted ones. Uneven surfaces and steep fields make complete autonomy more challenging for tractors relative to trucks and cars.

Poland lives in the shadow of Europe, bleeding outmigration. Two trends can be observed. First, the rising wages is attracting migrants from neighbouring Ukraine. Around 1-2m from the Ukraine work in Poland, morphing from guest workers to important customers. They also affect BoP, with remittances of zl11.7bn in 2017. Second, this low wage country is turning to robots. With 42 robots per 10,000 workers, it lags Hungary (84) and the Czech Rep. (135).

THE COORDINATION PROBLEM

The coordination problem entails the arrangement of groups of individuals with dissimilar goals in to a team with common goals. If uncontrolled, individuals will pursue personal objectives that may conflict with team goals. Thus, activity that requires collective behaviour requires the coordination of individuals. To subvert self-interest, co-operate or working interdependently requires an exchange of some sort: an individual must accept some satisfactory compensation. Moreover, a contract-specific task can be complex, mutually dependent and expensive to draw up. The individual contracting, coordinating and monitoring has *bounded rationality*. There is a limit to the entrepreneur's capability to envisage all possible problems associated with an array of contracts to perform a complex task. In general, it is possible that the risk of making an adverse selection will deter the information-poor party, whether they are a potential buyer, supplier or employer, from forging a contract with the information-rich party.

What are transactions cost problems?

An example of a contractual world in the news is insurance. Confused.com found that motor insurance premiums had risen from around £500 to £800 in the 4 years to June 2012. The industry provides its members with incentives to boost fees, which are ultimately paid by the culprit's insurer. Oddly, rather than acting collectively, the insurers bulk up the charges they levy on each other. A particular concern is the referral fee for injury claims.

Volkswagen withheld a payment of €385,474 over a dispute about €76.33. CarTrim and ES Automobilguss refused to deliver parts as a result. If production was brought to a holt it would cost €100m/week in profit. VW's relationship with the two soured after it commissioned CarTrim to develop new seat covers for high-end models and then cancelled the €500m deal in the aftermath of the diesel scandal, refusing to cover the €58m its suppliers had already invested. After 6 days, VW paid compensation of €13m. This shows *asset specificity* and weak negotiating position issues. These are strange ones to mention where JIT is prevalent.

A most awkward area with *opportunism* is the role of the financier when the business is close to failure. The business, by virtue of its dependence on the financier for forbearance, is an agent of the bank. Through access to the enfeebled business' books, the financier is in an unusual monopoly position, not subject to *asymmetric information*. The moral hazard is that it can force the business into receivership and acquire the business's assets on the cheap. RBS' Global Restructuring Group post 2008 was found by Promontory, a financial consultancy, to mistreat small businesses systemically. In other words, it was policy. Focusing on 207 of the 5,900 handled between 2008 and 2013, 86% were mistreated. Staff were coached in methods to extract fees and interest income from businesses that had already defaulted on loans.

Principal and Agent
Productivity is, in neo-classical terms, linked to [human] capital and incentives. Heterogeneity of the workforce and imperfect information are assumptions that lead to some practical realities:

- Workers differ in commitment and attitude, so their productivity is difficult to assess before appointment and often difficult to observe after;
- Productivity of a worker varies over time with a given level of human capital;
- Productivity per unit time is a function of innate ability, effort and the environment;
- Being highly productive can involve not following directives but acting on initiative.

The labour contract is split into two elements: Formal and Implicit. The former entails modes of direction and activity, and monitoring is often laid out: what is expected of the employee. These are challengeable in court. The textbook states that, as agents of the owners (shareholders), managers should seek to maximise shareholder value. The monitoring or oversight exercise by shareholders (principals) over their agents, the managers is often questioned. Specialisation is expected to improve productivity. Workers must be observed or monitored to prevent *shirking*. If this means that the worker moves beyond the monitoring capacity of their supervisor, the employer is forced to resort to other tactics to avoid opportunism. As monitoring and measurement can now be done by sophisticated machines or cameras, this observation may be virtual. GPS allows Deliveroo to monitor the performance of their couriers. Worksnaps will send regular screenshots from contractees' computers to contractors so they can check they are on track. Platforms, such as PeoplePerHour, allow entrepreneurs to address *monitoring* so that tasks can be auction to workers that may never meet their paymaster. The adverse selection is addressed by quality ratings from previous jobs.

Incentive schemes for workers can induce moral hazards: workers could behave badly where there is information asymmetry. In a drive to meet sales targets, between May 2011 and July 2015, 2m bank accounts or credit cards were opened or applied for by Wells Fargo employees without customers' knowledge or permission. Employees were trying to sell enough bank products just to keep their jobs. They were supposed to generate seven new chequing accounts and 42 other products every single day while making 100 phone calls each. Wells Fargo terminated 5,300 employees (about 1% of the workforce) in relation to the allegations. The bank was fined $185m; the CEO, John Stumpf, in September 2016, offered to forfeit $41m in bonuses; and in April 2017 $142m was offered to customers for fees and damage to their credit scores. In April 2018, it was further fined $1bn. The New City Agenda estimated that the 10 largest misconduct scandals cost UK banks and building societies £53bn in fines and other penalties, with PPI costing £37.3bn. Citibank was fined $425m as it employed Tom Hayes knowing he was a LIBOR manipulator and continued to do so whilst at Citi. The CFTC alleged that Citi was influenced by the possibility of $50-$150m profit from him.

Union Asset Management, based in Frankfurt, has found that litigation is a good tool to keep agents in line, suing Equifax over its cyber security breach in 2017 affecting 143m people in Georgia federal court. In May 2018, a class action lawsuit in the District Court in California alleged that the Wells Fargo made certain misstatements and omissions in disclosures related to its sales practices. The bank agreed to pay $480m to investors who bought stocks between February 2014 and September 2016.

Business Structures
Coase argued that one solution to transactions costs is the firm. The firm can be viewed as a nexus of labour contracts that are made loose and open-ended. Rather than specifying in a contract for each task or project for each artisan each day, the worker signs an incomplete contract. Workers are engaged on a 'permanent' basis and 'directed' by a supervisor to tasks that can vary from day-to-day. In other words, the contract is not task specific.

Coase addresses the bounded rationality problem, but what of opportunism, what stops the monitor behaving badly? From a Principal-Agent perspective, the owner is the ultimate monitor. For them the incentive to monitor is the profit. Everyone else receives a wage. Williamson, who took this further, suggested the monitoring problem where a team is involved will generate a *hierarchy* of bureaucracy. Assume that the owner or any other monitor can at best observe 4 people effectively. Once the business grows to 5 employees monitoring becomes less effective a deterring opportunism. By the time the business gets to 8 employees, the owner could employ another monitor. Indeed, there remains the opportunism of the employee-monitor. The owner could employ two monitors, and the owner monitors the monitors. The business could expand on this basis. With 64 workers there are four tiers. From this one can see how a management hierarchy can evolve. Interestingly, in this version all monitors could be paid the same. They are only observing/coordinating.

	Control	Flexibility
Internal Focus/ Integration	Hierarchy	Clan
External Focus/ Differentiation	Market	Adhocracy

In Economics we envisage two routes to resolving the coordination problem: market and hierarchy. The market entails drawing up the design before construction begins. However, in the table above, reflecting Mintzberg there are four resolutions to the coordination problem: the problem of organising people/workers to generate output.

To avoid opportunism, artisans are given formal, clear detailed, legally enforceable, written contracts. As mistakes happen, in this scenario all parties benefit from shifting risk; someone else carries the potential losses. One can see this issue with group of student renting a house from a landlord. Should the contract be signed by all and collectively they rent the house, or should there be individual lets? From the landlord's perspective, the former is better as the students must bear the risk of non-payment by one. Correspondingly, the latter would reduce the risk exposure of the student. There is no risk sharing. Here, the others could hold one party hostage on a job, but assuming repeat business, the 'cheat' will not be reemployed. But if there is low trust, the artisan may not see repeat business following and so behave **opportunistically**. This model works well where output is clearly associated with an individual entity. Measurement of output then is the mode of monitoring, reducing the scope for opportunism. However, this may only apply when the output is simple.

One dimension focuses on control. In the *market*, control comes through the contract. In *hierarchies* coordination and control comes from the supervision of the manager or principal. Output is a team effort, with no one entity being distinctive. Here a supervisor coordinates and monitors the team to address the problem of opportunism. Where the team member shirks, they run the risk of being fired. Monitoring can be becoming cheaper. Rewards are structured to encourage long-term relations, so that pay increments are based on years of service. The 'promise' of promotion will maintain the worker's motivation. So that there is long association, the wage is below what is merited in the early years and is over paid in the latter years. In effect, the MRP of an individual should reflect their wage in the long run.

A hierarchy fails when there is excessive ambiguity on performance evaluation. That is, a monitor cannot judge the quality of work. Under these circumstances an alternative mode of coordination is needed. Ouchi suggests the **clan** mode, which is based on self-control, is a solution. The opportunism that the expert can exploit is overcome through a *professional code of ethics*. The coordination problem, suppression of self-interest and the pursuit of congruent objectives, is achieved through socialisation. Here, the worker is pre-trained where traditions, customs, and a common way of thinking are inculcated into the worker. There is tight screening.

Performance monitoring is not possible so, as in a high trust world colleagues are left to self-manage. Clearly, a rogue partner/ employee could take advantage of this light touch regime.

A further business form is the adhocracy. Minzberg and Quinn (1991) outline two forms of adhocracy: the administrative and the operating adhocracy. At their core is a structure to deal with a rapidly changing environment. The structure is highly flexible, loosely coupled, and amenable to frequent change, where problems exist in highly complex and turbulent environments. Adhocracy comprises highly trained technical experts in teams that are fairly fluid. Examples include high-technology firms where being leading-edge with technologies and strategies that must be developed to respond quickly and effectively.

The notion of insurance has its heart hold a moral hazard. By sharing the risk of what you do with others, so they bear some of the cost, you are more reckless. By taking out a loan where you can default, it encourages you to borrow too much. Indeed, the recklessness during an asset price bubble is based on this risk sharing with banks. However, banks and other businesses also share risk. The notion of too big to fail is much of a focus for the BoE. But then without this insurance some socially desireable activity will not take place. A classic example is the entrepreneur. Although that are risk neutral in theory. In practice, the punishment for failure should not out-way the benefits of the pursuit of profit. Here, through the drift from entrepreneur to the corporation and the institution of limited liability proffers variation of that social contract. If corporates only exist because they are useful social instruments, the way they are managed shows a break or the social contract. Profits and management salaries are disproportionally large and wages correspondingly small. The distribution of tax and dividends is equally problematic. One can see why the populist movements believe that their supporters feel short-changed. What is ironic is that the nationalism associated with it is commonly about aliens when actually, it is their elite that has exploited them.

The Labour Arrangement – What is Self-Employment?
There are three types of employment status:
1. an employee, who enjoys the full range of employment rights;
2. a worker, who has less protection but is still entitled to the minimum wage and some other basic rights;
3. a self-employed person.
Platforms that represents a neo-classical labour exchange have been estimated by McKinsey Global Institute in the US, could add 72m full-time equivalent jobs or 2% to global output by 2025. According to the Freelance Union in the US there are 53m freelance workers, including 21m independent contractors.

Relations can be seen in principal-agent or transactions costs terms. A firm is viewed as a collection of loose contracts where the employee, in return for accepting direction, is given incentives such as permanence and stable income. From a Williamson hierarchy perspective, this is likely because production involves a team that needs coordinating on an ad-hoc basis and no single contribution can be assessed. In Coase/Williamson's world there is a trade-off between control and security. In forgoing free-will and accepting direction, the 'employee' (type 1) is given security. The employer accepts the responsibility of finding work to do and the risk of failing to do that. The obverse is the sub-contractor (3) who is contracted for specific tasks but the contract is the 'director' of effort, not an overseer. Are internet companies a *market*, where they act as an agent for both parties in bringing them together? Or are they *employers* where direction is given?

The UK Numbers

The TUC reported in January that, from 2008Q1 to 2017Q3 there were 895,000 new self-employment jobs and 1.65m employed (1.127+0.526m). In other words, 64.8% of job creation was in *employment* where 87% of jobs were located in 2008. Indeed, of the 2.52m new jobs 44.2% were permanent employee jobs.

	2008Q1	2017Q3	Δ	%Δ	% of totalΔ
EmpFT	19,122,857	20,250,428	1,127,571	5.9	44.2
EmpPT	6,459,020	6,985,036	526,016	8.1	20.6
SEmpFT	2,945,631	3,326,959	381,328	12.9	15.0
SEmpPT	931,944	1,445,860	513,916	55.1	20.2
Total	29,683,561	32,206,974	2,523,413	8.5	

The majority of self-employed was part time. The concentration of these new entrepreneurs is in the over 50-age bracket, making up half. They could be exploiting redundancy monies as well as their accumulated experience and contacts. The TUC pointed to a rise in non-regular employment and flexible labour markets.

In December 2016, the TUC estimated 3.2m workers (10%) were in some form of insecure work: 1.7m low-paid self-employment; 730,000 casual temporary or agency workers; and 810,000 on 'zero-hours' contracts. The ONS found that of the 848,000 jobs added to the total number of employees between 2012 and 2013, 34% were on zero-hours contracts and 36% were on flexitime. Only 16% were not classified as some flexible working. Sports Direct employs almost all of its 22,000 staff this way. But this is true of McDonalds and JD Wetherspoon as well. In the period April to June 2015, the LFS found that 744,000 were on a zero-hours contract, representing 2.4% of people in employment. This represented an increase is 120,000, or 19% up on 2014. The ONS survey in November 2017 of those on contracts that do not guarantee a minimum number of hours (NGHCs) indicates that around 1.8m are on NGHCs up from 1.4m in 2014. The Resolution Foundation reported that workers on zero-hours contracts doing similar jobs as part-time workers earn 6.6% /year less (£1,000).

Is this Temporary work Temporary?

The OECD suggested that the temporary job is no longer the stepping stone to permanent employment. It found that 49% of temporary workers in 2008 went on to permanent jobs by 2011 in the UK. In Italy (26%), Spain (20.6) and France (20.5), the movement is less fluid.

The TUC analysing the Labour Force survey calculated that of the 740,000 agency workers 420,000 had been with the same employer for over a year. Of these, 11,000 have been there for 20 years and an additional 39,000 for at least half that. The average agency workers was paid £1.50/hr less than permanent staff. Many employers are using agency workers not as a temporary stop gap. JLR is such a company. In part, it a long-term strategy to keep costs down. Agency staff can be let go at less

cost to the business. However, JLR treat agency staff like permanent, with the same pay progression. This gives them the advantage of long term association before they are converted to permanent (which takes 3 yrs, on average). This is more like an efficiency contract than an efficiency wage.

Research conducted by the Association of Independent Professionals and the Self Employed found that 37.3% of self-employed people did not earn a high enough income to be able to pay into a retirement fund. A further 9.1% were unsure of how to set one up. The RSA reported in February 2017 that 8% of the self-employed between the ages of 25-34 were enrolled in a pension, against 60% of employees. The typical earnings of the self-employed is £240/wk - 18.8% of them receive tax credits to make up their income; 10.6% of employees face this issue.

Unfair Wage or Competition?
JPMorgan's CEPS study of 260,000 respondents found a difference between physical and on-line work in the gig economy. As they are competing locally with people who face the same cost of living, physical taskers' wages, in countries such as the US, tend to be much higher. By contrast, on-liners are subject to wage depression. Average earnings per hour on Mechanical Turk are below the US minimum wage, but $14 \times$ the minimum wage in India.

Segmented Labour Markets
Segmentation occurs when the labour market is divided or structured in a way which is reflected in the forms taken by the employment relationship or contract. It is associated with the division between 'core' and 'atypical' employment in some contexts, and with that between 'formal' and 'informal' employment in others. In industrialised economies, a 'normal' or 'standard' employment relationship is full-time, indeterminate in duration, and based on a stable contract between the individual worker and a single, clearly defined employing entity. Atypical work takes the form of part-time, fixed-term and temporary agency employment, and casualised forms of work, such as zero-hours contracts, spot contracts and Uber or Deliveroo self-employment.

In developing economies, segmentation is identified with a distinction between a 'formal' sector in which employment is stable and regulated, and an 'informal' sector of casualised work relations which are, in varying degrees, undocumented, untaxed, and beyond the scope of collective agreements and legislative protections.

One can see several versions of segmentation
- employers' organisational requirements (internal labour market theory)
- labour-use strategies (efficiency wage theory)
- the responses of unions (insider-outsider theory)
- the outsourcing of risk (the flexible firm)

The first 'dual labour market' theories of the 1970s identified a division of the market into a 'primary' segment consisting of stable employment in firm specific internal labour markets, and a 'secondary' segment. The markets had the following characteristics:

1. Upper primary: Pre-trained, lightly monitored, task flexible. In ILM – highly paid, promotion, good working conditions – white collar
2. Lower Primary: On-the-job training, heavily monitored (time and motion study), machine worker in limited ILM, union security – blue collar
3. Secondary: Virtually no training, few rewards and low level of job security, high turnover/low wage – McJobs

In an era of Fordist Monopoly Capitalism employment within the vertically-integrated firm was widespread. The primary employment was based on formal, bureaucratic rules and procedures. **Internal labour markets** (ILM) are markets internal to a company, so that candidates only compete with others from within the company for the internally advertised vacancies. We can see these themes in other areas. Williamson's hierarchies used transaction cost to explain identified stable employment with a series of loose contracts and monitors. Human capital theory predicted that long-term employment relationships and seniority-based wages would be found in contexts where firms and workers made mutual investments in firm-specific training.

By contrast, the ILM approach views the secondary market as governed by unfettered competition and transactions approach views this market as low-skill and low-discretion jobs and associated with 'spot contracting'. Workers' wages are influenced by external conditions

Efficiency wage theory from the early 1980s posits that the higher wage paid by employers in the primary sector incentivises its workforce to remain with the firm, lowering turnover costs. With asymmetric information, employers cannot fully assess the qualities of workers. So with workers' aptitude and motivation difficult to assess and having invested in their skills, employers increase wages and other elements of the work bargain above the market-clearing wage. It is thought that this leads to [equilibrium] unemployment possibly in a Harris and Todaro sense. The reliability also would encourage greater investment in the worker, increasing their productivity.

Insider-outsider theory focuses on the role of trade unions in segmenting the labour market. Segmentation, at least partly the result of union activity, is geared towards restricting the labour supply, and bid up wages in the primary sector. With the decline of factory work and trade unions, this model may reflect little in the economy today. However, today the law may act in the same way.

Atkinson – Flexible firm

The entrepreneur in transaction cost terms is viewed as a risk taker whereas employees are risk averse. It follows that the entrepreneur should bear risk but take the rewards (profit). The flexible firm shifts the risk of changes in market demand onto the worker and the wage.

There are two types of flexible labour. Numerical flexibility entails adjusting hours or number of employees to suit demand. Here, we see the use of agency workers or causals. Functional flexibility involves labour that is task flexible (multi-skilled).

External workers are used for elementary work e.g. cleaning OR for highly specialised work. Outsourcing of government activities to the private sector places downward pressure on wages. To some extent, this is the dirty secret of the privatisation/ outsourcing agenda. If other costs are quasi fixed and economies are desired, privatising and lowering conditions of service fit the bill. The TUC and New Economics

Core worker:	FT, permanent, managerial, professional, Primary ILM Functionally Flexible
1st Peripheral group:	FT but semi-skilled Secondary Labour Market Numerical Flexibility
2nd Peripheral group:	PT Short term Contract Job sharing Public subsidy training
External	Agency workers Increased outsourcing Subcontracting Self-employment

Foundation reported in March 2015 that outsourcing had a detrimental effect on pay and conditions. In the case of residential care, a worker before outsourcing could have been earning £9.45/hr and a nurse, £15.18. In the private sector this dropped to £7.23 and £13.74. A specific case is G4S in Lincolnshire taking over back office activities for the local police force in 2012. At transfer, the pay ranged from £8.84 to £10.40. Two years later the same job was being offered at £7.36. But then this backfires. Serco runs a private sector prison HMP Thameside. A prison officer earned £17,350 rising to £21,000. A nearby public sector one paid £24,500. The inevitable move of officers left Serco struggling. It now uses inmates as 'violence reduction representatives'; prisoners manage prisoners.

The cutting of pay shifts part of the wage bill to the tax-payer. Unison found that council workers were just as likely to be in receipt of tax credits as retail sector workers (11%), with only the hospitality worse (17%). Local government workers' real wage fell 15% over the period from 2006. The tax-payer contributes £6bn/yr supporting low wage earners, with tax credits for the lowest paid amounting to £21m.

Wage Support Diagrams

In the figure right, a wage subsidy over the free market wage is considered. W_1 is the free market wage. The wage is deemed too low by society and a credit is made available increasing the reward from forgoing hours of leisure, rotating the supply curve downwards. The new equilibrium would be at W_2 Q_2. Credit $= W_{2+credit} - W_2$.

The cost of the credit provided raised = $(Q_2) \times (W_{2+credit} - W_2)$, which relates to areas A+C+B. Area B reflects the returns from working. Area C is the implicit employer subsidy and Area A reflects the deadweight loss.

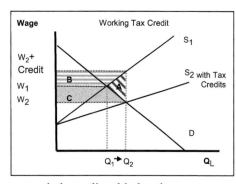

In theory, more hours should be offered, but the subsidy may not encourage workers to work longer hours. Also, knowing the State will provide the subsidy, the system encourages firms to pay wages below a liveable level.

It was reported by the Joseph Rowntree Foundation that those living below a threshold of income that could provide adequate housing food and clothing in 2014/15 stood at 19m, up from 15m in 2008/9. This group will be affected by the post Brexit devaluation which pushed up food prices. In October, food inflation was 4%.

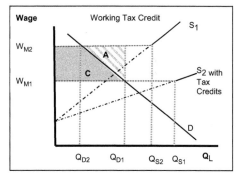

Assume the minimum wage W_{M1} is equivalent to £7.50/hr. At this level there will be Q_{D1} jobs and Q_{S1} looking for work. Unemployment will be $Q_{S1} - Q_{D1}$. Those in employment can claim a tax credit, which is a subsidy. The total subsidy would be areas C+A. Area A would be the welfare loss. If minimum wage was pushed up to W_{M2}, which is equivalent to £7/hr, this eradicates the subsidy, but at this level there will be Q_{D2} jobs and Q_{S2} looking for work. Unemployment will be $Q_{S2} - Q_{D2}$. The government has shifted the burden, but at the expense of fewer jobs.

Employment Subsidy
Rather than giving the subsidy to the worker, it could be offered to the employer in the form of an employer subsidy. In the diagram below, the demand for labour schedule shifts right as it is cheaper to employ the marginal worker. If the supply of labour schedule is upward sloping, there is a welfare loss of area A. The employer receives the subsidy directly. This time the policy drives up wages to W_2.

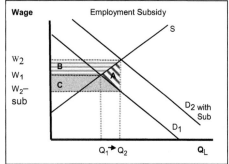

Sharing the Pain

A version of academic sharecropping emerged several years ago. Nearly half of universities and technical colleges in the US use Income Share Agreements. Students get money upfront in exchange for a share of their income. When administered by the university it aligns its interests with that of its students. In a sense, it is a signal of faith in their university education delivered by both students and lecturers.

Turnover Costs

One strand of Efficiency Wage theory emphasises turnover costs. Staff turnover is inevitable but it can prove a significant cost to employee morale, productivity, and company revenue. Recruiting and training a new employee requires staff time and money. In 2014, Oxford Economics estimated the cost of replacing members of staff was £30,614/worker. There are two main factors that make up this cost:

1. Lost Output whilst the vacancy exists
2. Training and absorption costs of a new worker

Costs of recruiting are shown right.

Once in, it takes on average, 28 weeks to reach Optimum Productivity, where one can do the job effectively. This cost is worth £25,181/worker. This time varies. For SMEs (with up to 250 workers) 24 weeks; over 250 workers, 28 weeks. Microbusinesses (1-9 workers) 12 weeks.

Hiring temporary workers before the replacement starts:	£3,618
Advertising the new role:	£398
Recruitment agency fees:	£454
Interviewing candidates:	£767
HR time spent processing replacement:	£196
Total	£5,433

Five sectors are considered - Retail, Legal, Accountancy, Media & Advertising and IT & Tech. Differences between the sectors are revealed in the table below.

	Optimum Productivity	Cost to replace worker
Accountancy	32 weeks	£39,230
IT & Tech	29	£31,808
Legal	32	£39,887
Media & Advertising	20	£25,787
Retail	23	£20,114

The time varies with experience. Joining from the same sector, time-to-optimum is 15 weeks; from another sector 32 weeks; new graduates 40 weeks; unemployed or inactive 52 weeks.

In the US, the Centre for American Progress found average costs to replace an employee are:

- 16% of annual salary for high-turnover, low-paying jobs (< $30,000/yr)
- 20% for mid-range positions ($30,000 to $50,000/yr)
- Up to 213% for highly educated, executive positions.

It was revealed by the National Foundation for Educational Research (NFER) in 2017 that teaching had a high turnover rate, particularly in their first five years. Between 2010 and 2015 about 10.4% of science teachers left the profession each year; 10.3% of maths; 10% of technology; 9.7% English; 8.4% art, drama and music; 8.5% humanities such as history and geography; and 5.9% of PE teachers. The government has claimed teacher retention figures in England remain steady. After 5 years about

70% remain. That would imply an attrition rate of 6.9%. A rate of 10% implies that 60% remain after five years and over half have gone after 6.6 years. Efficiency wage theory suggests a greater wage is needed.

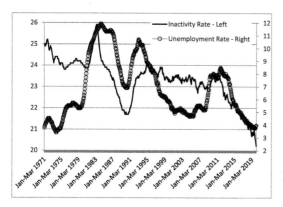

PARTICIPATION

Several factors have contributed to the rising demand for skills in the labour market: technological and organizational change, trade, deregulation of key industries, and the decline of unions. In contrast, reductions in the demand for labour appear to explain the participation decline especially for lower-skilled men. The graphic above shows the evolution of the unemployment and participation rates. The unemployment and the participation rate follow each other.

Households and Participation

The number of working age HHs was 20.682m in 2015Q2. This will include at least one person of working age. There were 3.269m HH where no adult of working age was employed (15.5%); 5.9m where some but not all work; and 11.55m where all worked.

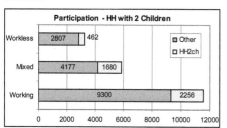

Of the workless households, 462,000 had two dependent children (10%), as opposed to 16% for all groups. The mixed category contains both working and workless members – probably a child carer. 1.68m or 29% of the total number of two dependent households fall into this category. Having 2 children may be a marker of a participant household. In 2019Q2, 75% of women with dependent children were in employment and if the children were under 2, it was slightly lower 67.5%. Around 13% of women born in the 1960s had a degree by the age of 33. Twenty years later this was up to 45%.

The male participation rate in the US of those in the prime age groups of 25 to 54 is around 88%. This compares unfavourably with the 1964 rate of 97%. A simple linear trend suggests that by 2050 a ¼ of US men will be non-employed: Larry Summers expects ⅓. ½ will experience at least a year of non-work out of every five. He was too pessimistic. From 2016 to 2018 5m jobs were secured by new and returning workers of all ages.

A Time Use Breakdown in 2014 for prime age males overall compared with non-participating males is instructive. The big difference in non-work time is in Socialising, Relaxing, and Leisure, in particular watching TV. The working male would watch 154 minutes of TV/ day. The non-participant would watch double that (335m/day).

As non-participating men could specialise in household management whilst their wife works, patterns for married and non-married men should be different. Those with children spent more time caring for household members (73mins vs. 58) and household activities (112 vs. 108).

One outcome of the US flexible labour model with a limited welfare provision is the crime rate. At around 1.5m, the US locks away 10× the number of criminals compared with the UK, with only 5× the population. The number of former felons is somewhere around 12-14m, which, given their record, makes them difficult to place in work. Another concern for the disadvantaged highlighted by Case and Deaton is that working-class white Americans have a

Prime age Men	Partic-ipants	Non Partic-ipants
Caring for Household Members	29	28
Caring for Non-Household Members	7	8
Education	8	25
Household Activities and Services	84	111
Socialising, Relaxing, Leisure	251	472
Watching Television	154	335
Work	316	7
Other (Including Sleep)	736	773

high mortality rate. Uneducated white Americans now die at higher rates than other ethnic groups. In 1999, white male and females aged 50-54 with a high school education had a mortality rate 30% below black Americans, by 2015 it was 30% above. Much of this excess mortality is down to deep social dysfunctionality. Characteristics include suicide, alcohol and prescription drug abuse. Opioid abuse is estimated to cost 2.8% of GDP in the US in 2015. Uncontrollable immigration and deindustialisation are possibly yesterday's problems.

US female participate is also a conundrum. Prime age female participation in the US is lower than in Japan. The concern for a drop in male participation was not great as household incomes were rising: female participate made up for the decline. With both in decline there will be a household issue. The US stands out as being less supportive of the home maker-worker. Paid-parental leave in OECD countries increased from 17 weeks to over a year since 1970. In the US it remains at zero. Trump promised six weeks of paid maternity.

World Bank participation rates 15+	1990		2016	
Income group	Female	Male	Female	Male
High income	49	73	52	68
Upper middle income	61	82	56	76
Middle income	52	83	47	77
Lower middle income	42	83	38	79
Low & middle income	53	83	49	78
Low income	69	85	70	83
United Kingdom	53	75	57	69
United States	56	75	56	68
India	35	85	27	79

In the UK, the DoE found that 53% of stay-at-home mothers would rather work if there was suitable childcare. It was also found that 80% of working mothers relied on child care of which ⅔ use formal childcare. However, 36% of working mothers would rather not work if they could afford to. So around 6.3m children receive some form of child care.

INTERNATIONAL POLITICAL ECONOMY

British foreign policy is organised for pursuing British interests (Douglas Hurd). How do we define what the national interest might be in any situation? Should we rely on politicians alone to define it? A fear here is they might serve their own (or groups') interests and ideologies. A fine example is who defined US national interest when prosecuting the Vietnam war? A major beneficiary was the Military-Industrial Complex. When the people voted for BREXIT politicians were acting in the National Interest? So, it is a flexible phrase which is often used to justify an existing policy but no real guide to generating new policies. Let's begin with a definition NI entails:

- preserving 'our' national territory against foreign threat
- encouraging foreigners to contribute to 'our' national welfare

Traditional IPE scholars emphasise three groups of ideas: Liberal, Marxist and Realist.

Liberal

Liberal trade theorists Ricardo and Smith challenged the Mercantilist view. The Neo-Classical position posits voluntary interaction/exchange between actors as being preferable whether in Economic or Political fields. Through choice, if there are no impediments, utility is maximised. So the liberal perspective envisages free trade and a small government provide public goods support such as education and provide good infrastructure. The state enforces property rights; defend borders; undermine monopoly power in the market; and regulate/provide sound money. Governments should manage international trade as they would their own domestic economies. Rules/regulations of exchange should be established to avoid unfair international competition. At the international level, liberals argue that all countries are best off when goods and services move freely across borders - free trade as opposed to protectionism. The mutual benefits of trade and expanding interdependence between economies will foster co-operative relations, hence a liberal international economy, according to this theory, will have a moderating influence on international politics. There is no economic basis for war or protectionism. Liberals are interested in maximising the overall benefits of exchange - the total creation of wealth - but have little to say how the total benefits are distributed.

Realist

With Realism the focus on nation states and politics determines economics. Nations States (NS) pursue power and shape the economy for this purpose too. It assumes that NS are the dominant actors within the international political economy with all other actors are subordinate to it. Realists are concerned about international power relations. Politics is a zero-sum game, there are winners implies losers. One can only gain power by others losing it. Based on such authors as Hobbes and Machiavelli, it entails a world of competition where you enrich your NS at the expense of others. Politics is a zero-sum game, there are winners implies losers. One can only gain power by others losing it. States are ultimately dependent on their own resources for protection. The emphasis on political power is what gives Realism its distinctiveness. Identify situations where a NS will sacrifice economic gain to weaken their opponent or to strengthen themselves militarily. Protectionist policies, which may reduce a country's income by restricting the market, may be adopted for reason of national political power.

Realist political economy is concerned with how changes in the distribution of power affects the type of international economy. For competition over wealth, hostility is inevitable. The key problem is maintaining order in the relations between states. The *Hegemonic Stability Theory* predicts that open international economy is most likely to exist when a single hegemonic power is present to stabilise the system.

Mercantilism advocates government regulation of economic life to increase State power and security. They are economic nationalists. Economic activities are subordinate to the interests of the State. Economic resources are the source of State power. Mercantilism shares much with political Realism. Both see the State as the principal actor, the international system as anarchical, where States and individuals conflict. The emphasis is on relative power, relative to other States, as opposed to absolute well-being that Liberals pursue.

Marxist
Capitalism and the market create extremes of wealth for capitalists and poverty for workers. Marxists rejected the view that exchanges between individuals maximises the welfare of society. Rather they believe that capitalism is an inherently conflictual system which would inevitably be overthrown by socialism. Classes are the dominant actors in the international system. Here capitalists, the owners of the means of production, struggle with workers in a political battle. Classes act to maximise the economic well-being of their class as a whole.

In IPE, Marxists are concerned with two issues. First, the fate of labour in a world of increasingly internationalised capital. Here, the growth of MNCs and rise of globally integrated financial markets have weakened the economic and political power of labour (and individual States). If workers in one country demand higher wages or better working conditions, the MNC can simply shift production to a country where labour is more compliant. Hence, labour's ability to negotiate with capital for a more equitable distribution of wealth has been undermined. Second, exploitation. The First world and MNC exploit the 3rd world just as on a domestic level the capitalist exploits the worker. Hence, autonomous development strategies for unaligned nations are a focus.

World Systems Theory
➢ In the NIDL, the machine replicated much of what the skilled worker offered the capitalist, freeing the MNC from the city and high cost regions.
➢ In the neoclassical world, an enhancement of labour productivity would shift the demand curve for labour to the right. However, a fall in the cost of capital relative to labour would lead to a substitution of capital for labour.
➢ In the world of the Austrian economics, technological improvements enhance the well-being of the consumers and the entrepreneur is rewarded with profits. The nature of deindustrialisation is evolving and accelerating.

The 5th Long Wave is associated with nanotechnology and biotechnology increasing the productivity of resources and energy. However, robots will feature strongly. The *second machine* age and thinking robots are about to make the future worse for many workers whose work is routine. This shift is permanent and will be divisive, further separating the high from the low-paid worker.

Regulation Theory
Central question here is how the production and growth processes are regulated. Using a Neo-Marxist framework, it assumes goal of capitalist production is the generation of surplus value and shows that capitalism is subject to crises. There are inherent contradictions within the system that eventually bring about these crises. However, between crises the system is regulated by institutions, rules and norms. Two key concepts *regime of accumulation* and *mode of regulation*

- *regime of accumulation*: set of rules at the national level enabling accumulation (growth); includes labour market norms/wage payment system, rules of management, distributional norms (profit, wages, taxes)
- *mode of (social) regulation*: the institutional (laws) and cultural rules that regulate and reproduces the *regime of accumulation* - rules of the game for individual and collective behaviour. Regulation secures cohesion of the accumulation process

plus

- *Industrial Trajectory*: the industrial, technological and human capital developments that influence the accumulation process (long waves)
- *hegemonic structure*: a specific, state supported strategy for accumulation, e.g. Keynesianism

Fordism and the 4th long wave analysed on 4 levels – (Jessop, Pathways)
1. Industrial paradigm - labour process involves mass production techniques and semi-skilled workers
2. Regime of accumulation - macroeconomic growth is associated with Keynesian economics, econs of scale, rising productivity > rising incomes > rising demand > rising profits, based on full capacity production > increased investment in production equipment & techniques. Growth is based on mass production and mass consumption
3. Mode of regulation - separation of ownership from control/large multi-divisional firms; Central control of the work process (Taylorism); Monopoly pricing,

collective bargaining; wage indexation (prices and growth); monetary policy aimed at full employment; welfare state; corporatism.

4. Mode of societalisation - patterns of institutional integration and social cohesion. With Fordism the system required the vast majority to receive a reasonable individual and/or social wage to satisfy needs. Here, we see a commitment to a welfare state, rise of significant social expenditure

Many of the things that politicians of the left argue about is part of the Fordist accommodation (Jeremy Corbin?).

Fordism promoted growing individual consumption of standardised commodities, and growing provision of standardised collective goods and services by the state. Trade unions and political parties were broad catch-all with a tripartite approach to regulating the system - corporatism flourished under this. Fordism also promotes a certain economic geography. Core industrial regions were dominated by large firms and their acolytes in cities in the North and West of the UK. This began to collapse under late Fordism in the late 1960s.

Misregulation or disequilibrium between mode of production and mode of social regulation, impedes accumulation process. Misregulation often spurs changes to the mode of production or mode of social regulation to prolong accumulation process. Crisis occurs when conflict within regime of accumulation cannot be mediated by the regulation process, possibly when the organisation of production reaches its own limits. There are disputes over the division between consumption and investment expenditures, wages and profit occur; institutions reinforce their positions. Conflict/strikes/elections of radical governments etc.. At this time productivity growth falls. The accumulation process breaks down.

Solution: a new combination of accumulation and regulation, which is likely to be locally and historically specific, commonly seen as being associated with new technologies. But social conflict precipitates institution change necessary for new phase of growth to be organised. The transformation between Fordism (4th wave) and Post-Fordism (Flexible Accumulation) (5th wave) in the 1970 saw the collapse of international (financial) regulation (Bretton Woods). Technological change: computer based, small batch assembly, information and communication technologies; facilitated a decentralisation of production. The mobile phone changed the way we behave.

Under Thatcher-Reagan, States abandoned full employment and corporatism decline in union power/large scale unions. Under post-Fordism the labour process is one based on flexible machines with a corresponding flexible workforce producing small batches, specialising in production and services. Clearly, the system does not work for too many so 2008 (well 2020) should also lead to a restructuring.

Hegemonic Stability Theory[4]
Since the beginning of the 19th Century the changes to the Structure of International Trade (*openness* to the movements of goods, not capital or labour) could be explained by the International Politics Approach. Assume the structure of international trade is determined by the State seeking to maximise its interests and power. Interests include: aggregate national income; social stability; political power; and economic growth. The relationship between these and *openness* depends on:-
1) the potential economic power of any given state; a proxy for this could be relative size (large/small) and development (developed/underdeveloped)
2) Relationship between different distributions of potential power (hegemonic, multipolar) to different trading structures

	Large number of highly developed small states	Small number of unequally developed large states	One state much larger and more developed (hegemonic system)
Aggregate national income	Increased	Modest gains	Enhanced for the large state
Social stability	instability mitigated by higher levels of development	more instability in developing	instability mitigated by the large state's low level of involvement in international economy
Political power	no loss: costs of closure are symmetric, all lose	for more backward, vulnerable	greatest for large and developed economy
Economic growth	Enhanced	for more backward, constrained; for more developed, enhanced	rapid growth; exploiting technological and size advantages (in ascendancy)
Trading Openness	Open international trading structure	Closed structure Unless advanced are more militarily powerful, developed cannot force developing to accept openness.	Open international trading structure Small states benefit from openness Medium-sized states – unclear

Theory of Hegemonic Stability holds that open international economy (free trade) is most likely to exist within a regime dominated by a single hegemonic power that can stabilise and regulate the system. The hegemonic state has the economic and military power to include or exclude others in the open trading system. It offers a large market to exporters and relatively cheap imports to others. It can be coercive, engaging in destructive direct competition and withdrawing grants/aid of non-compliant counties. It can provide the currency/liquidity necessary for an open trading system and support weaker members of the system.

---

[4] State Power and the Structure of International Trade - Krasner (1976)

Today, we exist in troubling times when the rivalry between the US, Russia, China and Europe suggests that the system is unstable and protectionism, nationalism and conflict should follow.

THE POLITICS OF THE LOW WAGE

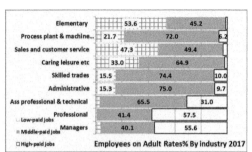

Employees on Adult Rates% By industry 2017

Perhaps fitting with a Marxist view, capital accumulation requires appropriate ratios of wage/profits and investment/consumption. The division between wages and profits determines the funds available for consumption and investment. Workers' income must grow at the same rate of the growth of output. Investor income and investment must grow as least as quickly as the output of capital goods. If workers' incomes are too modest, consumption will be inadequate to provide the rewards from production. If workers' incomes were too great, the funds available for investment will be insufficient to reproduce the necessary capital to generate the goods and employ the workforce. Real wage growth/year in the UK in the 1970s and 1980s was 2.9%; 1990s 1.5%; 2000s 1.2% but more recently the rate has been –2.2%.

In the US, the long-term average of wage/profit & interest is 63%. The labour share of the cake has been declining. Richard Lewis, on this theme, found that a decrease in the wage proportion in France, Germany, Italy, the UK, the US, Japan, Turkey and South Korea led to lower growth. But then Canada, Australia, Argentina, Mexico, India, China and South Africa saw higher growth. GDP fell 0.36% for every 1% fall in the labour share of the cake. Interestingly, the highest income earners are not rentiers; they are employees plus entrepreneurs. Moreover, lower wages had a negative effect on the proportion among trading partners: a low proportion infected other areas.

The division of the cake is central to the collapse of mainstream consensus politics, which can be characterised as the moderate left challenging the moderate right in liberal democracies – which constitutes part of the post war settlement and the triumph of the market economies over communism. Politicians were elected to moderate the excesses of the market and make is fairer for all. However, to a populist, this group was little more than a self-perpetuating elite that, as the agent of the people, was difficult to monitor and, in effect, ran the system at the expense of the people. A *populist* can be seen as someone that seeks to *challenge* this *'status quo'*. Thus, in old language, a populist can come from the extreme left or the right.

A populist sees the ruling elite as not supporting the neglected majority; those that see themselves as poorly treated relative to less 'deserved' cases (those tolerated minority groups); those that are victims of globalisation (see Vernon Bogdanor[5]). Those that fit the bill can be identified by their links to the past and place. The alternative group are most likely to benefit from the system that filters out non-member through exams. Yascha Mounk, from Harvard, is scornful of the current US political system describing is as 'undemocratic liberalism'. Economic elites and narrow interest groups succeeded in getting their favoured policies adopted about half of the time. The views of ordinary citizens, they had virtually no independent effect at all. When elites have sufficient power they have little interest in reflecting the preferences of the public at large. The burden of structural adjustment from the 2008 crisis is seen as the key marker. The internal devaluation (falling real wages and cuts in benefits) affect the squeezed middle (well the bottom of the pile) negatively.

The decline of trade unions goes hand-in-hand with the decline in the absorber of the traditional unskilled worker, manufacturing industry. Here, manual work could still bring home a solid wage that could be used to bring up a family and secure a roof over it. The decline of manufacturing from the 1980s left the less well educated exposed to a future of service sector work that was not well paid and not seen as clearly male-oriented. The wave of globalisation that followed in the 1990s and 2000s intensified this whilst the elite post Mrs Thatcher went further in reducing the transfer of wealth from those that benefited from globalisation to those that did not. Furthermore, those jobs and homes that the losers in the great scheme could compete for were moved further out of reach with waves of immigrants with more human capital following trade arrangements such as the single market or NAFTA. In effect, there has been three decades of eradicating the opportunity of work from the losers whist advocating the [profit] opportunities that free trade bring to the community [elite], much as the Regulationists see things.

Minimum Wage

The minimum wage rate, initially set at £3.60 in 1999, rose faster than inflation and average earnings. The minimum wage is of no consequence if it is below the clearing wage. In 2010, the wage stood at £5.93, when the median wage was £11.08 and the mean wages £14.65. The Low Pay Commission estimated the minimum

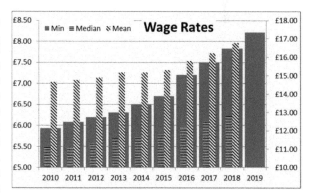

wage's 12p/hr increase introduced in October 2013 would have raised tax revenues by £110m and reduced benefit expenditure by £73m; assuming linearities, 50p/hr could save the exchequer about £750m/yr. Card and Krueger, found that a higher rate did not

---

[5] https://www.youtube.com/watch?v=_6Kc16BpbBs

destroy jobs. Their 1994 study of fast-food restaurants in two neighbouring US states showed a rise in jobs.

In 2013, 5% were on minimum wages and a further 10% were earning within 50p/hr of that. Of this 10%, ⅓ had been stuck there for 5 years and 20% for 10 years. The Resolution Foundation found that number of those earning less than the 'living' wage has increase from 3.4m in 2009 to 4.6m in 2013. In other words, the wage-wage spiral that the minimum wage could cause had not materialised. The Low Pay Commission reported that only the lowest 15% of earners (3.8m workers) saw a real wage increase over the 2007-2016. The pay dominated by the minimum wage of those working 26 hrs/wk rose by £180/yr in real (£400/yr nominal) terms. For the whole of the UK, the real wage fell by 1%.

Minimum Wage – at a Cost
In April 2016, mayors of California and New York signed in to law a minimum wage of $15/hr to be introduced in 2023 and 2018, respectively. The then Federal minimum of $7.25/hr is found in states such as Texas. Normally, a minimum increase is absorbed in price and profit. Alan Krueger sees $12 as beneficial but $15 as potentially introducing undesirable consequences to replace labour with capital. The Congressional Budget Office projected that a Federal minimum of $10.10 would cost 500,000 jobs, or 0.3% of the workforce, or 2 month's job generation. The consequence of pushing minimum wages too far are below.

In manufacturing, rising labour costs would provoke greater mechanisation. Labour intensive industries such as care homes cannot replace labour. In November 2018 Allied Healthcare, which supports 13,000 people, admitted it was struggling with debts. The Care Quality Commission issued a notice saying it had serious doubts about Allied Healthcare's future. In April 2019, Four Seasons Health Care went into administration. With about 322 homes, 17,000 residents and patients and employing some 20,000 staff, it was the biggest care home group to have gone into administration since Southern Cross in 2011.

In 2018, the Joseph Rowntree Foundation reported that since 2008 the minimum income standard had risen by 30% for a nuclear family but 50% for a pensioner couple. With 19m people in a household below this minimum, the increase of 3.4m over a decade is consistent with other measures of growing inequality. Concurrently, the Resolution Foundation found that between 2003 and 2016/17, the lower bicentile household real income adjusted for housing cost had dropped from £14,900 by £100.

Following the introduction of €8.50/hr wage, inequality in Germany fell more than anywhere else in the EU. Eurofound, an EU Agency, found no effect on employment. In the UK the minimum wage helped pay rise by 10% in real terms between 2015 and 2017 whilst employment rates were at record highs and falling unemployment rates. In June 2018, it was announced that German minimum wage would rise to €9.19/hr.

AN UNEMPLOYMENT PROBLEM?

In December 2006, John Hutton, the Work and Pensions Secretary, announced a review of the benefits system. He stated that: "the hardcore 'that can work but don't work' benefits claimants... [should] ...compete for jobs along-side the growing number of migrants who arrive in Britain especially for work." Over 66% on job seekers allowance were prior-claimants and 12% (100,000) of them had claimed for 6 of the last 7 years. These are really on the margins of the labour market and may cause some interpretive problems for policy makers.

When presented with an unemployment rate of 7% one should be asking, what does this mean for policy purposes? It is likely this headline is a measure of **involuntary unemployment**. The number of [involuntary] unemployed is defined as *those of working age but without work and willing to work AT THE GIVEN MARKET WAGE.*

Those that are not willing are **voluntarily unemployed**. This group, which could include those that retire early, choose not to participate in the labour market. They were not of major concern. However, their capacity to switch when wages rise so adding to the capacity to produce is now making this group a focus of attention.

Those that participate form the labour force: they comprise the employed + self employed + unemployed.

Unemployment rate = Involuntarily unemployed ÷ Labour force

In an effort to reduce the use of illegal migrant labour, the Alabama State legislature in 2011 passed a law requiring proof of immigration status. It is one of 5 States that have acted to reduce the incentives to stay in the US. It was a great success. The number of illegal Hispanic immigrants was estimated at 120,000 in 2010; by 2013, ⅓ to ⅔ had left. The cost to the local economy was estimated to be $2.3-11bn, according to the University of Alabama. The illegal workers contributed both hands and mouths. The legislation should shift the supply curve of labour to the left, boosting the local wage. Unemployment fell from 9.3% to 7.1%. What also emerged was that some locals were not prepared to undertake the arduous work available for $9/hour, so Alabama producers faced a labour shortage. For example, for every 15 workers hired to undertake basic factory labouring, 11 would quit immediately. This looks like voluntary rather than involuntary unemployment and the claim about immigrants stealing jobs sounds hollow.

Full employment is where the number of people that want to work = the number of jobs available *at the given market wage*, so a marker of full employment relates to vacancies and unemployment. **Disequilibrium** unemployment occurs when there are more people looking for work than there are job opportunities for them.

U-V Analysis

A *U-V* curve traces an inverse relationship between vacancy and unemployment rates. In times of low demand, one would expect vacancies to be relatively scarce and unemployment correspondingly abundant. The figure right shows the ratio of the number of unemployed (by ILO) to the number of notified vacancies. You would have thought that, as there would be a job for each unemployed participant, a 1:1 ratio would imply full employment.

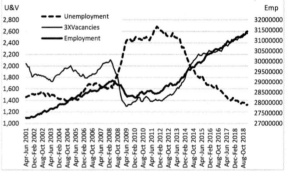

However, it is estimated that only about ⅓ of vacancies are notified, so a ratio of 3:1 would be nearer the mark. The graphic then implies that disequilibrium unemployment emerged in the summer of 2008 and disappeared in summer 2014.

In the figure right, employment, unemployment and vacancies×3 are displayed. From 2013 the numbers of unemployed (left-hand scale) seem to fall in tandem of the number of vacancies and the number of employed (right-hand scale), but not before which is a puzzle in itself. Employment appears to follow real GDP. The *U-V* switch is evident in 2008, just before Lehman's collapsed. 'Normal levels' change. There is a mirror image suggesting that vacancies fall and unemployment levels rise. It is argued that the *U-V* locus shifted outwards in the 1970s and 1980s, indicating that there was an increase in the number of unemployed workers for every vacancy in this period. This would be consistent with a hysteresis, where new norms are established, very much like a structural change. Full employment can occur at a higher level of unemployment.

Equilibrium unemployment occurs when there are at least as many job opportunities are there are job seekers. Thus, at full employment rate there is equilibrium unemployment. This notion is captured by Friedman *et al.* and the natural rate of unemployment. The natural rate occurs because there are impediments to the labour market working perfectly. The natural rate encompasses Frictional + Structural + Geographic/regional unemployment.

Frictional unemployment describes the continuous flow of individuals from job to job in and out of work. As jobs are available, these potential workers are engaged in 'job search.' Frictional unemployment occurs because change happens: productivity improvements forever destroy jobs; innovation creates them. So, jobs are being lost here and generated there. If this creation/destruction rate increases, so does frictional unemployment. Also, life issues play a role. Some find that they change their job for family or career reasons. To reduce frictional unemployment, the State needs to speed up the rate of matching of vacancies with job seekers.
POLICY SOLUTION
Information:- The seeker may not be sufficiently well-informed about job opportunities, so more job information would speed up matching.
Incentives:- Job search can be expensive and disheartening. Indeed, the longer someone is unemployment, the more likely it is they become 'discouraged' and withdraw from the labour market. To support the job search, the State may provide some financial assistance or advice to improve the searching process.
Punishments:- it could be that the seeker has greater aspirations than the State views as appropriate - they could be too choosy. If so, the State may threaten to restrict their access to the benefits system.

The Dept. for Work and Pensions is keen to weed out false claimants. If someone is not looking for work, they are not really a job-seeker, so evidence of job seeking is an important indicator that they comply with the requirements. In December 2013, the Universal Jobsmatch website was launched. Employers could advertise vacancies, linking them with qualified seekers. This system could scan remotely job-seekers' efforts. Also, if they are throwing interviews, this could also suggest that they are not happy to take the job. If someone is willing to work at a higher wage, they may participate under more favourable circumstances, but currently, they are voluntarily unemployed.

Job Centre managers exhibited an unrealistic view of the sort of the matching function they play. A Job Centre in Hull was found to be advertising vacancies in Surrey, Watford, and North London as well as France and Turkey. These were viewed as 'local.' These far-a-field jobs were less skilled work, such as part-time cleaner or assistant aromatherapist. The reality, as ONS found from reviewing a 3-month period in 2009, is that commuting is really the domain of the well-paid executive. 9% of commuters outside and 36% within London spend longer than 45-minutes on their journey to work. The median pay of Londoners commuting for over 60 minutes was £18.80/hr and £14.30 outside. By contrast, commuting less than 15 minutes, the corresponding figures were £9.60/hr and £8.30. Moreover, in Britain, 36% of managers and professionals but only 12% of low skilled jobs engaged in long distance commuting. Thus, frictional could be redefined as geographical unemployment beyond a certain distance.

In a sense, at full employment all the involuntary unemployed are in-between jobs. However, 'time taken' to change jobs may entail geographical and occupational shifts. We describe these below:-

Structural unemployment is where there is a mismatch in the skills set between the jobs and the job seeker. As mentioned above, jobs are destroyed and created continuously. If the skill difference between jobs lost and created is significant, structural unemployment can become a major problem. Declining industries will be releasing workers with sets of skills that are not transferable to growing ones. Moreover, it is likely that while employed the worker skills capability is refreshed. Once unemployed, this is less likely: the longer someone is unemployed, the more likely it is they become structurally unemployed.

POLICY SOLUTION

Training:- A mismatch in skills suggests training is a solution. More drastic action, such as a change of career, will be costly. The State could provide subsidise training courses in preferred skills areas.

In the US, the probability of becoming discouraged and exiting the labour market is doubled if unemployed for 15 months. However, if these do secure employment, they tend to return to the industry for which they had previously worked, which, if it is a declining industry, points to a structural problem.

The ONS found that in 2013Q2 87% of those with a degree were in employment; 83% with 'A' levels; 76% with passes at GCSE level and 47% with no qualifications.

The CIPD reported in August 2017 that low-skilled vacancies had 24 applicants for each one; 19 for medium-skilled jobs; and 8 applicants for each high-skilled job.

Punishments:- It could be that the seeker is not that keen to retrain. If so, the State may threaten to restrict access to the benefits system.

Regional Unemployment is where there are job vacancies of the right task set but they are elsewhere, far from the job seeker's locale. There is a mismatch of location.

POLICY SOLUTION - relocate the work or the work seeker

Incentives for firms to set up/relocate to the area have been a standard approach for local and regional authorities. Providing soft loans, grants and tax holidays to multinational enterprises to locate direct foreign investment (branch plants) has led to competitive bidding. Ireland uses a low corporation tax rate of 12.5%.

Incentives for workers to move are less commonplace. There are pecuniary and non-pecuniary costs of moving. Housing is commonly a major pecuniary cost. If the cost to live in an area where the jobs are advertised or the costs to commute to that area outweigh the benefits, then job seekers will not resolve the regional unemployment problem. Key worker housing is often touted as a policy solution, but this needs to be subsidised by the State. A private buyer or builder will want a good price for the property, so building it at an affordable price and retaining it for key workers are problems that require State intervention. The right-to-buy policy of the 1980s has gone this way. In April 2013, the GMB reported that, of the 15,874 former council homes bought by their tenants in the London borough of Wandsworth, private landlords then owned 6,180. In other words, they went from State to private renting, and along the way someone extracted Ricardian rent. Their value had increased by a factor of 20.

Punishments:- it could be that the seeker is not that keen on commuting or relocating. If so, the State may threaten to restrict access to the benefits system.

Structural unemployment can be focused in an area leaving it persistently depressed. Labour immobility is often blamed, but for those with limited skills and unemployment being relatively high for all, the non-pecuniary costs plus being unemployed elsewhere are major disincentives to relocating to improve the likelihood of finding work.

Disequilibrium unemployment has two elements:

Cyclical (demand deficient) unemployment is related to the business cycle. Business conditions fluctuate - recessions, depression etc.. Reducing the intensity, duration and frequency of ups and downs of business activity can lessen cyclical unemployment. **Demand Deficient Unemployment** as explained by Keynes fits here. Persistent or mass unemployment is caused by a lack of demand (particularly in the downswing of the business cycle). The *economy can be in equilibrium but the labour market does not clear* so the economy could occupy an underemployment equilibrium caused by insufficient aggregate demand.

POLICY SOLUTION - Government can smooth out fluctuation in economic activity by manipulating aggregate demand. Instruments include government spending and taxing (fiscal policy) or the monetary authority (central bank) can alter money supply or interest rates.

Real wage or neo-classical unemployment occurs when too many workers are enticed on to the labour market and others are priced out of work. The real wage is too high for the market to clear.

POLICY SOLUTION - Reduce the wage towards the clearing wage. This could involve reducing the power of Trade Unions and disbanding wages councils and minimum wages.

The topics above can be captured by the following figure. *WP* reflects the working population (q4), which is dictated by demographic, cultural and migration forces. Changing school leaving and retirement ages, extending the working week/ year and encouraging in migrants, can shift it. *N* represents the labour force at any given wage, and S_{eff} and D_{eff} are the effective supply and demand for labour. Here, effective supply means those that are employable now. Effective demand means there is a job that can/is filled. The number of people in work is the lesser of the

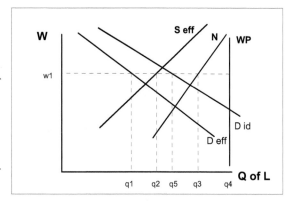

two. In this case, demand is the constraint. The gap q2 − q1 is *real-wage* or *demand deficient unemployment* (disequilibrium forms of unemployment). These appear the same if the wage $w1$ is sticky downwards. Full employment occurs when the number of jobs equals the number of (full-time equivalent) workers wanting work at the given market wage. The gap between D_{eff} and D_{id} (ideal demand) represents vacancies. As with the supply of labour, there will always be a number of vacancies reflecting the frictions in the labour market. At $w1$, the number is q5 − q1. The difference between S_{eff} and N captures *frictional, structural and regional unemployment*, which is q3 − q2 (equilibrium unemployment). At full employment the number of vacancies equals *frictional, structural and regional unemployment*. The *rate of unemployment* is (q3 − q1) ÷ q3.

In addition, there are some who do not want to participate in the labour market. As a result we can derive a *participation rate* q3÷q4 (the proportion of the population participating in the workforce). There are three more rates: the *natural rate of unemployment* is (q3 − q2) ÷ q2; (q4 − q1) ÷ q4 is the *rate of non-employment*, (those that could physically work but do not); and the *rate of employment* is q1 ÷ q4 (those that do physically work as a proportion that could do).

Male inactivity numbers are growing steadily, due to a rising number not interested in work. In the table right, in 2020, there were 3.3m males that were inactive.

Dec to Feb 2020 '000	Women	Men	Aged 16-64	Aged 65 and over
Full-time employment	9,336	15,119	31,687	1,386
Part-time employment	6,391	2226		
Unemployment	601	763	1,331	33
Economic inactivity (aged 16 to 64)	5,089	3,381		
Economic inactivity (aged 65 and over)	5,862	4,794		

The estimated employment rate for all people was at a record high of 76.6% and for women again a record high of 72.7%.

Inflexibility in Europe
In the 1980s, it was proposed that the natural rate of unemployment in Europe was subject to hysteresis. Authors have provided commentaries on the unemployment 'puzzle', where, unlike in the US, European unemployment continued to rise after the energy (supply side) shocks of the 1970s had past, where the natural rate follows the actual rate. Krugman argued that the welfare-state was partly to blame for the rise in the natural rates of unemployment in Europe. It discourages those on low incomes from working by raising the reservation wage and, through the taxes imposed on those working, reduces the reward from pecuniary focused toil. Krugman's 'solution' to the puzzle is that poverty and low wages on one side of the Atlantic is mirrored by greater long term unemployment for the corresponding low skilled worker group on the other. What would unite the two is the low net rewards from labour market participation. What distinguishes them is greater wage flexibility in the US. Thus, the fall in demand for labour, a shift of the demand curve to the left. In the US, the wage falls; whereas in Europe, the quasi-fixed wage is sticky-downwards leading to an increase in unemployment.

Hysteresis can result from a major shock inducing the scrapping of geographically or industrially specific productive assets, reducing the economy's potential output, so shifting the production function downwards. We could label this phenomenon *production hysteresis*. The 1974-79 period had a lower rate of growth than from the mid-1980s. One could argue that the

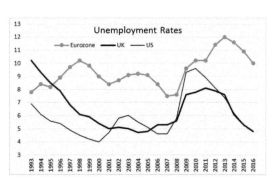

Lehman's collapse was the largest shock for 60 years and the Corona virus for centuries. This analysis need not be confined to a large shock. Restrictive activities, possible enshrined in law, negotiated by Trade Unions, were blamed – inflexible labour market. Prolonged unfavourable conditions in the labour or goods markets may provoke or enlarge an output gap. Persistent and large gaps between actual and potential output may eventually prompt a re-evaluation of expectations and initiate the scrapping of capacity, or production hysteresis, and a change in the equilibrium rate of unemployment, or *unemployment hysteresis*. Consequently, there is a range of potential equilibria that the economy could move towards. Either a supply or demand shock may force manufacturers to change their expectations about the future, leading to the adjustment of capacity. Any subsequent stimulation of the economy could quickly lead to price and wage inflation as, once hysteresis has set-in, excess capacity in both the production and labour markets will be much reduced. Thus, the government may be left severely constrained by events. To reinvigorate the economy, the government ultimately needs to change both firms' and workers' expectations so that they respond to an increase demand by expanding output and employment.

Anderson in *Business Economics* Vol. 49 pp.2-30 proposed a new source of unemployment – *policy cost uncertainty hypothesis*. Here, political uncertainty provokes rational private sector managers to restrict the number of employees they hire because of the potential cost of employing them due to future changes in government policy. So the possibility of a new future payroll tax, greater paternity leave or a high minimum wage would deter employers from taking on the staff they need today. Moreover, the uncertainty affects employment through investment indirectly.

The firm is a value-maximiser. Managers maximise value over a longer run rather than maximise profit over a succession of periods. This implies that there is a multitude of economic conditions that could prevail at any time. The manager has some idea of likelihood of the current state changing and in what direction. These assumptions allow the manager to pre-empt a perceived change in the environment. Potential cost avoidance can lead to not recruiting someone when it is profitable so to do. This was evident in manufacturing output.

A case in point where political uncertainty affects expectations: a trade war for a global business can be seen in Caterpillar, the mining machines and construction bulldozers. In May 2018, it was evident that it could not keep up with a boom in demand. Like heavy trucks construction is a bellwether of economics conditions. Over a year its East Peoria plant saw orders jump, in general, three-fold. However, it did not respond. The plant was running just one shift, only four days a week, and its CEO, Jim Umpleby, won't invest in factory capacity. Rather, he will invest in new technologies, expanding its parts business and selling more rental and used equipment. This, in part, reflects the recent restructuring where it closed or restructured more than 25 factories and its full-time workforce was smaller in 2018 than it was at the end of 2012.

Kevin Murphy and Robert Topel[6] argue that these disturbingly high rates of unemployment are a result of inflexible labour markets. The labour market *insiders*, protected by union contracts, may gain from higher wages. *Outsiders*, those looking for work, are less fortunate. They pay with more than their jobs opportunities: they also lose the chance to accumulate skills and experience that would raise their future earning power. Flexible labour markets in the US and UK yield lower wages for some workers, but they are much better at putting people in to work. Without labour market flexibility, young workers are especially hard hit, and suffer permanent scars. Their employment prospects forever curtailed. The US youth unemployment rate was 12.3%, whereas Italy's (43.1%), Portugal's (33.8%), Spain's and Greece's (50.1%) were over twice that. Even if the economy and employment are growing, when growth in the demand for labour is outpaced by growth in the number of people looking for work, real wages will fall.

A reduction in benefits lowers the level of unearned income, possibly below the reservation wage of the non-job seeker. Also, it increases the opportunity cost of seeking rather than working. So, a cut in benefits should focus the mind of homo economicus. However, Jan Eichhorn of Edinburgh University argues that State benefit levels across the Europe 28 had 'no effect' on jobseekers' motivation to find work. There was a positive relationship between benefits and despondence. Luxembourg and Sweden were in the top quartile for both benefit levels and dissatisfaction amongst the jobless. The German unemployed were more dissatisfied than elsewhere in Europe, more than 50% higher than in Hungary. Romania and Poland, by contrast, were in the bottom quartile for benefit levels whilst the unemployed were the least and third-least affected by being out of work, respectively. In some countries, such as Spain, Poland and Romania, benefits had 'little effect' on perceived well-being.

---

[6] FT.com August 15, 2014 6:42 pm Raising the minimum wage is the wrong way to deal with low pay

INFLATION

Inflation is technically defined as a sustained rise in a weighted average of all prices, or a persistent increase in the general level of prices. Deflation is technically defined as a sustained fall in a weighted average of all prices, or a persistent general decline in prices. Disinflation is when the inflation rate is positive, but declining over time.

Traditionally, when discussing inflation, we consider the costs to society. Standard considerations are outlined below:
- There is a slot machine cost, where stated prices must be altered to reflect changing costs. As well as slot machines, it will also cover menus and brochures that must be altered or reprinted;
- The shoe leather cost concerns liquidity preference. Holding cash entails an opportunity cost. With higher inflation the holding of cash becomes more of a cost so one will visit the bank more frequently wearing out the shoes;
- As price rises are not uniform across products, inflation changes relative prices and, indeed, injects uncertainty into anticipated prices. This should deter entrepreneurs from investing, reducing potential growth. Also, one is spending more time gathering price information, wearing out shoes;
- Inflation pushes up interest rates, also reducing investment. The banks will be less clear about their returns from lending, so as to share some of the risk, the bank will offer the loan on a variable rate or on a fixed rate with a higher rate of interest;
- Inflation disfavours those on fixed incomes and favours borrowers. The purchasing power of those on fixed incomes will fall with inflation. In the developing world, food riots have occurred as the prices of essentials make them unaffordable. Also, the real value of debt will decline so that the real cost to the individual of repaying the loan declines;
- Inflation discourages saving and favours consumption. It shifts resources from the old (fixed income) to the young. Strangely, the government, usually the largest debtor in the system, benefits the most from inflation. So, there is a bias which credit rating agencies are keen to discourage.

Unanticipated inflation comes as a 'surprise', whereas anticipated inflation is the rate expected to occur. A means of reducing the risk of real values being undermined by inflation can be to index-link it or to share the risk. In a sense, the reward to the capitalist is based on risk taking, but some entrepreneurs may shift the rise in price on to the consumer. As inflation affects the purchasing power of money, the lender loses and the debtor gains. To compensate for the loss of the value of capital a greater interest rate is charged to the borrower by the lender, such as through a variable interest rate on a loan rather than shouldering all the risk with a fixed.

Measures of UK inflation are shown below. In 2017, CPIH was introduced. This adds owner-occupier housing costs and council tax to CPI. In April 2015, the CPI was negative, but CPIH was not. One way of boosting demand is to give the impression that prices will be higher.

Deflation

Deflation should have the reverse effects.

❑ The real value of debt rises, disadvantaging borrowers. The purchasing power of the fixed income rises and, by implication the stock or saving (wealth) is enhanced;

❑ Slot machine costs remain – so it is price *changes* that impose a cost;

❑ Nominal interest rates, instruments of monetary policy may become impotent. With inflation, nominal interest rates can move in line. Until 2015, one would claim nominal interest rates cannot be reduced below zero. But they can. It is not clear though what this means;

❑ Consumption is reduced. If prices are expected to be lower tomorrow than today, consumers will reduce their discretionary spending. Current consumption will fall, weakening enfeebled companies. (The standard view is that excess capacity puts a lid on price rises.)

Given the perverse world of Japan's deflationary pressures, a 40% phone charges drop was estimated to drive core consumer inflation down by 0.96 and education fees 0.9 percentage points in 2018/19. In October 2018, Japan's inflation rate of 1% was boosted by the oil price. However, the price falls meant that this would taper off. BoJ believes Japan's inflation expectations are adaptive so 'negative price shocks' are remembered. This was compounded by the report that in 2018Q3 the output gap was −0.2%, falling from 0.7% above trend in Q2. In March 2019, Coca-Cola Japan raised its prices for the first time in 27 years, by ¥20.

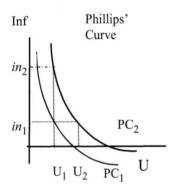

Shift or Shape - the Phillips' Curve Unpacked

The PC originally related money wage growth to unemployment. When unemployment was high, trade unions would be in an enfeebled bargaining position or employers could easily find staff without the need to offer a greater wage incentive. Tighter labour markets would see higher wage increases. As an *X*-efficiency wage perspective, once staff began to leave in large numbers, the employer would raise wages for all to retain some. Alternatively, when unemployment is high, there was the threat that those outside the firm could replace the insider, making the insider more compliant. Let us go through possible breaks in the argument.

1) The outsiders are not a threat

Krueger, Cramer and Cho argued that the long-term unemployed do not affect wages and inflation so they should be stripped from the unemployment figures. In effect, this implies the Phillips' curve *shifts* outwards. Unemployment needs to be higher to place downward pressure on prices. It also means there are more in the labour market that are structurally unemployed. The workforce schedule shifts to the right relative to the supply of labour. It also can be interpreted as hysteresis. There is a higher level of unemployment for a given rate of inflation, or higher inflation for a given level of unemployment. If these are removed from the equation, full employment will be met at a higher rate of non-employment.

2)   It is machines, not people, that threaten

The Phillips' curve in this sense could be flat for much of it away from full employment – and as Keynes envisaged, money wages are sticky downwards. TODAY from a Marxist perspective capital is not constrained by labour. Hines modelled wage increase based on trade union power. The number of workers involved in labour disputes in the UK in 2017, at 33,000, was the lowest ever recorded. This reflects a decline in TU membership to 6.23m or 23.2%. Alternatively, the threat of money wage increases results in substituting in capital. Wage-wage and wage-price spirals might have been a function of the era of the manual worker. A Spar manager, facing an increase in the living (minimum) wage to £7.20, let some staff go, others working harder to make up the gap. At £7.50, they installed a self-service checkout machine. Sainsbury's announced in March 2018 that it would raise the base wage to £9.20 from £8/hr. The cost is that the workers lose bonuses and paid breaks. With that threat to benefits and jobs, market power has shifted to the capitalist. Thus, there is also the possibility that it has *flattened* so that the rise in wages/prices is not as pronounced as unemployment declines. Yellen was seeking to explain how the fall in unemployment was not putting the usual pressures on wages and inflation, signifying less of a need to raise interest rates.

3)   Non-Participation is rising

The problem with skills and the labour market arise in the US. Long-term unemployment is defined as that over 26 weeks. Between August 2008, before Lehman's and February 2014, the count doubled to 3.8m. The proportion of long-term unemployed in the unemployment figures rose from 19.8% to 37%. The long-term unemployed are very much at the margins of employment. Their likely spell of non-participation could be prolonged but temporary, implying that the output gap becomes smaller and the Phillips' curve *shifts* inwards. The US unemployment rate dropped to 3.5% in September, the lowest since May 1969. The participate rate was 63% shifting the divide between unemployment and non-participation – non-employment remains the same.

4)   Wage Increase are suppress by Monopsony Employers

Another reason to suggest the Phillips' curve had *shifted* in the US is based on profit margins pushing prices up at every level of unemployment. Corporate profit margins before depreciation are inflated when price is high relative to labour cost. As corporate output makes up 52% of US GDP, producer prices are estimated to be 350bps (3.5%) higher than they would be if the profit margin was at its long-term average of 31.3%. Goldman Sachs estimated that US wage growth since the early 2000s was 0.25%/yr slower because of corporate and union concentration. The Resolution Foundation reported that in 2003/4 the top five companies in 600 sub-sectors in Britain had a market share 39%. By 2015/16, this had risen to 43%.

5)   Wages are not a good indicator of compensation

Japan faced an unemployment rate of 2.3% in February. This low level is lower than in 2018 but wages still remain stubborn. In March 2016, Japanese wages were rising at half the rate they were in 2015: in 2017 they were lower again. Without wage inflation, price inflation >2% was not possible. Toyota paid a ¥4,000/month basic wage increase in 2015. In 2016, it awarded ¥1,500, ¥1,300 in 2017 and ¥10,700 in 2019. By contrast, Honda agreed a ¥1,400 deal, up from ¥1,700 in 2018. The wage system is highly structured so that a basic wage increase affects all layers of a company. This wage growth may reflect a desire not to increase costs. The BoJ believed that compensation in terms of holidays and family friendly polices (see day-night shift) is off-setting the wage rise. Cutting out wasteful unproductive hours of work will increase productivity per hour. In December 2017, hoping for a wage-wage spiral Abe called for a wage rise of 3%. A bid of 4% was expected to provoke a 1.98% outcome. In 2018, according to Rengo, the trade union federation, wages rose by 2.07%.

6)   Unemployment is Not a Good indicator

Blanchflower proposed that the pay puzzle what not a sign of the Phillips' curve not working, but that the spare capacity indicator was poor. The underemployment in the economy is increasingly related to constrained hours rather than job access.

In the quarter to May 2015, the ONS reported that both wages and unemployment in the UK rose. The unemployment rate rose from 5.5% to 5.6% when there was a notable 3.2% increase in average weekly pay. In effect, this conflicts with a Phillips' curve analysis or the PC shifts outwards. It could be that some shifted from non-participation to offer themselves on the labour market. However, employment fell 67,000 as well. There could be a restructuring. The number of people working as full-time employees increased 45,000 but there was a much bigger drop in the number of self-employed, part-time and temporary workers.

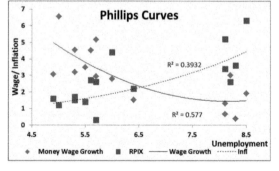

7)   Firms only need to Attract

Haldane argued that wage increases went to job shifters. With fewer shifters, the fear that others would move jobs is not the same threat to employers to retain staff that it once was.

AGGREGATE SUPPLY AND DEMAND

The Aggregate Demand Schedule plots the quantity of real GDP demanded at any given price. It slopes downwards because of:

- the real balance effect:- As prices rise, a consumer's money wealth and income will buy fewer goods. Therefore, less will be demanded as prices rise. Correspondingly, as prices fall, a consumer's real wealth and income will increase. As people become richer, they purchase more goods/services;
- interest effect:- as prices rise, consumers demand larger money balances. This will lead to an increase in the rate of interest. As the interest rate rises, investment expenditures fall. This will lead to less aggregate demand in the economy;
- international effect:- as UK prices rise, British goods become relatively expensive compared with foreign imports resulting a fall in the purchase of goods/services by both British and foreign citizens.

A change in the average price level will lead to a move ALONG the AD curve. The AD curve will shift when there is a change in demand conditions at any given average price level. The AD schedule will shift outwards to the right when:

- the nominal money supply increases - this would lead to a fall in the rate of interest in the money market and so an increase in investment expenditures;
- there is an increase in government spending or cut in taxes;
- there is an increase in the income of foreigners. This would increase the demand for normal and luxury UK exports.

The Aggregate Supply Schedule plots the quantity of real GDP supplied at any given price. It has three phases.

Keynes assumed that, under the conditions of huge under-employment, with an increase in aggregate demand, average price does not rise – it is fixed. This is important. This means that we assume that the government can spend money without increasing prices, i.e. no inflation. In this phase, the AS is horizontal. By contrast, neo-classical economists believe that the economy has flexible wages and prices in the short-run. This implies that the economy automatically operates around the natural rate (full employment) in the long run. Any pump-priming can increase output but only in the short-run: in the long-run it will lead to an increase in prices only. This occurs at the natural rate of unemployment. (Q_n full employment output.) In this phase, the AS is vertical and occurs in the long-run - hence LRAS. In the third phase, the AS slopes upwards because of:

- prices of factors:- if firms wish to increase output, they will demand more factors of production. This increases wages and prices of raw materials. Thus, the increased output will be accompanied by an increase in the costs of factors of production;
- general prices:- change in the average price level will lead to a move ALONG the AS curve. A price rise will present more opportunities to make profit. Firms expand output but costs rise limiting this expansion.

This third phase is associated with the Phillips' curve. This phase can shift more easily relative to the other two. It is the short-run trade-off and is labelled SRAS.

When there is a change in supply conditions at any given average price the AS curve will shift. That is, prices are fixed but firms change output. This includes:
- a wages fall reduces overall costs and, therefore, increases profit. We would expect businesses to expand output: SRAS shifts to the right;
- a fall of the costs of raw materials or the non-wage costs of employing labour falls. These will reduce overall costs and, therefore, increase profit of firms. We would expect businesses to expand output: SRAS shifts to the right;
- an increase of the output per man will increase GDP output for given input. In other words, the AS has shifted to the right. The same applies to the application of new technology. These are incremental changes;
- a supply shock, such as a natural or institutional change in supply conditions, which usually shifts the LRAS to the left. Examples of this are the OPEC oil price shocks of 1973/4 and 1979. One could include the banking collapse of 2008/9 and now Corona. Hysteresis is associated with this shock. Labour market participants may change their attitude to work fundamentally, perhaps withdrawing permanently; moving from employed/unemployed to non-participant.

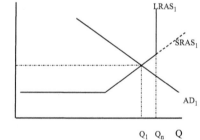

An AS/AD diagram is shown below. The AD intersects with the SRAS at Q_1, which is to the left of Q_n. A fiscal stimulus should shift the AD curve to the right, reducing the unemployment rate but at the cost of higher prices. This is the trade-off portion of the SRAS schedule.

Demand pull inflation

Keynes made particular assumptions about an economy when in a deep recession. He suggested that the economy would be in equilibrium significantly below full employment. The theoretical forces moving the economy back to full employment (later interpreted as the natural rate), flexible wages and prices, do not exist. He suggested that wages were *sticky downwards* and as the under-utilisation of capacity would prevent factor prices from rising. So, an increase in aggregate demand would not lead to an increase in prices. In the diagram below, the starting position is P_1Q_1. A collapse in demand shifts the AD curve to AD_2 at output level Q_2. The price level and output have fallen. However, the depth of the recession means that a stimulus package could shift the AD curve to the right to AD_3 and output to Q_3 without prices changing. Demand pull inflation is a necessary evil to be accommodated if the policy is to move the economy to Q_1. Keynes presumed no inflation until full employment, so this is related to a different theory.

Keynes advocated a counter-cyclical policy based on running a budget deficit in a recession [G > T]. Thus, one measure of a government stimulus package is the extent of the borrowing requirement to cover the deficit. Government borrowing could have a counteractive impact. Fully funding the deficit requires increase borrowing. This could raise interest rates or at least crowded-out private sector borrowing. Alternatively, it could support the fiscal stimulus, by increasing the money supply (print money). Note that Keynes did not project the upwards sloping AS curve and he was not focused on a structural deficit.

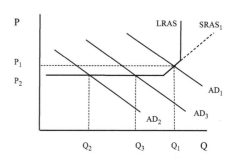

Demand pull inflation entails too much money (demand) chasing too few goods. In the diagram right, the initial position at P_1/ equilibrium real natural output Q_n.

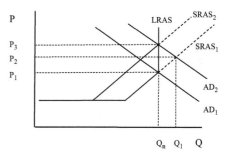

An increase in aggregate demand to AD_2 leads to an increase in output above real natural output. Here, there is excess demand. This could be viewed like an inflationary gap (but isn't). Keynes would suggest a reduction of government expenditure would resolve this problem. The AD would move back to the left. An EAPC model would see movement back to Q_n as those workers fooled on to the market in the hope of a real wage increase withdraw. The fall in the numbers in the labour market will shift the SRAS to the left, to $SRAS_2$.

Cost Push Inflation
Cost push inflation entails an increase in prices when the economy is not close to full employment. It involves an increase in the costs of production, leading to the shift in the AS to the left. In the diagram right, the initial position is P_1Q_1. Under these circumstances, prices rise and output falls (implying unemployment rises).

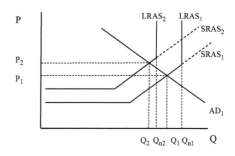

A **supply side shock** shifts both the long-run and short-run AS schedules to the left or right. Importantly, the full employment level of output, Q_n, also moves. In other words, the capacity to produce goods and services is persistently reduced and the natural rate of unemployment increases. The output gap decreases from $Q_{n1} - Q_1$ to $Q_{n2} - Q_2$. Why? LRAS can shift to the left as a result of:

- prolonged unemployment;
- a collapse in demand for certain skills;
- an increase in the rate of technological change;
- a rapid and significant change in costs.

With deep recessions firms and workers become more cautious/ pessimistic, which lowers the investment rate and willingness to look for work. Firms scrap productive capacity. The collapse of manufacturing industry in the north and west of the UK in the 1980s left many structurally/ regionally unemployed. Moreover, the longer someone is frictionally unemployed, the more likely it is that they become structurally unemployed.

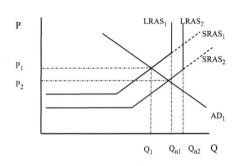

Not discussed often, but must be the case, is the supply side change that increases the capacity to produce goods and services. In other words, the LRAS shifts right. The initial position is at P_1/Q_{n1} with an output gap of $Q_{n1} - Q_1$. With a shift in productive capacity and prices do not fall, the output gap will increase to $Q_{n2} - Q_1$. However, lower prices with a fixed wage increase the real wage, participation and output.

Oxford Economics estimated that for every \$20 fall in the price of oil, after a 2 to 3 year lag, leads to an increase in growth of 0.4%. One could suggest the shock is not symmetrical. There is not a restructuring, so the change costs are not there. A fall in costs does not have to lead to a fall in prices. A fall in the oil price in 1986 led to a rise in growth to 4.6% in 1988, a figure not again seen until 2000.

As discussed under unemployment, there is such a concept as the non-employment rate. This will vary with:-

- Benefits:- higher benefits will deter some from seeking work;
- The recent rewards from job search:- lack of reward from job search will discourage workers from seeking work;
- The rate of job generation: a more dynamic economy will generate more jobs but increase the dislocation between the unemployed and skills. More will be in training, shifting the supply of labour curve to the left;
- The greater the number of women of child bearing age;
- The greater the number approaching retirement:- some will retire early;

- The greater the rate of female participation:- this point can be cultural see participation;
- The reward from working:- if the after tax, real wage is falling, this will lead to workers withdrawing from the labour market. This would be consistent with the EAPC and participating only if the reward is sufficient.

A Macro Policy Nightmare
As noted with a negative supply side shock firms and workers become more cautious/ pessimistic. Firms scrap productive capacity. With a negative demand side shock consumers are less willing to part with their money. They fear the future is fraught with uncertainty. They may have or about to lose their job, so they up their precautionary funds – save more. The Corona virus imposed both. It would not allow workers to work or shoppers to shop in sufficient numbers. As the US death toll from the outbreak hit 65, the mayors of New York City and Los Angeles ordered restaurants, bars and cafes closed, with takeout and delivery the only options for food sales. Movie theatres, small theatre houses and concert venues were also ordered closed. The Trump administration was on the horns of a dilemma that others missed. Which is worse; more people die but the remainder are richer, or fewer die and the survivors are poorer? Lockdown will force many firms into receivership and workers in to hardship. With a weak support system these resources may become permanently idle, shifting the aggregate supply curve left - a supply side shock. Deaths and despair will follow, anyway.

Against the advice of medical experts, Trump was considering *removing* guidelines to avoid large gatherings and other measures on the 30th March. In the US system the president cannot lift the order that applied to more than 100m Americans to remain at home and non-essential businesses closed. As in the UK, without restrictions the healthcare system would be overwhelmed. With about 93,000 intensive-care hospital beds, and a death rate of 10% 1.1m US deaths estimated by Imperial College would imply 11m cases.

Let us examine the issues in simple terms. The AD/AS diagram below is drawn with a very flat Phillips curve section. The output gap of $Q_{n1} - Q_{e1}$ is relatively small.

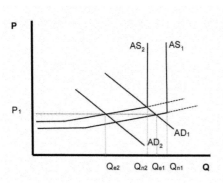

Suddenly, both production and consumption is affected; both consumers and producers become more pessimistic/ ordered home. AS and the AD schedules shift to the left. Importantly, the full employment level of output shifts as firms collapse, lay-off workers and scrap machinery to Q_{n2}. The AD shift left. Shoppers cannot shop. The output gap decreases from $Q_{n1} - Q_{e1}$ to $Q_{n2} - Q_{e2}$. Keeping businesses afloat will not help if there are no shoppers. Keeping consumers optimistic is of no use if there is no job for them or goods to buy. Both aggregate supply and demand must be supported. The stark reality of the problem was revealed on the 26th March and 2nd April 2020. Despite unemployment at a near 50-year low and a steadily growing economy, many Americans were struggling before Corona. Almost 40% of adults had less than $400 in precautionary cash holding. The top 10% of household income earners hold nearly 70% of US wealth while the bottom half had only just over 1%. As recently as February, the US unemployment rate was hovering near historic lows at 3.5%, with jobless claims about 210,000. On the 26th March it was reported by the Department of Labor almost 3.283m people registered to claim jobless benefits for the week ended 21st. The 3m increase was nearly five times more than the previous record of 695,000 set in 1982. Over the following 6-weeks the total rose to 33.3m. Economic Policy Institute found an additional 8.9-13.9m were unemployment but 'shut out of the system' as they did not qualify. But 19-26% unemployment rate is mass unemployment. The US had *not* implemented job retention programme, reflecting perhaps a more fluid labour market – so this was temporary. They implemented a Payroll Protection Program of forgivable business loans, instead. In the UK, the Dept. for Work and Pensions had 2.5m applications for Universal Credit between 16th and 5st May. Normally, there would be 100,000 claims in a two-week period.

Two countries' responses will be explored. In July, the Reserve Bank of Australia's (RBA) reduced interest rates to all-time low of 1% in part to meet its target of pushing unemployment down to around 4.5%, down from the prevailing 5.2% so the economy was in need of a boost. As a major exporter of materials to China, it would be exposed to China's reaction to the Corona virus. However, it kicked into action in March both fiscal and monetary initiatives. The RBA bought A$18bn in sovereign government bonds between 20th to 26th March as part of a A$2tn strategy to keep three-year yields around 0.25%. Thus, this would affect borrowing costs of both firms and consumers. But, if worried about job loss, this would not work. On 29th Australia announced a six months wage-subsidy plan for possibly 3.5m works worth A$70bn. The "job keeper" allowance provided eligible companies with A$1,500 every fortnight for each employee. Any company that lost 30% of its revenue was eligible. On the 1st April, it offered free childcare for six months as part of a bid to keep businesses operating. Included in the A$200bn, was a A$1.6bn subsidy over the following quarter to keep about 13,000 childcare centres open. It also made sense to support indirectly critical workers from medical professionals to cleaners and food deliverers. These would affect the capacity (Q_{n2} vertical AS) and the upwards sloping part of the AS, reducing the movement left shifting. Also, helping to reassure consumers they would have an income close to normal times the detrimental precautionary effects (the drift of AD_2 leftwards) would be reduced.

The US was also engaged in novel fiscal and monetary policies. On the 17th March US Treasury Secretary Steven Mnuchin announced that he would put to Congress a helicopter fund of $250bn as part of a $1tn stimulus package. Helicopter money is a term for giving consumers free money for them to spend as they see fit. Separately, the government also allowed companies and individuals to delay their tax payments for 90 days. A fiscal measure to reduce the leftward AD shift.

The FED initiative on 23rd March was an unlimited bond purchase scheme and backstop direct loans to companies. On 24th the NY FED announced that it hired BlackRock to help it execute the purchase of commercial mortgage-backed securities, secured primarily by multifamily home mortgages guaranteed by housing entities Fannie Mae and Freddie Mac. Having announced on 15th a bond-buying programme the NY FED on the 19th would purchase \$32bn in OMO. In the event, it bought \$17.398bn. An increase on \$878m the week before, but clearly it was still short. This is odd. A measure of the demand for money during the panic running up to the bailout bill on 27th could be gauged by the Libor-OIS Spread. It is an imperfect measure of extra interest big banks pay for longer-term financing than the cost of overnight funds. On the day, the spread was 138bps, twice as high as anytime in the previous decade, but short of the 350 seen in 2008. This could be due to banks being unable to borrow (as in 2008). Here, it was an indication of demand for cash as companies and individuals try to stay afloat while the Corona virus pandemic chokes off income. Vivek Juneja of JPMorgan estimated that up to 26th March major public corporations announced new loans and draws on credit lines of \$208bn during the coronavirus panic, almost half of that from 22nd. A crisis for money market funds would will follow. Redemptions in March of \$102bn constituted 31% of the money market funds. These marked a shift to intervention beyond financial markets into the real economy. Here, to reduce the collapse of firms due to weak or no cash flow and no easy access to short term funds (so a leftward LRAS shift), the FED would act as lender.

When approved by Congress came to it on 27th the package was worth \$2.2tn. The helicopter element worth \$290bn was a direct payments of up to \$1,200, with additional payments of \$500/child. Payments would be phased out for those earning more than \$75,000 a year. A further \$260bn in payments was allocated to the displaced worker & employer. The jobless workers would see increase of \$600/wk. Laid-off workers would get those payments for up to 4 months. Regular benefits, which typically run out after six months in most States, would be extended for 13 weeks. The self-employed workers, independent contractors and those who typically do not qualify for unemployment benefits would be eligible. The government would also partially make up wages for workers whose hours were reduced. A vulnerable group, the gig economy, were captured. Most government safety net benefits including health insurance, sick pay, workers' compensation and unemployment insurance are attached to an employment relationship. State authorities use data on wages submitted by employers to calculate unemployment pay. Gig economy companies do not report that information, making it difficult for drivers to claim unemployment benefits.

Loans for businesses with < 500 employees were to be forgiven, partially, if they are used for employee salaries, rent, mortgage interest and utility costs. With this and emergency grants for small business, the loans and grants element amounted to \$377bn. A refundable 50% payroll tax credit for businesses for employee retention was also available. Within two weeks $349bn was allocated so that the fund ran out and only replenished on 27th by another $310bn.

The FED opened a 'Main Street Lending Facility' programme limited to those with 10,000 workers and $2.5bn in turnover on 9th April. On April 30th this was extended to firms of 15,000 employees and $5bn turnover. The programme of $600bn operated through banks with $75bn underwritten by the Treasury.

The poor were not entirely forgotten. There was a ban on foreclosing on federally-backed mortgages through mid-May, and a four-month ban on evictions by landlords who rely on federal housing programs. There was additional spending for food stamps and child nutrition ($42bn), child and family services ($45bn) and housing programs ($12bn). So, the US and Australia appeared to be shoring-up demand using a Universal Income approach. This was reviewed last year….

Universal Income
McKinsey Global Institute reported in 2018 that global executives expect to replace over a quarter of their workforces by 2023, along side the possibility that 30-40% of jobs being replaced by technology. The latter has enormous political implication. One solution is to offer a Universal Income. In May 2018, Finland was half way through a 2 year programme when it was abandoned. Rather than €500 unemployment benefit, a candidate received €560 in a monthly basic income. This does not require someone to be a job seeker, which reduces stress. Interestingly, a recipient did not lose it if they worked.

Clearly, with 40% possibly persistently without work, a universal income is socially desirable. Five arguments have been mounted against UBI:
1. it is expensive if everyone gets it. Deficits and so interest rates will mushroom.
2. it will increase inequalities. Those getting targeted benefits will get less whilst the rich get more.
3. work offers a social capital, structure, meaning: it trains, challenges and rewards: along with pensions, it is the key means by which income currently disbursed. Delinking work from income, as we see from the US male, tends to be associated with dysfunctional societies.
4. it undermines the incentive to participate in work and possibly society. It encourages dependence.
5. it deflects from looking for alternative solutions to the distribution of work issue. Rather than calling it part time, a full working week could redefine 16 hours/wk as full time. This is not so fanciful. IG Metall and Sudwestmetall agreed a 2-year deal covering 900,000 workers that entailed a 28-hr week in February 2018.

In Australia, rather than laying off, some large firms in March were hiring. Seen as doing their bit under CSR, one could see this as long term profit maximisation from a Ford(ist) perspective. But their actions will also likely protect profits by taking customers from rivals, minimising loan defaults and a change in work-styles. Telstra, the largest telecom, was in the process of cutting a fifth of its workforce. It brought forward A$500m capital spending, froze redundancies and advertised for 1,000 contractors to handle customer calls as people worked from home. It removed internet data limits. Long term it could see a cultural shift in working, and wanted to be well-placed for that change.

Woolworths and Coles were hiring more than 30,000 people between them to cope with the supermarket rush. People's long term shopping habits could also change. With restrictions on the numbers in supermarkets, shoppers would make a smaller number of larger shops, returning to the one-stop-shop, favouring the larger supermarkets.

Even though the initiatives were backed by State guarantees following the RBA emergency ¼% interest rate cut, the Commonwealth Bank of Australia, cut fixed-interest mortgages by 0.7% and 1% for small business borrowers. It also deferred business and property loan and interest repayments by six months. That said, most are on variable-rate mortgages, which it did not change. This, along with the other initiatives, is also about reputation. Having have very 'bad presses', coming out well from the Corona period could improve their standing in the community.

What Happens to Price?
In the AS/AD figure above the price level is arranged as fixed. This is, in part, because the price level could shift either way. I would expect it to shift on the upside. Much of theory relies on the smooth running of the system with swift adjustment between (some) equilibria. However, in a bid to stem the spread of the virus governments placed severe restrictions on movement and key workers have fallen ill. Logistics and supply chains break down as air-freight capacity, trucking and shipping crews are depleted. Moreover, as China was hit first, Europe and the US were short of tens of thousands of freight containers, while shippers were also struggling with quarantines at ports and crew shortages.

The head of the British Retail Consortium, Helen Dickinson, observed on March 21st that there was £1bn worth more food in people's houses than there was three weeks previously. The global supplies of the most widely consumed food crops were adequate when wheat was projected to be at record levels in the year ahead. The UN's Food and Agriculture Organisation warned that any rush by importers to buy staples could fuel global food inflation, despite ample reserves of staple crops. Let us look as five examples in March:
1. In the two weeks to the 26th wheat futures surged to two-month highs. Here, there is a shift in demand to the right for bakery and pasta goods.
2. As restrictions on movement were imposed in Argentina, logistical issues reduced shipments of soymeal, raising global prices. Thus, here, the supply of soymeal to the market is reduced, not due to crop production but distribution. This being an

input to the price of meats, it will shift the supply schedule of beef production to the left.

3. Maize, which in the US is grown as a biofuel, was exposed to the price war in oil, which sent WTI to $19/b. The corn price hit a low not seen since December 2017. Here, the issue is substitute in supply. The price of oil shifted buyers of fuel to purchase a derivative of crude rather that a biofuel.
4. Fresh produce, like fruit or fish, reflects short term market issues. In France, the agriculture minister called on sellers not to hike prices of produce like asparagus facing seasonal difficulties. At the same time, he encouraged households to buy fish. With a drop in demand because restaurants are closed, the price of fish dropped.
5. In an effort to maintain supplies, Vietnam banned rice exports in February. It wanted to stockpile 270,000t to ensure food security. Using the same food security argument, the Philippines planned to boost rice imports to boost stocks by 300,000t. The Philippines became the world's biggest rice importer in 2019 usually buying from Vietnam. Benchmark Thai white rice prices hit their highest level in eight years.

Policy RIP?
By the end of the 1970s, the problem of stagflation, where the recession is accompanied by rising unemployment and inflation, left demand management advocates in a policy paradox; whatever target the government pursued, another would worsen. This led to a rejection of Keynesian policies and a switch to Monetarism. Stagflation, associated with a supply-side shock, would affect the natural rate of unemployment and the long-run growth trend. A short-run deviation from trend becomes ossified with the scrapping of capacity to produce and, hence, induces a long-run effect. Oddly, it could be that the quantity theory of money, the cornerstone of Monetarist theory, was abandoned in July 2009, as the MPC found the relationship not reflected in the results of Quantitative Easing. One could say Keynesian demand management was shelved in 1975/76 following the oil crisis of 1974. It is interesting that the furlough and helicopter money, Keynesian notions returned as a much larger shock than the others is leading us into new territory.

INCOME MULTIPLIER

The Keynesian model uses terminology and symbols as follows:

Y (national income) = E (expenditure) = Q or O (output)
J (injections to the economy) = I (investment) + G (government expenditure) + X (exports)
W (leakages from the economy) = S (savings) + T (taxes) + M (imports)
Y_d = disposable income = $Y - T$ Marginal propensity to consume $c = \dfrac{\Delta C}{\Delta Y}$
Marginal propensity to pay tax $t = \dfrac{\Delta T}{\Delta Y}$ Marginal propensity to import $m = \dfrac{\Delta M}{\Delta Y}$

Average propensity to consume $= \frac{C}{Y}$. The income multiplier shows that an increase in an injection will feed through to create a much greater increase in income than the stimulus that induced it. This will not happen instantly, but will build up over a period of time.

The derivation of a multiplier in an open economy
The model is in equilibrium when $E = Y$ or $J = W$. The general expression for expenditure in an economy open is $E = C + I + G + (X-M)$. The consumption function can be written as $C = cY_d$ i.e. consumption varies with disposable income. The level of import varies with disposable income $M = mY_d$. Disposable income will be income retained after taxes $T = tY$. Substituting in produces the expression:

$$Y = \left(\frac{1}{1 - (c - m)(1 - t)}\right)[I + G + X] \quad \Delta Y = \left(\frac{1}{1 - (c - m)(1 - t)}\right)[\Delta A]$$

Where $A = I + G + X$ $\Delta Y = k\,\Delta A$ where k is the multiplier

The simple multiplier discussed in text books would have it that the stimulus, represented by ΔG, would be spent on employing workers to dig holes, build hospitals and roads etc., which should put money into workers' hands. This is spent on domestically produced goods. Domestic firms, seeing a fall in inventories, will employ more domestic workers, reducing unemployment and increasing output.

In an open economy $(c - m)$, the addition to the model of the consumption of non-imported goods, strongly influences the magnitude of the impact of a stimulus package. With an MPC of 0.8, a simple multiplier, where savings are the only leakage, is equal to 5, but this is reduced to 2.78 if the average income tax rate is 20p in the pound, and is reduced further to 1.47 once imports are taken into account. A larger the gap between MPC and MPM induces a larger multiplier. Giving money to those with a high MPC should boost the multiplier. But if that group's preference for overseas' goods counters this, the strategy would be undermined.

MPC = 0.6	K	MPC = 0.7	K	MPC = 0.8	k
MPT = 0 MPM = 0	2.5	MPT = 0 MPM = 0	3.33	MPT = 0 MPM = 0	5
MPT = 0.2 MPM = 0	1.92	MPT = 0.2 MPM = 0	2.27	MPT = 0.2 MPM = 0	2.78
MPT = 0.2 MPM = 0.2	1.47	MPT = 0.2 MPM = 0.3	1.47	MPT = 0.2 MPM = 0.4	1.47

Cambridge Econometrics estimated that for every £1 invested in super-fast broadband by the government the UK economy benefited by £20. A short-term gain of £1.5bn and 11,000 jobs in network and construction would grow by 2024 to £6.3bn/yr, associated with 20,000 jobs and because some could work from home, an additional £45m/ year in savings. The government would provide an initial subsidy of £530m to the private sector to induce this.

HOUSING

Rent

With a perfect capital market, people should consume property services up to the point where their utility is equal to the rent paid, subject to a budget constraint. As a capital good, property ownership, though, whilst it is being utilised, possibility bestows a capital gain. As a result, renting and buying a home are not perfect substitutes; there is no Modigliani-Miller notion of indifference. However, as the price of a property falls, one would expect the rent to decrease correspondingly. Following from the basic idea that the value of agricultural land (agricultural value) is based on the present value of discounted agricultural rent $r^a \div i$ where i is the discount factor, the same relationship holds for housing rents. House prices and rents should move together in the long run. Of course, this is predicated on perfect capital markets. If the buying and renting markets are segregated in some way and the arbitrage / adjustment is very slow, it could leave the two market prices moving in opposite directions for some periods.

Market Rent

Using supply and demand analysis, we consider the market effect of rent controls and vouchers. First, rent controls. The diagram right is for an idealised market for rented accommodation, where the dwellings are homogenous and have common locational characteristics. The short-run supply schedule for dwellings (S_{SR}) is vertical. As we know from a discussion of elasticity of supply over time, landlords are able to switch accommodation from alternative uses into renting over the long-run (LR). The demand for housing services will be downward sloping.

If the market is allowed to allocate rented dwellings, the market rent would be R_1 and the quantity supplied would be Q_1. It is decided that the market rent is too high for some
$$P\varepsilon_S = (+)\frac{\%\Delta Q_S}{\%\Delta P}$$
poorer members of the community and a 'fair' rent is imposed. This controlled rent R_2 is below market rent. As this alters the price and not supply or demand conditions otherwise, there are movements along each schedule. Now, the demand for accommodation increases to Q_2. Under these circumstances, landlords would filter out the less desirable tenant; the more-likely non-payer.

Over the longer term, landlords will switch some accommodation from the rented to the home owning market or some other land use. Thus, switching to the long-run supply curve (S_{LR}), the number of units that landlords make available drops to Q_3. The result in the long-term of rent controls is that there is excess demand of $Q_2 - Q_3$ Those that find rented accommodation are great gainers from the system and so are less likely to move for a job opportunity elsewhere. With a smaller reward, landlords

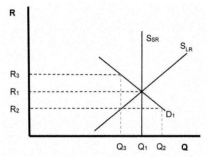

have less of an incentive to maintain their properties, which means a worsening of the housing stock will follow. Also, the owning market will see a fall in price either because the discounted rents income stream is lower or because the number of properties in that market increases.

We can see this in the following work. In 2012, Autor, Palmer and Pathak, analysed the abolition of rent control in the mid-1990s in Cambridge, MA. Having introduced controls in 1970, the first movement was up. This was followed by price. The former explained about only ¼ of the $7.8bn of price appreciation between 1988 and 2005.

Landlords converted substantial numbers of rental units to condominiums. To prevent the controlled rental stock from being depleted, in 1979 the city council passed the Removal Permit Ordinance, which substantially restricted the removal of controlled units from the rental stock and complicated the conversion of controlled units into owner-occupied condominiums. It is normal for cities to have zone of affordable rents close to the CBD. The authors found market rents were much higher, afforded by significantly more affluent group than the tenants they replaced.

A shadow market may arise where some renters, so desperate for accommodation, pay R_3. Landlords could charge for elements not normally associated with the renting of property, such as key-money or a non-returnable deposit, etc..

An alternative to rent controls is the rent subsidy or voucher. Again, the short-run supply schedule for dwellings (S_{SR}) is vertical and the starting point is R_1 Q_1. It is decided that the market rent is too high for some poorer members of the community and they should be in receipt of a rent voucher, or housing benefit. Assume it is a lump sum subsidy, so shifts the demand curve to the right to D_2. In the short-run, this drives market rents upwards from R_1 to R_2.

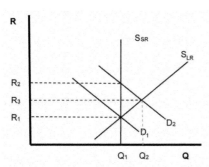

Over the longer term, landlords will switch some accommodation to the rented sector from the home-owning market or some other land use. With the voucher system, the long-run rents fall back to R_3, which is above R_1. Also, the dwellings in the rented sector increases to Q_2. Those that had a contract at Q_1 may find landlords seek to renegotiate the rent or they attempt to evict those on 'low' rent and re-lease the accommodation to higher payers.

According to Dept. for Communities and Local Government, the end of a tenancy has been a common cause of homelessness. In 2009Q4, 1,060 households in England became homeless after their private tenancies were ended. In 2014Q1 it was 3,330 and two years later it was 4,650. With a greater reward, landlords have more of an incentive to maintain their properties, which means an improvement of the housing stock will follow.

A third possibility is for the State to build 'affordable' housing or more rented accommodation. Again, the short-run supply schedule for private rented dwellings (S_{SR}) is vertical and the starting point is R_1 Q_1. The new property takes out some of the demand for private rented accommodation so shifts the demand curve to the left to D_2. In the short-run, this drives market rents downwards from R_1 to R_3.

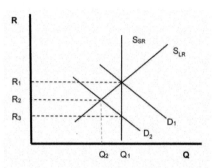

Over the longer term, landlords will switch some accommodation from the rented to the home owning market or some other land use. Thus, switching to the long-run supply curve (S_{LR}), the number of units that landlords make available drops to Q_2.

AirBnB

PwC reported that in London, average monthly private rents increased by 35% from £1,095 in 2011 to £1,473 in 2018. In Amsterdam, rents rose 64% in the 5 years from 2013 when real disposable incomes rose by 4.4%. Rents in Ireland rose 40% over five years when average earnings rose by 14%. After the bubble burst in 2006 Ireland stopped building houses. Since 2012, one house has been built for every 7 new residents. Many young people in the capital are spending more than half of their income on rent. Across Germany, one-fifth of tenants in the private rented sector say they spend more than 40% of their disposable income on rent. In October, Berlin imposed a five-year freeze on rents on around 1.5m apartments. This follows Catalonia and The Hague. This is likely to be a more widespread trend.

The Update points to a new issue. In primary cities like London we see: a rising population, including migrants; a lack of house building; a rise in property as a major investment vehicle for corporates; people living longer, unprepared to move out of large houses; Buy-to-Let landlords fishing in the same pool as FTBs; a house price accelerator pushing up prices as more (socially-useless) lending goes toward housing; an age group shift towards young qualified workers (Locational Conveyor Belt); and, we add one more – AirBnB.

Started in 2008, it is yet another on-line marketplace for arranging or offering lodging, primarily homestays, or tourism experiences. In effect, it is an alternative source of income for the home owner, skirting round legislation on other types of lets. The homesharing site's rapid growth has encouraged some owners and landlords to focus on this very short term lets. If more can be made from short terms lets, there should be a shift of properties from owning and long term lets to short term, Airbnb.

A way to imaging this illustrated right. The original position is $R_1 Q_1$. There is an increase in demand for short term lets. Rents rise to R_2 (with fixed supply Q_1). Over time more accommodation is made available and rents fall back to R_3. Substitute markets in supply are adversely affected. It was reported in February 2019 when Greek hoteliers complained a boom in homesharing properties via Airbnb for tourists in the capital Athens was hurting hotels. They should see a drop in demand. More worrisome perhaps is that that some owners in some neighbourhoods were evicting local families in order to rent their properties via Airbnb. Situated near the Acropolis, in Athens, the suburb of Koukaki saw 83% of

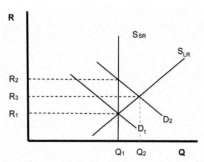

available rental properties as registered for short-term lets. Rents in Athens rose over 9% in 2018. This is a problem elsewhere. The number of not permanently occupied dwellings in Paris has risen by 30,000 in 5 years. At close to 60,000 listings, Paris has more Airbnb listings than any other city in the world.

Depopulation is an issue. Paris saw 15 inner city schools merged or closed because pupil rolls have dropped by 13,000 in 2012. New York lost 37,700 in 2017 and 39,500 in 2018. The ONS estimate that 18% of 35-39 year olds left London between 2014 and 2016. In 2009, 51,000 of 30-somethings left London; in 2015, 66,000. Overall, 283,000 migrated from London to the rest of the UK. By contrast, 4% of the borough of Epsom and Ewell were interlopers from London. City depopulation has been a problem in Eastern Europe. However, the problem seen during the deindustrialisation, has reemerged in Western Europe. This time it is due to the cost of renting.

Airbnb's model for short term lets and lockdown was not well placed. Bookings dropped off a cliff. Landlords that require the income that Airbnb provide would collapse. In a message on its website, the company acknowledged the decision to offer guests a refund had caused hardship for many hosts and it would pay £200m to help cover the cost of these cancellations.

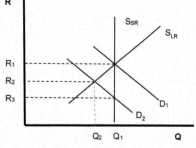

Desperate for a new model Airbnb in April focused on 'connecting 100,000 healthcare staff and first responders with places to stay that allow them to be close to their patients – and safely distanced from their own families.' This followed on the "dangerous and irresponsible" marketing tactic of during the lockdown listing homes as being "Covid-19 retreats" and "perfect for isolating with family" in the British countryside. Individuals and businesses could face fines of up to £960 for breaking lockdown rules. In May, the 7,500 staff were told that

1,900 were to go as the company is forecasting its revenue for 2020 to be less than half of what it took in 2019.

In December, with echoes of Uber, the Court of Justice of the European Union (CJEU) deemed Airbnb to be an on-line platform that connects people looking for short-term accommodation, rather than a full-blown estate agent, which meant it could avoid some legislation. However, in April, the CJEU advised that a shortage of long-term housing constitutes an overriding reason of public interest capable of justifying a national measure, which requires authorisation to be obtained for the repeated letting of residential accommodation for short periods to a transit clientele. In other words, Parisian apartment owners need permission for letting out their homes on Airbnb.

Whether the Corona virus or the courts forced this or not but in April, Airbnb changed its main landing page to highlight longer-term stays. In 2019, one in every seven nights booked was for a longer-term stay. In the last two weeks of March 2020, the company saw the number of guests booking longer-term stays within their same cities nearly double. 80% of Airbnb hosts now accept longer-term stays and about half of the company's active listings now provide discounts for stays of one month or longer. It was seeing students, doctors and nurses in residency, or others in long term work assignment turning to Airbnb to find housing for six to nine-month stays.

Cities from Amsterdam to New York and Paris, which have accused Airbnb of worsening housing shortages and pushing out lower-income residents, are unlikely to make Airbnb's transition easy. Moreover, the rising population of youngers is likely to favour policies like rental control. The current situation for many entails sacrificing large portions of their incomes to landlords and repopulated housing (see Vauxhall, Islington)/gentrifying all parts of the urban area.

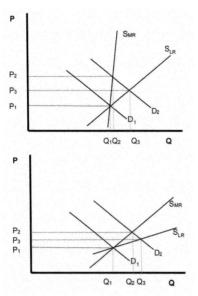

Delving into the realm of price elasticity of supply and house prices further we can follow Malpezzi and Wachter, Journal of Real Estate Literature. The diagrams are examined over two periods: the medium term and the long term. Assume a demand side shock to the housing market, so the demand curve shifts from D_1 to D_2. In the short-run, the supply of housing is vertical so we consider the medium run S_{MR}. As the construction, industry is not that price responsive we apply a steep supply curve. So a demand shock leads to modest increase in the number of dwellings built Q_1 to Q_2, suggesting that the accommodation is in a large rise in price P_1 to P_2. Over the longer run, S_{LR} is more elastic. There is more scope for the higher price (and so profit) to drag in more builders: make more land available for building; more time for planning permission to be granted. The price drops down to P_3. But it is ratcheted up over P_1. Compare this with an environment where the building sector is more price sensitive. Here price is lower and more dwellings have been added to the stock. Now reconsider these two and a housing bubble. The steeper supply schedule leads to a greater price bubble in the short-run. These bubbles can last 2-3 years. Below is a graph of the HPE or house price earnings ratio. HPE = HP÷Y. Loan-to-value LTV = Loan ÷ HP. The loan-to-income ratio LTI = Loan ÷ Y. Therefore, HPE = LTI ÷ LTV. If the LTV remains fixed, what emerges is greater prices are associated with greater loans or greater income. From 2002 to 2019 gross median incomes rose from £20,596 to £30,504 or 1.48 times. Median house prices rose from £104,000 to £235,000 or 2.26 times. In other words, people have to borrow 50% for the same dwelling they did in 2002.

House Price Accelerator

It is argued that the prices of homes bought by those already owning a house would be more volatile than those in a starter home market. Assuming a LTV of 80% and a steady growth of loan funding, a €20,000 deposit would merit a maximum loan of €80,000 for a property worth €100,000. Also, assume the annual average house price growth is 9%. If a capital-constrained buyer purchased a house on that basis and during the subsequent year it rose in value by €9,000, the price increase would be 9% but the home-owner's equity in the house would rise by 45%. The leveraged property has an implied equity multiplier [of 5]. The now repeat-buyer has a €29,000 deposit, which puts a €145,000 within grasp. Increasing house prices boosts equity and fortifies purchasing power. By frequently revisiting the market, the borrower, operating at the limit, accelerates house price rises. This price acceleration is a function of the LTV.

The HPE will mollify the acceleration of price. With a ratio of 4 and an income of €20,000 the maximum mortgage that could be offered is €80,000. The buyer initially jumps both ratio hurdles. If income grows by 5%/year, the maximum they could borrow after year 1 is €84,000. Combined with the €29,000 equity, the house price they could qualify for is €113,000. This is a 13% increase in the value of a house within the grasp of a second time buyer. Hanging on for a second year generates a far greater capacity to buy. The house is now worth €119,000; and the income of the buyer is €27,560, with a maximum loan of €110,000. The second house that is affordable within two years is worth €149,000.

Kennedy and Stuart of the Central Bank of Ireland proffered an analysis of the complementary goods of house renting and owning. In the short-run, the supply of accommodation is fixed, shared between the renting market and owner occupation. The cost of buying = mortgage costs + taxes + depreciation + maintenance costs −

expected capital gains = user cost of capital. The cost of renting = rent. Assume no transactions cost. In the diagram left rent = P_{1r} on the right-hand scale. The demand curve = D_{1r} slopes upwards. This intersects with the demand for buying schedule = D_{1b} which slopes downwards.

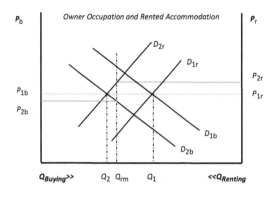

The quality rented is Q_1 running from right to left. The quantity owned is Q_1 running from left to right. Suddenly, buying is made more challenging (e.g. LTV, and/or the LTI ratios are lowered). This shifts the demand for buying to the left to D_{2b} and the renting demand curve D_{2r} also to the left so that Q_2 is the intersecting quantity. Assuming a one-for-one transfer, neither price changes. However, not all switch so that the demand curve does not move as far as D_{2r}; dropping out of the hunt for a house purchase so both price of renting and buying, falls. An alternative question is that some owned properties cannot be rented so that the max quantity that can be rented is Q_{rm}. Now, the renting price rises and buying price falls. This is a short-run problem. The return for renting is relatively high.

A Child of Forward Thinking
Hungerman and Buckles found that, rather than coinciding with the business cycle, pregnancies appear to be a forward indicator, with a lead of 6 months. The explanation is that pregnancy is an indicator of consumer confidence. In effect, planning to expand the household is similar to consumer durables; you engage when you feel you can afford to. The Royal Economic Society reported in 2017 that fertility was associated with home ownership. A 10% rise in house prices was linked to a 2.8% increase in child birth. But this was offset by the 4.9% drop in fertility among renters. Overall, from 1995 the birth rate has dropped 1.3% - or 9,000 births/yr.

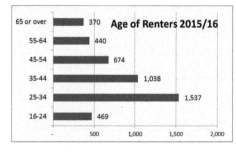

Rent-not-Buy
There were 4.528m in the private renting sector identified in the table below. 1.537m or 34% of those in the private sector were aged 25-34. One can glean movement from rent to renting and from renting to buying from the table below. Of the 1.828m moves, half were within the renting sector. Indeed, 13% of renting households moved in that sector in 2015/16, against 3% in the owning sector.

Renting has become more expensive, rising from 14.2% across 2002/4 to 25.1% in 2012/14 in the North East. Despite its relative poverty and the low cost of renting it is still high relative to income.

One cannot be sure but there appears to be an outbreak of unreasonable indignation with risk. Deposit-free renting is a phenomenon that allows tenants to pay a smaller, generally non-refundable fee in place of a traditional deposit. The indignation comes when tenants claim they do not understand the

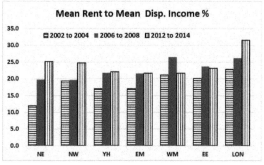

Mean Rent to Mean Disp. Income %

costs involved. The same can be said of selling. Trading Standards in January warned home sellers that they could be at risk of losing large sums of money when using quick-sale estate agents to find a buyer. Consumers are naïve if they presume that can get a quicker sale or a lower/no deposit to rent. As risk is being shifted onto the provider they will need a return.

Total value of tenancy deposits protected in England and Wales (March 2008 to March 2019) is left. Information about deposit dispute adjudications, if a regression is run:

	No. of Deposits	£ Total Deposits	£ Ave Deposit	Disputes
2008	924181	885098501	958	458
2009	1553130	1406482263	906	8098
2010	1888532	1661896693	880	20363
2011	2220543	2104219832	948	18156
2012	2374385	2325317355	979	20279
2013	2659301	2637843361	992	24448
2014	2848110	2865824221	1006	25029
2015	3066130	3187501867	1040	27816
2016	3425718	3566784769	1041	28100
2017	3691242	4017045899	1088	30742
2018	3840216	4159663783	1083	31865
2019	3949202	4408543068	1116	35513

Disputes $= -4922 + 0.0102 \times$ Deposits. In other words, around 1% of deposits are disputed. Closer analysis suggests this is stable since around 2010.

Of the stock of 14.33m home owners, there were 60,000 joiners and 400,000 OO move home but remained owners. Of these, 58,000 moved to own outright. A further 156,000 (38+9+97+12) shifted to the renting sector. Going the other way, 191,000 changed from renter to owners. Variance compares tenure changes over 2014 and 2015 with moves. 262,000 households not accounted for. These include deaths and migration.

	Own		Renting		Join
From	Outright	Mortgage	Private	Social	
Out	128	14	38	9	5
Mort	58	197	97	12	57
Private	21	151	787	84	196
Social	1	18	52	158	60
Variance	232	-325	123	-87	-55
Total	7,732	6,598	4,528	3,918	262

The proportion owned outright passed 50% in 2012/13. 78.1% of those owned outright are either occupied by an individual or a couple without dependent children. In other words, the OO market is made up of retired people, without children, living in large houses. Then again the lone person need not be retired. The number has risen in 10 years from 7.23m to 7.74m out of 26m. One would expect this to be an aging population problem. However, it is more a 45-64 problem, where there is a 470,000 growth. This could reflect the rise in divorces.

'Generation Rent' characterised 48% of households of those aged 25-34 in 2013 up from 21% in 2003. Private rental accommodation rose from 11.9% of tenure choice to 18%, whilst social renters fell from 31.4% to 16.8% between 1980 and 2013. The former year is when the right-to-buy legislation came in. Private renters comprised 4m HHs, of which 987,600 were

Household Income Quintiles	Own '000		Rent '000
	with mortgage	Outright	
1	296	1,535	2,725
2	628	1,806	2,122
3	1,224	1,638	1,692
4	1,940	1,459	1,158
5	2,511	1,295	749
Tot 22.8m	6,598	7,732	8,446

on housing benefit. The housing benefit bill of £21.1bn was 117% higher than in 2001 and the number on benefits was up by ⅔.

Surveying 15,000 Europeans, ING reported in September 2015 that 80% believed that it was becoming increasingly difficult to buy a first home, with 89% baffled as to how a first time buyer would ever buy a property in the UK. 72% of respondents, particularly renters, believed that society would benefit if house prices fell. The Resolution Foundation estimated that ⅓ of Millennials (born 1981+) owned their own home in their late 20s compared with 52% for Generation X (1966-1980) and 60% of Baby Boomers (1946-1965). GenX had real incomes 54% higher than the Boomers in the early 30s, but Millennials are only 6% better off than GenX. The CML found that 65% of households born in 1970 were homeowners when they were 35. Due to the rising unaffordability, 44% of households born in 1980s were homeowners at age 35. One reaction to prohibitively high mortgage costs is to spread the load over a longer period, so that the monthly outgoings are affordable. The Halifax revealed that repayment mortgages, which account for 88% of new lending, was being repaid over a longer period. In 2015, 26% of FTB took out a 35-year mortgage when only 15% were taken out in 2007. By contrast, 30% had a mortgage term of 20-25 years, when in 2007, 48% of loans were of this duration.

	1996/98		2014/15		%Δ
	With parents	% of all 20-34s	With parents	% of all 20-34s	over 96/98 14/15
NE	117.1	21.96	139.8	25.78	17.40
NW	323.4	22.76	399.5	27.62	21.36
YH	207.6	19.16	240.4	21.78	13.65
EM	164.6	18.69	198.3	22.68	21.33
EM	237.5	21.33	306.4	28.11	31.82
EE	211.5	19.71	3.8	26.99	36.90
LON	309.4	16.77	530.6	23.69	41.25
SE	299	18.63	402.9	25.54	37.06
SW	173.9	18.19	217.1	22.29	22.56
ENG	2,044	21.20	2,735.8	26.29	24.05

Civitas reported that there has been

a decline in the proportion of single-person households among younger adults, most notably because of a marked increase in the proportion of young adults living with their parents. In the table right comparing 1996/98 data for households with non-dependent (i.e., adult) children, there was an increase in the number of 20-34-year-olds living with their parents across the UK of 791,600. This represented in England an increase of 24.05% but in London (41.25%), and the South East (37.06%). Oddly, in the North East, it was only 17.4% and Yorkshire Humberside 13.65%.

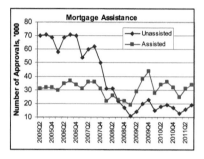

With the assistance of parents, FTB can continue to join the housing ladder when normally out-priced, so that equity growth can be self-refreshing. It is conceivable that a housing ladder can be maintained without many FTBs. Clarke of the Council of Mortgage Lenders (CML) suggested that intergenerational transfers make up a significant but stable volume of mortgages. There were an estimated 31,000 UK FTBs that were 'assisted' in the second quarters of both 2005 and 2011, and yet the number of unassisted FTBs dropped by 78% to 16,000 over the same six years. So, whilst the number of 'assisted' FTBs remained stable, the 'assisted' proportion rose from 31% to 66%. Clarke estimated the proportion of unassisted FTBs stood at 38% in 2014, which is around the rate post-2008.

	2018	2019
NE	£12,000	£13,900
NW	£12,900	£24,200
YH	£16,900	£17,200
EM	£17,300	£16,000
WM	£14,700	£13,700
EE	£17,900	£25,500
London	£30,600	£31,000
SE	£21,700	£29,000
SW	£19,300	£29,700
SC	£10,800	£16,400
WA	?	£30,600

In June 2019, L&G reported that, in the UK parents and friends gave house purchase supplements to the tune of £24,100, £6,000 more than in 2018. As this represented £3,000 more than the average UK house price rise over the same period, they were making greater contributions proportionally. In part, this increase in lending to £6.3bn from £5.7bn in 2018 may reflect a fall in affordability and a 20% drop in property purchases compared with 2018. That said 259,400 (19%) were supported down from 316,600 in 2018. L&G project that the shift in loan size could reflect the purchase of larger properties, with 3-bedroomed being the mode (44%) followed by 2-bedroomed @ 38%. Millennials (below 35) make up 62% of recipients with 22% aged 45-54 have received financial assistance.

Undertaking something similar in the US L&G reported in February 2019 that in 2018 20% of purchases worth 1.2m involved a gifts or loan of on averaged $39,000 (= $47bn). The median housing prices in the US was over $300,000 for most of the preceding three years. As in the UK, home ownership rates have fallen from a pre-Lehman crisis peak of 69% to 64.4% in 2018Q3. Those under 35 had an ownership rate of 36.8% while those over 55 had a rate over 75%. 51% of prospective owners under 35 expected help to buy from family or friends. Without the loan/gift L&G put the delay buying for at least three years without it. 43% of home buyers under 35 received help whilst 6% of over-55s were assisted.

The added complication in the UK was two Help-to-Buy programmes providing additional support. Notably, the assisted FTB in 2014 bought a more expensive abode (£175,000) with a smaller loan (£120,000) than the unassisted (£147,000; £129,000). Weale takes a rather sanguine view of intergenerational transfers. Rising prices represent a transfer of wealth from future generations. If parents feel this is wrong, they can adjust their planned bequests. Savills estimated that in the year to September 2016, £2.8bn of family financial support was injected. 34% of FTBs relied on it in 2013/14 and a further 9.6% used inherited monies. This allows purchase to occur 2.6 years earlier (London 4.6) compared with the unsupported. In June 2019, the National Audit Office reported that 63% of recipients could have bought a home without Help-to-Buy funds. Between 2013 and 2018 over ½ of the sales in England made by Redrow, Bellway, Taylor Wimpey, Barratt and Persimmon involved Help-to-Buy. Persimmon the biggest beneficiary increased their profit on each house from roughly £20,000 to £60,000. Fran Boait of Positive Money argued that Help-to-Buy has mainly been a subsidy for a housing bubble, benefiting property developers and existing home owners.

Pryce and Sprigings find that, as buy-to-let (BTL) purchasers occupy the same portion of the housing market as FTBs, purchasing a dwelling for rent sucks cheap housing out of the owner-occupation market, possibly being rented to those that would have bought. BTL might be the significant blockage to the FTB. The Resolution Foundation estimated that over the 2014-16 period there were 1.9m BTL landlords. Additionally, 1.4m own second homes. Between them, they absorbed at least 0.9m (=0.5+0.4m) dwellings, over 8 years. 1.1m were newly built in that period in England.

Housing Ladder
A simple housing ladder entails a small number of distinct dwellings placed in a hierarchy of quality. The discussion above implies there is a flat, a [terraced] house and a [family] house. A first time buyer (FTB) household is one just joining the property-owning sector for the first time. Given wealth, income and credit constraints, the FTB is limited to the lower end of the housing hierarchy. Through a series of acquisitions and disposals, the serial buyer household, injecting fresh capital, exchanges a smaller for a larger dwelling, rising up the ladder, likely to be affected by mismatches between family housing requirements to dwelling characteristics. Once the children have left the family home, to complete a life-cycle, the household could trade down back into a flat or into a bungalow. The buyer's age is an important indicator of their income, family unit and the relative value of their property.

Moving, what Moving?
Jamei & O'Brien (2017) reviewing the FTB in both Ireland and the UK, find that they have accounted for a very stable share of housing transactions since the early 2000s,

with a rising proportion of cash buyers. The decline in the RB market is notable. Between 2004 and 2012 across the British Isles, movers accounted for more than half of property purchase mortgages. By 2016, movers' share of new purchase mortgages had fallen for six successive years in the UK and two in Ireland. Hudson & Green (2017) suggest that there has been a dearth of around 400,000 transactions each year since the bubble burst in the UK compared with before. Of these 80% are mortgaged movers. There is a shift to cash and there is an older population, who are less likely to move, which explains much. However, they highlight 140,000 missing moves that can be attributed to a decline in the rates of moving among mortgaged home-owners. Positing three factors: their desire to move; sufficient funds; and the availability of a home they want to buy, *they find insufficient equity is the dominant factor* holding back the mortgaged mover rate. Interestingly, they find the period between 1990 and 2008 is the unusual one, not the current phase. In an era of financial deregulation, falling inflation and interest rates, although there was modest income growth, home-owners could borrow and service more debt to buy or move up the housing ladder. Real house price increases bestowed equity windfalls onto those in home-ownership. Those who bought in the 1960s through to late bubble in 1989 saw high nominal interest rates and high inflation. In the post 2008 period, there has been little house-price growth and little wage growth.

Unfortunately, the relative decline of movers may suggest reduced market liquidity. This limits the supply of second-hand properties for sale, possibly because movers have low or negative equity, they have an attractive mortgage rate that they do not want to lose or because of relatively high transaction costs. This has a knock-on effect on sales where those willing or able to sell may struggle to find a suitable property to buy. Between 2014 and 2017 the number of transactions in London dropped by 20%, while sales across the UK had fallen by 1% in 2018. A casualty of this is the estate agent. Accountants Moore Stephens, reported in July that more than 7,000 (27%) of UK High Street estate agents were struggling to survive. In August 2018, Countrywide Estate Agents announced an emergency equity raising of £111m. This effectively wiped out the value of existing shareholders. Struggling with net debt of £212m, income was down 8.7% to £306.6m. Losses were £218m in 2018, compared with a £207m in 2017. On-line agents Purple-Bricks and Emoov had been an additional factor.

Lloyds-TSB found that the average age of a second time buyer (trading up to their second home) had risen from 37 in 2002 to 40 in 2012. The type of house buyer changed between 2007 and 2013. The number of cash buyers fell from 417,000 by 18%; first time buyers from 360,000 by 31%; home movers from 654,000 by 50%; and the buy-to-let buyer from 183,000 by 57%.

The dwelling of preference of the well-educated retired owner is the four bedroomed detached, which presents a blockage issue. The International Longevity Centre argue that there is not a suitable supply of dwellings for the retired to move to; stamp duty makes it costly; but in the main, people could not see the benefits of moving. Older folk do not move out of larger houses, in part because they own the property, are rich, and want somewhere for the family to stay when they visit. Savills estimated that 2.9m homes are occupied by over-65 year olds with two or more extra bedrooms. The exit rate of 90,000/yr is just too low and needs boosting.

Affordability and Moves

Stamp Duty	£2,019
Estate Agent	£4,815
Surveyors	£600
Conveyancing	£1,619
Removals	£1,079

Compiled by the Centre for Economics and Business Research, the Post Office Money's Cost of Moving study, reported in November 2018, found that both renters and buyers were using the majority of their cashable savings to cover the cost of moving. Renters need £944 for the next security deposit and spend £525 on moving costs such as rental van fees, childcare and agency fees. Homebuyers require £10,132. The breakdown is seen right.

The same research unit found that the average property across 20 of Britain's largest cities in 2018 took 102 days to sell, 6 days longer than in 2017. London slowed, taking 126 days, when it took 111 in 2017. Properties in Edinburgh and Glasgow spend the shortest time on the market, with homes typically selling in 39 and 48 days respectively, quicker by 2 days. Other cities away from London, although taking over 100 days, also speeded up: Liverpool 106 (112) and Belfast 111 (119) days.

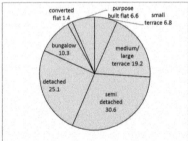

25.1% of OOccupied dwellings are detached and a further 30.6% are semi-detached. Despite terraced housing and flats making up a relatively small proportion of the housing stock in 2011, they accounted for 47.5% of sales.

In the figure below, the pattern of sales by type of dwelling shows the Terraced to be the most traded. This is consistent with the housing ladder discussion. As a relatively affordable type, households will acquire this and then trade up. As price increases the owner's equity in their (Terraced) property (the value above the outstanding mortgage) increases. Thus, the credit-constrained household has their budget limitation relaxed. As with other asset markets, the amount that

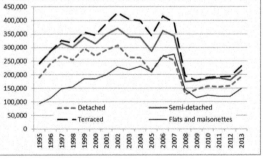

can be borrowed increases, leading to pro-cyclical lending. If the home owner is already participating in the housing market, their borrowing and so purchasing power is enhanced, leading to an acceleration of house price inflation. In an accelerating era the repeat buyer (RB) is priced *in* to the market. More sellers join with little time or cost constraints, adding turnover volatility to the markets when prices are already accelerating. The seller may have no urgency to move, so need not price-to-sell. In a low demand era the seller may engage in 'fishing', where they continue to participate in a thin market with a high asking price hoping for a match with a buyer. Moreover, loss aversion may prevent the vendor from reducing price in the face of falling demand.

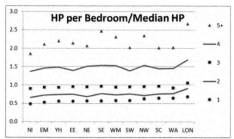

The price of an additional bedroom varies from region to region. In the figure left, the median house prices for each size of dwelling is benchmarked against the median dwelling price of the region. The median price is just above that for three bedrooms for all but London and the four bedroomed dwelling is around 50% more than the median. As a guide, any dwelling with more than 4 bedrooms is around double the median. However, this factor is more unstable than others mentioned.

The average new home was described as a rabbit hutch. A typical semi-detached in 2013 had 3 bedrooms and covered 925sqft. In 1920, there would be an additional bedroom and a further 622sqft. The equivalent numbers for a new terraced of 645 sqft are again a loss of a bedroom and 375sqft. At least there is still approximately the same space for 3 bedrooms. Affordability is the key. If land is expensive, then to utilise it more intensively, what is built is smaller.

Productivity	Lincolnshire	UK
Wheat	1	2
Cloth	3	4
Output 1		
Wheat	50	25
Cloth	16.67	12.5
Output 2		
Wheat	87.5	0
Cloth	4.17	25
Output 3		
Wheat	75	0
Cloth	8.33	25

INTERNATIONAL TRADE

Returning to the Primitive Society in Lincolnshire, assume Lincolnshire and the rest of the UK have the same levels of productivity. As the opportunity costs would be identical there would be no benefit from trade.

In the table left one can see that it takes Lincolnshire one unit of labour to produce one unit of wheat but the UK requires two units of workers. To produce one unit of cloth takes four hours of labour in the UK but only three in Lincs. If there is demand for an additional unit of cloth, two units of wheat must be foregone in the UK. This is the opportunity cost. In Lincs, it is worse. Three units of wheat must be foregone. Surely it is better for the UK to forgo the wheat? Assuming a 50:50 split in both regions and 100 units of labour, Lincs initial output of wheat is 50 and cloth is 16.67. The rest of the UK produce half that. Thus, without specialisation, wheat output is $50 + 25 = 75$ bushels and cloth output is $16.67 + 12.5 = 29.17$ units (Output 1).

Although we might teach that Lincs should specialise in one and the Rest the other, it is not clear with the figures we have. The maximum output of cloth that can be achieved by the Rest is 25. To stay within the tradable zone there are then two extremes. One can maximise wheat output given the total cloth output should be 29.17. This would require 4.17 units of cloth to be produced by Lincs. This needs $4.17 \times 3 = 12.5$ hours of labour. Thus, 87.5 remain to produce 87.5 bushels of wheat (Output 2). Alternatively, the maximum output of wheat should be 75, harvested by 75 workers. The remaining 25 workers in Lincolnshire should produce some cloth as well ($25 \times 0.33 = 8.33$) (Output 3).

We have not mentioned prices. In the event of an improvement in productivity, the price of wheat and/ or cloth should fall, even if there is no trade. It is not clear that all benefit. Prices come down in both regions but incomes may fall as well.

A sign of changing times is evident in trade figures. For the first time since the 1930s, global GDP growth was outstripping trade growth. With expanding trade, there has been a 2 to 1 ratio of trade to GDP growth. Between 1980 and 2011 the figures were 7% and 3.4% annually. The IMF and WTO estimated growth in 2013 should be 2.9% when trade should expand by 2.5%. The trade consultancy, Delta Economics, estimates that 40% of global trade is now south-south trade. This is associated with capital movements. By the end of 2013, McKinsey estimated that capital flows across G20 borders had fallen 68.5% from the 2007 peak. However, China-African trade in 2013 ($200bn) outstripped US-African ($110bn). India now supersedes the EU as the largest exporter of agricultural products to the very poorest countries. The price of its exports undermines producers in the poorest countries.

From Ricardo's theory of international trade, countries benefit from specialisation and trade. The Marshall Islands in the South Pacific is not the best example of trade. After WWII when they became a US trust territory, the inhabitants changed their diets. Out went domestically produced coconut and fish. In came flour, white rice, fatty meat and sugar. This is financially and physically crippling. Not only was it expensive to import but the Islands had the 3rd highest prevalence of diabetes in the world. The preference for a western diet over what a coral atoll could muster could be viewed as a choice failure.

In the diagram below, the free movement of goods and the welfare changes that follow can be analysed. The initial position entails no trade so country M operates at a higher price than country X. With free trade, there is an equalisation of price at P_e. The export schedule XS is derived from the differences between the supply and demand curves in Country X (excess supply). The import schedule MD is derived in a corresponding manner using differences between the supply and demand curves in Country M

(excess demand). Trade drives down price in country M as consumers purchase the cheaper version from country X.

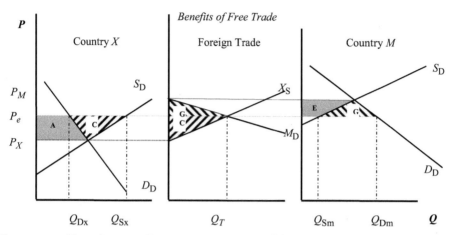

There are welfare changes. Consumers are worse off in X (area A) but better off in M (E+G). Producers are worse off in M (E) but better off in X (A+C). The free movement in goods has resulted in a net welfare gain of G+C.

It is customary to analyse the movement of goods only. Trade theory and Customs Union theory presumes labour does not move so as to preserve relative productivity or relative labour costs. The free movement of labour can be analysed in the diagram below. The initial position entails no movement of factors so Country B operates at a higher wage than Country A. With free movement of labour, there is an equalisation of price at W_e. As the wage rate is higher Q_M (= $Q_{SA} - Q_{DA}$) workers relocate from Country A to Country B. This drives wages down in B and up in A. Correspondingly, there is a shift of production from country A to country B. Employers in Country B gain E and G because labour is cheaper and there is more of it. Employers in Country A lose area A in higher wage costs and B in lost output. Workers that migrate gain B+C in rent (higher wage). Those that remain in Country A gain A. Country B workers lose E as the wage has fallen. The free movement in labour has resulted in a net welfare gain of G+C.

As implied above, free movement of goods means the production is reduced in country M (the US?) and an equalisation of prices. The movement of labour to country B (the US?) leads to an equalisation of wages. This can be seen to be operating in the US labour at the bottom end of the skills and wage hierarchy. Forbes estimated that the median wage in Beijing of \$329.53/wk is just below what a fork lift operator at \$12.75 is making (\$382) in a warehouse in the US. Asian economy wages grew by 5.7% annually from 2006 to 2011. In the developed world the rate was only 0.4%. Euromonitor estimate that Chinese wages had tripled between 2005 and 2016. Thus, those at the bottom of the skills hierarchy more than any other group are affected by globalisation. Their work has gravitated to China (demand curve for labour, left) and migrants from Mexico have moved to the US (supply curve for labour, right) driving wages down.

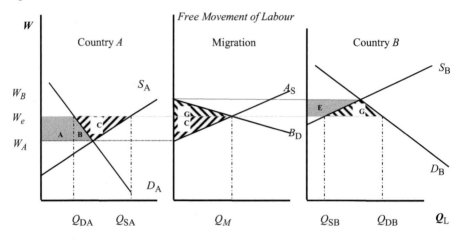

The car industry has moved east in Europe, but migrants have moved west, to where wages are higher. This has led to growing labour shortages in the east and a huge interdependence with Germany's car industry. In January 2019, employees at Audi's plant in Gyor, which employs 13,000 people, were awarded an 18% pay increase. Industrial action led to a suspension of engines produced in Gyor, causing Audi's plant in Ingolstadt had to halt production for two days. This victory is within a country where its parliament passed a labour law in December 2018 allowing employers to seek up to 400 hours of overtime/yr. Hungarian union focused on wage relatives with comparable production units. Audi and VW workers in Poland (39%), the Czech Republic (25) and Slovakia (28) earned at least a quarter more.

TRADE PROTECTIONISM

A standard theme in International Trade Programmes is the issue of trade protectionism and the question, why protect an industry? In previous *Updates* there has been a wealth of diagrams showing trade protectionism outcomes with the conclusion that interference leads to a net welfare loss for a small country. As we know from the discussion of international trade theory, in a Ricardian world, free trade leads to country specialisation and an improvement in the allocation of resources. However, the outcome will not favour all sectors in all countries; some must lose resources for them to be reallocated. This means that various sectors in every country will experience restructuring costs, some difficult to bear. It is common for countries to advocate free trade when it is to their advantage, but squeal about unfair competition when it is not (America first?).

Protectionism leads to a greater misallocation of resources:

❑   The large lobbying supplier extracts economic rent, so it redistributes wealth from the consumer to the producer in the small importing country.
❑   A key outcome is that it raises domestic price
  ○   production expands in protected markets – Producer Surplus increases (PS↑)
  ○   consumption decreases in protected markets – Consumer Surplus decreases (CS↓).
❑   Less competition may foster inefficiency – this point is relevant where the market is dominated by oligopolies – but then Ricardo is based on perfect competition.
❑   It increases (less efficient) employment in protected markets.
❑   It reduces the volume of imports (but not necessarily the value).
❑   A tariff raises revenue for the State.
❑   It may encourage firms to relocate to the protected market.

Explanations for Protectionism
Standard explanations for trade protection revolve around the avoidance of the disadvantage of international trade. These include the defence of infant or senile industries; maintaining a diverse industrial structure, which can include possibly being self-sufficient in a sector where security of supply is vitally important; or there is a wish to retain a way of life worth protecting. The loss of jobs in certain sectors can be highly emotive in many countries and governments might step in to protect those jobs by restricting access to the domestic market, such as agriculture. Moreover, an importing country will face external balance issues. As any trade disadvantage grows, either a balance of payments deficit or an exchange rate deterioration develops. Where an exporting country subsidises its exports (dumping) both jobs and trade balances are put under pressure in the importing country leading to domestic producers losing market share in the home market. To counter act this, under WTO international trade rules, the importing country is permitted to use countervailing measures, including an antidumping duty.

Another reason why protectionism might emerge is that the advantages of international trade fall thinly on the many (consumers) but the disadvantages fall heavily on the few (producers). Producers, having more power in the market place, are better placed to lobby the government for special treatment, either individually or collectively through associations. Market power is related to the last set of points. Countries with market power could exploit it by engaging in trade protection domestically in such a way as to alter world price, imposing the costs of trade protection on others.

Welfare Changes
In a discussion of the disadvantages of trade protection, it is common to review welfare changes. An economy can be seen as a combination of three groups: consumers; producers; and the exchequer. The change in price due to the imposition of a tariff or a quota leads to a redistribution, and a loss, of welfare. A rise in price

benefits producers in the form of greater profit and output whereas a fall in price benefits consumers. Welfare changes can be explored by examining what some food exporting countries have done in the recent past; imposed an export ban.

In the diagram below, we begin with a small exporting country, that, when operating at world price, P_{w1}, exports the gap between domestic production Q_{S1} and domestic demand, Q_{D1}. If the world price increases to P_{w2}, domestic prices and supply increase as do exports to $Q_{S2} - Q_{D2}$. The higher domestic/world price precipitates domestic disquiet, leading to the banning of exports. The result will reduce the domestic price to P_D, now the only market for home producers. The fall in price from P_{w2} to P_D, which is below the original world price, results in a rise in consumer surplus corresponding to area 1 and a loss in producer surplus of areas 1+2. There is no export tariff revenue as there are no exports. The net change in welfare is a loss of area 2.

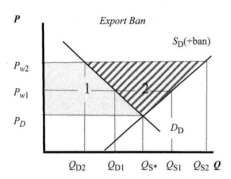

Importantly, domestic production falls from Q_{S2} to Q_{S*} leading to potential problems when exporting becomes more acceptable.

Subsidy

A producer subsidy is cost reduction designed to increase domestic employment and improve the balance of payments by either, reducing imports, or boosting exports. A Deficiency Payments system entails providing an incentive to local producers to producer more. This could be applied to either net exporter or importer industries. In Fig4 below, the subsidy to domestic producers, represented as the gap between the world price P_w and the target or support price P_{w+s}, leads to an increase in domestic output Q_{S1} to Q_{S2} and reduces imports, without raising price. As discussed above, this can be applied to net exporters of goods (Fig6). Again, domestic output is increased without the corresponding loss of consumer surplus associated with a rise in price. Deficiency payments supporting agriculture were used by the UK government before it joined the EEC in 1973. The EEC itself used a variable import levy, which resembles an import tariff.

For protectionist purposes, the exchange rate could be employed to reduce imports or expand exports. If the world price of the good is in Dollars and the importing/exporting small country uses Sterling, a depreciation of the Pound against the Dollar would make UK exports more, and imports less, price competitive. In Fig1 the world price is reflected in the vertical schedule $w. At exchange rate £1:$, domestic price is $w = P_{w1}. However, at exchange rate £2:$, the imported goods appear to be more expensive, so domestic price rises to $w = P_{w2}$. This leads to a boost in domestic output, Q_{S1} to Q_{S2}, and a reduction of imports to $Q_{D2} - Q_{S2}$. In other words, the outcome is similar to that of a quota.

With export-orientated countries, such as China, a depreciated exchange rate would boost exports. China has been accused of maintaining a low exchange rate to boost the price competitiveness of its exports. A low exchange rate acts like a subsidy, without government expenditure and without the need for WTO approval. See Fig7.

The relative welfare changes are outlined in the table below. It is evident that, with small importing countries, the exchange rate and quotas lead to a greater welfare loss than an import tariff. Moreover, the least-worst situation is the deficiency payment, which is targeted at domestic producers. In all cases, there is a net welfare loss.

With small exporting countries, export subsidies induce the greatest welfare loss whereas the deficiency payment results in a relatively small loss. The interesting outcome of this analysis is that, whilst being an exporter, an exchange rate depreciation induces a net welfare gain. Unlike the traditional analysis concerning tariffs and quotas, deficiency payments do not affect domestic price and, hence, consumer surplus, and exchange rate depreciations do not entail government expenditure directly.

Rich economies seeking to reduce trade barriers in services have shifted to plurilateral agreements. These are not made available to all WTO members, so contravene the most favoured nation clause.

F i g	Form of Protection	Consumer Surplus Loss	Producer Surplus Gain	Tax Gain	Welfare Loss
1	Exchange Rate Depreciation (importer)	1+2+3+4 +5	1+2	0	3+4+5 = A+B
2	Import Quota	1+2+3+4 +5	1+2	0	3+4+5 = A+B
3	Import Tariff	1+2+3+4+5	1+2	4	3+5 = B
4	Deficiency Payment (importer)	0	1+2	−1−2−3	3 = B*
5	Export Subsidy	1+2	1+2 +3+4+5	−2−3−4 −5−6	2+6 = B
6	Deficiency Payment (exporter)	0	1+2 +3+4+5	−1−2−3 −4−5−6	6 = B*
7	Exchange Rate Depreciation (exporter)	1+2	1+2 +3+4+5	0	−3−4−5 = −A−B

Fig4

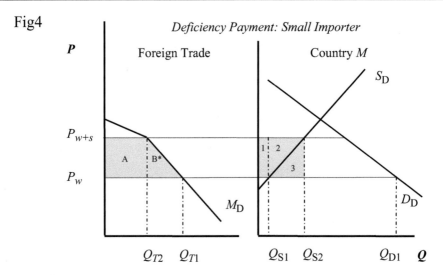

Deficiency Payment: Small Importer

Fig1

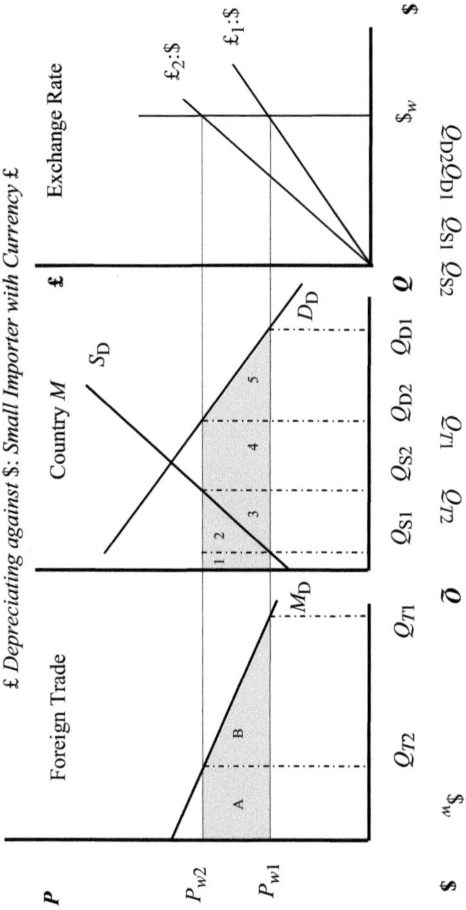
£ Depreciating against $: Small Importer with Currency £
Exchange Rate
Country M
Foreign Trade
£₂:$
£₁:$
$w
$
£
P
Q
SD
DD
MD
Pw2
Pw1
QD1
QD2
QS2
QS1
QT1
QT2
A
B
1
2
3
4
5

Fig7

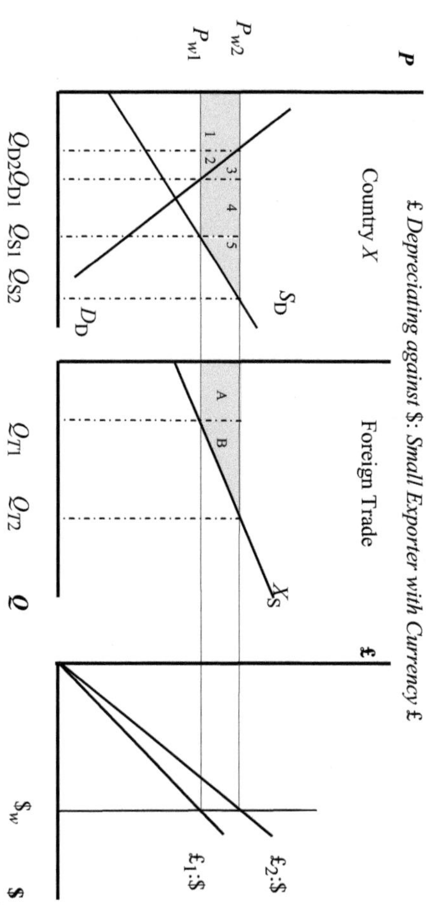
£ Depreciating against $: Small Exporter with Currency £
Country X
Foreign Trade
P
Pw2
Pw1
SD
DD
XS
QD2
QD1
QS1
QS2
QT1
QT2
Q
£
$w
£₂:$
£₁:$
$
A
B
1
2
3
4
5

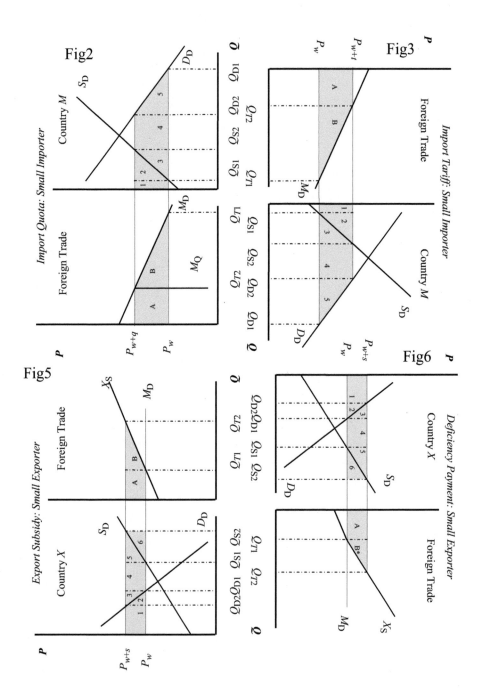

Market power, where the impact of a tariff or quota falls partly on other countries, can be explored. The next four diagrams represent a two economy model where one acts as large exporting country imposing a tariff and quota, followed by a large importing country imposing a tariff and quota. In Fig8, the foreign trade demand for exports schedule M_D is constructed by assessing the horizontal distance between S_D & D_D in the importing Country M. World price and the level of imports/ exports can be assessed. P_{w1} is determined where M_D intersects X_S; Country X exports what Country M imports, i.e. Q_T. The **export** (lump sum) tariff, represented by the vertical distance between P_M and P_X, shifts the export schedule upwards from X_S to X_{S*}. The intersection of M_D and X_{S*} results in a lower level of exports $Q_{T*}(= Q_{S*} - Q_{D*}$ in the exporting $= Q_{D*} - QS*$ in the importing diagram). Country X sees a fall in price from P_{w1} to P_X, however, world price is inflated to P_M. Thus, the importer bears some of the burden of the tariff.

The welfare changes in the exporting country are as follows: the exchequer gains export tariff revenue areas C+C*; the fall in price results in a rise in consumer surplus, corresponding to area A; and there is a loss in producer surplus of areas A+C plus the two upwardly striped areas. The net welfare change depends on whether the gain in area C* offsets the loss of the two upwardly striped areas. The welfare changes in the importing country are as follows: the increase in price results in a rise in producer surplus, corresponding to area E; and there is a loss in consumer surplus of areas E+G plus the two downwardly striped areas. The net change in welfare is a loss of the two upwardly and the two downwardly striped areas, so society is worse off. The two upwardly striped areas on the export country diagram combined equal the upwardly striped area on the foreign trade diagram and the downwardly striped area on the foreign trade diagram equals the two downwardly striped on the importing country diagram.

The allocation of the tariff burden can be seen from the foreign trade diagram. The deadweight or net welfare loss equals the upwardly and downwardly striped areas combined. Areas C+C* (=I+H) represent the total tax of which C*(=G) is extracted from the importing country.

The **export quota** diagram Fig9 is similar to the export tariff diagram. The export schedule X_{S*} is vertical at the quota level, Q_{T*}. The quota forces down domestic price and elevates world price. The key difference is that there is no direct benefit to the exporter's exchequer with a quota. Instead, area C*(=G) is extracted from the importing country in the form of higher profit for exporting firms (rent). Whenever a large country implements a small restriction on exports, it will raise national welfare

The **import tariff** diagram, Fig10 entails an import (lump sum) tariff, represented by the vertical distance between P_M and P_X, shifting the import schedule downwards from M_D to M_{D*}. The intersection of M_{D*} and X_S results in a lower level of exports $Q_{T*}(= Q_{S*} - Q_{D*}$ in the exporting and $Q_{D*} - Q_{S*}$ in the importing diagram). Country M sees a rise in price from P_{w1} to P_M, however, world price is pushed down to P_X. Thus, the exporter bears some of the burden of the tariff.

The **import quota** diagram Fig11 is similar to the import tariff diagram. The export schedule M_{D*} is vertical at the quota level, Q_{T*}. The quota, plus domestic supply S_D, provide the effective domestic supply curve, S_{D*}: the gap represents the quota that is exported. The effective domestic supply and demand schedules determine the domestic price. The quota forces up domestic price and elevates world price. The key difference is that with a quota, there is no direct benefit to the import's exchequer. Instead, area G (=C*) is transferred in the form of higher profit for exporting firms.

Assuming the level of trade is the same, as it raises revenue for the exchequer whether the country is large or not, a tariff is preferable to a quota when imposed by the importing country. When imposed by the exporting country, tariffs and quotas produce the same welfare change for the home nation as either revenue is raised for the exchequer, or exporting firms earn greater profits.

From the small exporting country's perspective, the worst situation is where the importer is large and imposes a tariff. Commonly, in international trade texts the issue of new forms of trade protection are reviewed. A 'new' form, Voluntary Export Restraint (VER), entails, through bilateral agreements, the exporting country agreeing to restrictions to the quantity of exports to avoid the wrath of the importing country. That wrath could result in a severe penalty (say an anti-dumping duty). However, from our discussion, the VER, which is a quota, results in a transfer of revenue to the exporter. Thus, one could argue the concern is not necessarily as severe a penalty as the imposition of a tariff by the importer. The exporting country is large. Having said this, if the exporting firms are compelled to buy a licence, the profit can be appropriated by either the importer or exporter. Perhaps the exporting country needs to get its tariff or quota in first so there is less pressure in the importing country to engage in this practice.

Who Bears the Cost of Free Trade in General?
Larry Summers argued that it is hard to see today how some in the West benefit from free trade:
1. The benefits of reduced tariffs and quotas are now very small. Protectionism in the textbook sense remains in areas steeped in cultural symbolism, such as agriculture. Trade agreements now are more about regulatory harmonization and the protection of investment, such as in intellectual property.

Fig8   Fig9

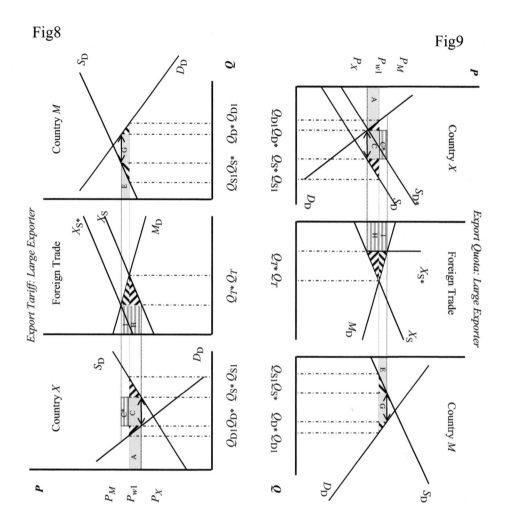

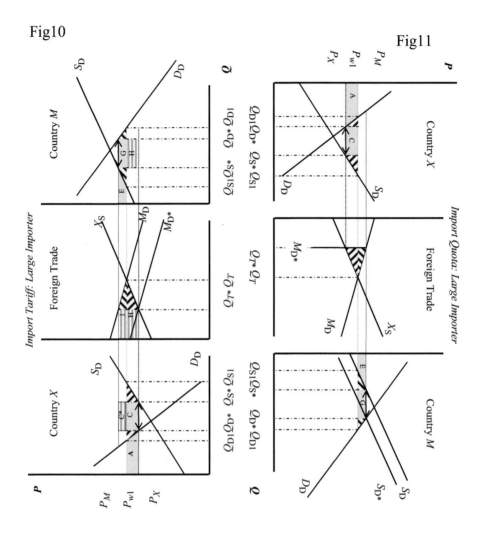

Fig10

Fig11

2. The benefits of freer trade have assisted the developing countries spectacularly. In the West, freer movement of factors has benefited the owners of capital and a cosmopolitan elite. The losers have been the poor, where wages, harmonizing with those in factories in the developing East, have fallen in real terms, so much so that reshoring is viable. Worse for politicians, the middle class are feeling the costs rather than the benefits, with the US median real wage unmoved for four decades. Inequality is shifting from a developing to a developed nation issue. The benefits of free trade by-pass the less-skilled [American] worker. Between 1979 and 2013, the top 1% saw their income rise 188%. The middle and lower income brackets grew by 18%. The protection of intellectual property benefits the skilled elite. An innovation may boost employment in both developed and developing nations – such as the iPad. The influx of migrants into the rich West from the poor East is of benefit to capital but a threat to less skilled labour. The Euro elections in 2014 and in the US and UK in 2016, 2017 and 2019 revealed discontent.

3. REAs that make sense geographically or have a clearer strategic purpose are more likely to succeed. Trump cancelling REAs as soon as he took office and GSP two years later is making a statement about his view on trade. Interestingly, China takes a different, more inclusive approach.

If Trump was appealing to an electorate that feared migration and globalisation; where working-class Americans were looking for someone to blame, it has a strong upside. Trump makes pronouncements and then the Democrats protest free trade issues, alienating the Blue-Collar vote.

The complaint that freer trade costs jobs is not unreasonable. An MIT study estimated that rising Chinese imports of all good from 1999 to 2011 cost up to 2.4m American jobs. The Economic Policy Institute in Washington estimated that the granting of market economy status to China would endanger between 1.7m and 3.5m jobs in the EU. Competitive disadvantages are found in aluminium, bicycles, ceramic, glass, car parts, paper and steel; with 639,000 jobs vulnerable in Germany; 416,000 in Italy and 387,000 in the UK. Aegis Europe (30 industry bodies in numerous sectors including the vulnerable sectors) was campaigning against China's WTO market economy status.

Growth in the US between 2009 and 2013 may be seen as jobless. The export - jobs multiplier can be assessed in the following way. In 2009, exports created 9.7m. Each additional billion dollars of exports created 6,763. Although exports generated more jobs in 2013 (11.3m), the jobs/$ exported fell to 5,590. This could mean that the US is shifting towards capital-intensive exports - perhaps overturning the Leontieff paradox. This may be due to the cost of production in the US. Thus, Trump is hoping to reshoring US jobs through trade restrictions – overturning Vernon's product life cycle thesis and the NIDL. Automakers are unlikely to uproot billions of dollars of investments in plants and supply chains. Rather those that cannot comply with standards for passenger cars could simply pay tariffs of 2.5% (around $800 to $900 per vehicle) and buy low-cost parts from Asia to offset the cost. Trucks are different. More than 40% of GM's 2017 U.S. pickup truck sales were built in Silao, Mexico (400,000). 75% of the vehicle's content should be made within North America, with 40-45% at $16/hr wage, to qualify for tariff-free import from Mexico or face a 25% tariff. That said Ball, State University estimated of the 5.6m US manufacturing jobs lost 2000-2010 85% due to automation and only 13% due to trade. The use of automation is related to capital intensity, facilitation the reshoring of output. Klaus Kleinfeld, CEO of Alcoa, argued that [Lean] production requires production to be close to the R&D unit and customers. However, the labour needed is likely to be highly skilled, so not addressing the concerns of those blue-collar workers left behind.

ECONOMIC ASSOCIATIONS

REAs encourage trade among a subset of the world. As such, the benefits of free trade should be bestowed on member countries and this should off-set any distortions. The benefits from specialisation and an improved allocation of resources should produce a welfare benefit. This should be gauged against the pre-trading arrangements. In Custom Union theory, if the group of countries constitutes a high cost group, trading among themselves rather than using the lower, world price, could result in trade diversion and so possibly a welfare loss. By contrast, if the group operate at the lowest cost of production as the rest of the world, it should lead to a welfare (static) gain. This corresponds to trade creation.

Additional benefits of a REA include scope to exploit further economies of scale. Assume that 10 countries of similar size and stages of development form an REA, so that, from expanding output, each firm can lower unit cost whilst serving a market of 10 countries. Clearly, not all can grow; some can expand whilst other, high cost producers, become uneconomic. Economies of scale are not part of the H/O and Ricardian worlds. Krugman's geography and trade thesis predicts a core-periphery outcome where economies of scale ideas produce much the same outcome as perfect competition and free trade: there will be a spatial division of labour, specialisation and more trade.

Another argument concerns the nature of manufacturing. It is common for oligopolies to emerge in an industry, leading to exploitation of the consumer, X-inefficiency, etc.. Moving from one country with 3 producers in the industry to 10 countries with 30 producers collectively should increase the degree of rivalry among oligopoly suppliers, driving firms to be more cost sensitive and innovative. However, the above point about economies of scale applies. The tendency to exploit economies of scale should lead to a shakeout, mergers and a smaller number of larger producers again. If one aim of forming a greater governing unit is to exercise greater power over large firms, this strategy of enlarging the political grouping, such as the EU, should succeed, but only in the short-run, as the firms grow larger also.

Particularly when reducing unnecessary duplication, developing countries should be well placed to exploit economies of scale. Resources necessary for growth could be pooled, such as a jointly funded power plant by Brazil and Argentina. Here, the group of countries might be interested in import substitution or export promotion. These could apply to both primary and secondary goods. Import substitution could be seen as part of a self-sufficiency strategy. The infant industry argument for developing nations is a strong one. Additionally, outward looking policies, such as export promotion, would appeal to an export base model as the explanation for growth. Here, from a Thirlwallian perspective and an export base model, income elasticity matters. Agricultural staples, which have income elasticities around zero, are likely to leave the country or group as part of the periphery. Furthermore, from a balance of payments constraint perspective, the developing country cannot grow beyond certain limits. Also, such a policy may hit a trade barrier from developed countries. The multi-fibre agreement and agricultural barriers have prevented free access to developed economies' markets. So an export-led growth strategy is not an automatic choice for a developing country in a non-neo-classical world.

Importantly, for the welfare gains to be made, countries should be at the same stage of production and produce the same goods. For many REAs involving developing countries, they operate at different stages of the development process and produce different goods. The benefits of specialisation must come after, not before, joining. If they already have specialised, trade diversion is likely to emerge. Worse, commodity-exporting countries are less likely to find the intra-union trade will grow much. If they already have a focus on more lucrative international markets, boosting demand in a low growth area may not be worthwhile.

Trade Creation

Upon joining a REA, a small importing country removes a lump sum duty. The REA operates as a low cost producer (= world price = £20). This lowers domestic price by £20. Imports are increased by 30 units and domestic production is reduced by 20 units: 10 units more are consumed. The balance of payments is harmed and so is domestic employment. But what

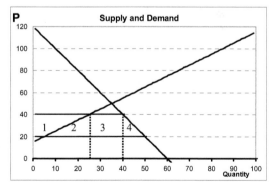

about overall well-being? CS↑ £900 (1+2+3+4) PS↓ (1) £300 Gov't Rev↓ £300 (3). Combined, well-being ↑£300 (2+4). Centre for Economic Policy Research (CEPR) estimated the welfare gains from the TTIP for the EU as up to €119bn/yr, or €545/yr for a family of four. For the US, the values were €95bn/yr and €655/yr.

Trade Diversion
Below the REA is a high cost producer (EU price = £30). Domestic price drops from
£40 to £30. At this price
domestic production = 15,
domestic demand = 45, so
imports = 30. Imports
increase by 15 units and
domestic production decrease
by 10 units, but 5 more units
are consumed. Breakeven
occurs when well-being from
joining a CU does not change
(2 + 4 = 5). This occurs at EU
price = £27.64. If EU price >
£27.64, there is a net welfare
loss. If EU price < £27.64,

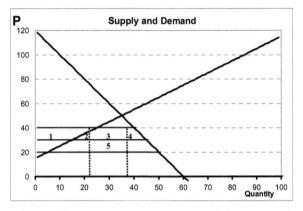

there is a net welfare gain. Leaving a high cost arrangement should lead to trade
creation. If Europe is a high cost car producer, it could make cars more expensive, but
this form of trade diversion could boost demand for UK-made components for UK
cars. The percentage of British parts in a British-built car has risen from 36% in 2011
to 41% in 2013 to 44% in 2017.

CU theory does not address factor movements. Free movement of labour is predicated
to produce good outcomes, but cumulative causation may suggest otherwise. A core
may grow at the expense of the periphery. In a Krugman sense, countries could
concentrate on (be a core country in) a narrow range of goods, so that all could
specialise and trade. However, cumulative causation is a non-product model that
implies resources in general could be surrendered by the periphery to the core, so that
national/ regional unemployment may get worse. Labour, capital and goods may flow
in the same direction.

Increasing integration comes at the cost of a loss of sovereignty. In the case of
monetary or tax harmonisation, the country loses control of the levers that can be
pulled to steer it along an independent road. In effect, the country ceases to be a
separate entity and becomes part of a super-state. However, it must be stressed that up
to 1973, one could put a case for the EC membership of a CU. With the inclusion of
poorer states, the case for EC/EU membership really became one of political influence
and control of borders, rather than an economic one. Moreover, allowing free
movement of labour with very large disparities in national wages without a robust
regional policy would lead to mass exoduses from poorer, smaller countries. The core
would become over-crowded, leading to congestion problems, and the accusation of
stealing a generation of skilled workers; the periphery would become an economic
backwater or home for the elderly. As this appears to have happened between Spain
and Germany, one must conclude the politicians were not concentrating on the ball.

In June 2019, The European Union signed the EU-Vietnam Free Trade Agreement (EVFTA) resulting in tariff reductions on 99% of goods over a 10-year period and other goods, notably agricultural products, will be limited by quotas. Vietnam had already signed about a dozen free trade pacts, including the Comprehensive and Progressive Agreement for Trans-Pacific Partnership (CPTPP). In 2018, Vietnam exported $42.5bn worth of goods and services to the EU, while the value of imports from the region reached $13.8bn. It would boost EU exports to Vietnam by 15.28% and those from Vietnam to the EU by 20.0% by 2020. Moreover, Vietnam's GDP would be growing by 2.18%-3.25%/yr by 2023 and by 4.57%-5.30%/yr between 2024-2028.

June also saw a free-trade treaty between the EU and Mercosur. The draft free trade agreement took 20 years to complete and the EU has described it as its biggest so far. However, by September, MPs in Austria demanded a government veto on the deal. This followed France and Ireland who were disappointed in Brazil's attitude to fires in the Amazon rainforest. In April 2020, Argentina withdrew from negotiations.

In July, fifteen West African countries agreed to adopt a single currency, the eco. Eight countries already used the CFA franc, which is pegged to the €, and is guaranteed by France. To join 6 criteria must be met including: a budget deficit of not more than 3%; an average annual inflation rate of less than 10%; central bank financing of budget deficits should be no more than 10% of the previous year's tax revenue; and gross external reserves worth at least three months of imports must be available. The group of Benin, Burkina Faso, Cabo Verde, Cote d'Ivoire, The Gambia, Ghana, Guinea, Guinea-Bissau, Liberia, Mali, Niger, Nigeria, Senegal, Sierra Leone, and Togo, is likely to be dominated by Nigeria.

In August despite its independence, Nigeria's President, Muhammadu Buhari, instructed the Central Bank to stop providing funding for food imports. This is consistent with policies from 2015 to stimulate growth in the agricultural sector to reduce dependence on oil. In July, there was a foreign exchange ban on import of milk. Those policies included a 2015 ban on access to foreign exchange for 41 items that the bank felt could be produced in Nigeria. This conflicts with signing up to the African Continental Free Trade Agreement (AfCFTA) in July. Import controls on rice, imposed even as local farmers fail to meet demand, kept prices artificially high and led to smuggling from neighbouring Benin into Nigeria. Indeed, 90% of the traffic through Benin's main port Cotonou was destined for Nigeria.

UK's New Regime
On 19th May 2020 the UK Government set out new post-Brexit global tariff regime. The key points are: rounding tariffs down to standardised percentages, and gets rid of all tariffs below 2%; but it maintains tariffs on strategic sectors such as lamb, beef, and poultry, the vast majority of ceramic products, and cars where there is a 10% tariff. The UK will not use EU's Meursing table for agricultural goods, avoiding "unnecessary tariff variations on products". This results in 60% of trade being on

WTO terms or through existing preferential access. Interestingly, the government focused on the withdrawal of tariff on £30bn-worth of supply chain imports entering UK supply chains including copper alloy tubes (moving from 5.2% to 0% tariff) and screws and bolts (3.7% to 0%).

WHAT IS MONEY?

Money is an indirect claim on assets. Money can be exchanged for a wide variety of other assets. It can itself be based on an underlying asset that has intrinsic value, such as a cow or a camel. Alternatively, it has little intrinsic value but users have faith in its value in exchange, such as a rock or a piece of paper. Mostly, it is guaranteed by the State (fiat currency) and has a single source of supply: the central banks, such as the Reserve Bank of India, hold the monopoly on producing this paper money within the borders of a Sovereign State.

To some extent, money is what money does. Importantly, money can be seen as any asset that is *generally acceptable as a means of payment*. In effect, a trade or exchange process entails a swap. The parties sacrifice one set of things for another that should provide them with equal or greater utility. Money acts as a temporal intermediary in this exchange. Without it the volume of exchanges will be lower. As such, we presume that the most important function of money is that of being a *medium of exchange*. For money to act as an intermediate asset, there is an incompatibility between what the two parties to an exchange 'want.' One is willing to accept money on a temporary basis. This money is then exchanged with a third party for what is desired. There is a time delay between the exchanges. For money to facilitate the exchange process it must hold its value. If it did not, why accept money in exchange for goods when that money would be worth notably less in a short space of time. Thus, money must act *as a store of value* to make future purchases. Interestingly, cash withdrawals on Fridays was, typically, 5 to 6 times greater than other weekday nights.

A variant on this is the *standard of deferred payment*. Investments, where there are returns but over an extended period, are central to the growth process. The investments are funded by the sacrifice of current consumption, in favour of greater future consumption. If you purchase a bond, you want some notion of the benefits of such a sacrifice.

We presume that people make the best use of their endowed assets. To achieve that, they exchange one set of goods for another. Those choices are made on the basis of relative prices. That is, they need to know how many of good A is acquired compared with good B for a given endowment. Money provides that rank ordered set of prices. In other words, it provides a *unit of account*.

Cash is not disappearing but there are reasons to expect it to. Cash represents only 3.7% of GDP in the UK. Mobile phone apps and debit cards for the youngster are the norm. The older consumer may not trust banks and prefer cash. Millions of US residents do not have accounts. Criminals and the informal economy rely on cash. The total value of goods and services purchased in 2018 in the UK, according the BRC, was £381bn, up from £366bn in 2017. 9.3bn transactions were made by debit card by volume [56.8% by value], 7.7bn cash [20.4%] and 2.6bn credit and charge cards [21.5%]. The average value of a cash transaction was £10.21. This is less than the £31.71 for credit cards. Each card transaction costs retailers an average of 5.85p in third party fees. In May 2015, card overtook notes and coins for the first time. Transport for London stopped accepting cash payments on the London bus network in 2014, claiming this would save £24m/yr in handling costs.

India scrapped the R500 ($7.60) and R1,000 notes in November 2016. The reason given was to reduce the size of the black economy (23.2% of GDP in 2007). As these represented 86% of India's cash supplies, this led to a cash shortage, reducing GDP growth by possibly 1.2%. The ratio of currency to GDP in India of 12.2% is higher than countries such as Russia (11.9%), Brazil (4.1%), and Mexico (5.7%), indicating the dependence on cash.

Crises stimulate the holding of notes. In Greece in May 2015, cash in circulation was at €45.2bn, a level last seen in June 2012. The holding of larger denominations reflects the urge to hoard cash in the face of bail-ins and bank failures. Not wanting deposits, banks will penalise the retail consumer, encouraging them to hoard cash.

As a generally accepted medium of exchange, a dual currency has to provide the holder with additional returns compared with the primary coin. Examples include Lewes, Ambridge, Brixton, Totnes, Stroud, the Lake District and Lambeth. The multiplier effect is much reduced by leakages; monies leaving the locale. A local currency boosts the local multiplier. Ultimately, people need to be paid in the currency, particularly their salaries. Shops not only need to accept but be able to buy their produce from local suppliers using that currency. They should have work done on their business units by local artisans so, the currency allows for some indirect monitoring of the supply chain. A bank, acting as a key intermediary, needs to take deposits and issue loans. Local authorities have been key in the buy-in or the accepted aspect of the currency. If you can pay your local taxes in the local coin, you are more likely to accept the currency rather than pounds.

A credit card is not money. A credit card has no intrinsic value. What it offers the user is credit. Cash or even electronic money does not require the owner to forgo any future consumption to clear any debt, whereas credit must be repaid. But money is credit of a sort. Alfred Mitchell-Innes argued that money is a promissory note or IOU that circulates or is exchanged in a trade. A sale is an exchange of a commodity for a credit. Bills of exchange were the effective currency of Victorian Britain. When bank loans replaced bills, the notion of a credit note was lost. However, when banks create money they are creating a credit. March 4th 2018 election in Italy brought anti-establishment parties together who wanted to have tax cuts and aggressive spending.

To pay for this the proposed issuing non-interest-bearing Treasury bills in branded as MiniBOTs. These would be printed, rather than electronic, using the State lottery's ticket presses – but it claim they are not money. This parallel currency may be accepted by customers as they can pay back the government, for example through taxes or fines. Shops may not be so willing. It was anticipated that there would be a market for them operating at a discount, whereby pensioners and state creditors lose say 10% of the value in exchange for €s. This would redistribute wealth from those on benefits to financiers. As a means of circumventing Article 106 (only the ECB can issue the €), if MiniBoTs are introduced on a large scale, political strains could eventually force either Italy or Germany out of the €.

Although a Bitcoin is called a currency it behaves a lot like oil and gold. As a commodity, it can be bought and sold in cash markets or via derivatives such as futures. Securities are typically subject to more rules on price transparency, trade reporting and market abuse. Commodity markets operate with relatively little regulatory oversight. It was originally conceived as a means of payment, but it is not generally accepted. As a store of value, it fails as its volatility is too great. As a means of exchange, it is hampered by its slow network and high transfer costs. However, Bitcoin lending is its key growth area. Genesis Capital, one of the biggest lenders in the market, had outstanding loans of around $545m in 2019 compared with $100m in 2018.

When consumers lose faith in money they seek other means of exchange. Barter is one of those standard market failures corrected by the facility of money. The double coincidence of wants makes barter inefficient. However, this double coincidence is an information thing. An increasing number on-line could being together those who could, through exchange, improve their well-being without the need for cash. Two cases where barter is getting easier are reviewed:

- Across 78 municipalities, the Asturian network of barter communities has 1,500 users. It creates digital money, equating a 'copin' with one Euro. The community network's platform enables users to barter directly, or to accumulate copins to spend on goods and services from others in the community.
- Inflation in Argentina drove many to revert to barter clubs. These existed in previous crises of 2001-2002 and 2009. However, the double coincidence of wants problem is eased by Facebook. Trades before exchanging goods in person take places in places like the railway station. A chart posted on the San Miguel group's Facebook page outlined a points system for certain goods. A 1 kg (2 lb) pack of flour served as the central currency or reference = 1 point or hypothetical value of 30 pesos. One bottle of sunflower oil = 2 pts. One cake = 4pts, and adult jeans = 3pts. Barter can lead to consumer surplus extraction so the Facebook recommended 'prices' seek to ensure fairness in trades.

MONETARY POLICY INSTRUMENTS

One of the Bank of England's two core purposes is monetary stability. Monetary stability means stable prices and confidence in the currency. Stable prices are defined by the Government's inflation target (of 2%), which the Bank seeks to meet through the decisions taken by the Monetary Policy Committee (MPC). Monetary policy in the UK usually operates through the price at which money is lent – the interest rate. In March 2009, the MPC announced that in addition to setting Bank Rate, it would start to inject money directly into the economy by purchasing financial assets – often known as quantitative easing (QE).

Recently, the BoE reviewed the monetary system. It makes seven points:

1. Banks are more than financial intermediaries. Their liabilities are generally accepted means of payment (money). Bank deposits make up 97% of broad money.
2. The money multiplier is a myth; there is no strict relationship between money stock and bank deposits. Central banks can create reserves at will (e.g. QE). It supplies these reserves to banks if demanded and at a price.
3. Credit creation is based on risks and rewards. Banks will only lend if they see a profit in it and only take deposits accordingly. Borrowers cannot be made to borrow. If borrowers or lenders are more risk averse, lending drops.
4. The central bank can alter the returns that banks hold with it. As the bankers' bank, the central bank intermediates between the banks to facilitate settlements so all have accounts with the central bank. Each regulated bank is obliged to hold deposits with the central bank. It could, lending elsewhere, receive a higher return. Thus, market interest rates should be at a premium over bank deposit rates.
5. Lending can be influenced by other regulatory requirements, such as reserves and liquidity requirements. If, as is common, lending by banks is secured against an asset, this boosts its demand, and price, increasing the scope for more lending. This risk needs to be moderated with lending restrictions.
6. QE entails swapping bonds with bank reserves at the central bank. The money multiplier has been possibly zero, so QE has boosted bank reserves and also lowered yields across a range of assets.

Banks do not need to lend out their reserves, they can create loans without that need, by the stroke of a pen. Money is created at that point. It is destroyed when a debt is repaid. Credit easing, where corporate bonds are purchased, will cut out banks as intermediaries in the first instance, but the corporates will increase their deposits at the bank.

The Reserve Bank of India's roles are to operate the currency and credit system of the country to its advantage; to regulate the issue of Bank notes and keeping of reserves with a view to securing monetary stability in India and generally to operate the currency and credit system of the country to its advantage; to have a modern monetary policy framework to meet the challenge of an increasingly complex economy, to maintain price stability while keeping in mind the objective of growth. Norges Bank, the Norwegian central bank:-

- promotes price stability by means of monetary policy
- promotes financial stability and contribute to robust and efficient financial infrastructures and payment systems
- manages the portfolios of the GPFG and the bank's own foreign exchange reserves in an efficient and confidence-inspiring manner.

The South African the constitution, requires the Reserve Bank to protect the value of the currency in the interest of balanced and sustainable economic growth.

The Central Bank of China's monetary policy objective is to maintain the stability of the value of the currency and thereby promote economic growth. Nationalbank, the central bank of Denmark, operate a peg of 746.038 DKr per €100 ± 2.25%. Denmark is the sole member of the ERM II.

A central bank may have a number of interest rates that it can manipulate. The deposit rate is what banks receive from deposits at the central bank. Some monetary authorities compel domestic banks to deposit a minimum amount, possibly under the heading of a *cash ratio*, related to the extent of the banks' deposits.

Bank Rate
Bank rate, or discount rate, is the rate of interest that a central bank charges on the loans and advances that it extends to commercial banks and other financial intermediaries. Changes in the bank rate are often used by central banks to control the money supply. Bank Rate is a long-term measure and is governed by the long-term monetary policies of the Central Bank concerned. NB. the **repo rate** is a short-term measure. The repo rate has been the Riksbank's policy rate since 1994. The repo rate is the rate of interest at which banks can borrow or deposit funds at the Riksbank for a period of seven days. In February 2020, Sweden raised its Policy Repo Rate from -0.25% to 0%.

Reserve Ratio Requirement (RRR)
The reserve requirement is the minimum reserve each commercial bank must hold (rather than lend out) as a proportion of total customer deposits and notes. The reserve ratio (RR) can be used as an instrument, influencing the country's borrowing and interest rates, by changing the amount of loans available. The FED had not altered the RR for 20 years until March. The use of ratio requirements is more the domain of the developing nation with less sophisticated capital markets. On the 13th March, PBoC cut target-compliant banks' reserve requirement ratios (RRR) by 0.5%-1% releasing RnB550bn to shore up the economy.

Statutory Liquidity Ratio
Statutory Liquidity Ratio is the amount of approved liquid assets that a financial institution must maintain as reserves with the central bank. SLR Rate = the liabilities of the bank which are payable on demand, divided by those liabilities which are

accruing in one month's time due to maturity. In May 2020, India's was 18%. The Swiss National Bank can require banks to hold up to 2.5% of their risk-weighted assets, in a buffer. This is preferable to raising interest rates, which would affect the value of the Franc.

Open Market Operations
Controlling the money supply in the West is more likely to rely on OMO as commercial banks work on low excess reserves. In the US, the FOMC manages the money supply, through OMO.

The Transmission between the Money and Real Economies
The rate of interest is seen as the price that has to be paid to persuade people to forego the advantage of holding money. It is the price that must be paid in order to overcome people's liquidity preference. As interest rates rise, as there is an opportunity cost from holding cash, people will hold less cash and visit the bank more often. Keynes was interested in using the inverse relationship between bonds and interest rates. If a bond (e.g. Government Stock or Gilts) offered the owner a fixed sum of money per year regardless of what s/he paid for it, then the cheaper it is, the better the yield (or rate of return on the investment) for the owner. The price of the bond follows the laws of supply and demand. If consumers wish to buy more bonds, demand shifts to the right, the price rise and the yield falls. Keynes' model implied that there were two types of assets; money and bonds. The speculative demand will vary with expectations about future changes in interest rates. For example, if interest rates are high and bond prices are low, speculators, who expect interest rates to fall, will buy bonds. Speculators will hold cash if they anticipate a rise in interest rates i.e. an expected fall in bond prices should result in holding cash. Thus, the Money Demand schedule MD is downward sloping.

Indirect Transmission Mechanism
Keynes' indirect transmission mechanism entails increasing the Money Supply MS from MS_1 to MS_2 in the diagram below. With this additional cash in idle balances, speculators buy bonds. As the price of bonds rises, yields fall. As a yield is a rate of return, interest rates in the economy falls from i_1 to i_2. This *may* have an impact on the real economy.

For investment to be worthwhile, its rate of return must exceed the opportunity cost of investment (the rate of interest). Thus, as the interest rate falls, the level of planned investment will rise. There will be an increasing number of projects that yield a rate of return sufficient to cover the cost of capital. The relationship between the level of investment and the rate of return on investments is called the marginal efficiency of investment (MEI). This schedule is downward sloping. The fall in interest from i_1 to i_2, lowers the costs of borrowing leading to greater investment from I_1 to I_2. Investment is an injection into the circular flow of income. The aggregate demand schedule shifts to the right. Assuming some unemployment, greater output, employment and growth follow.

Liquidity Trap

A liquidity trap occurs when interest rates have reached, what is perceived as, their lowest level, i.e. where bond prices have attained their maximum level. Any purchase of bonds will result in a capital loss on irredeemable bonds, so speculators will hold cash. If the Money Supply schedule is to the right of

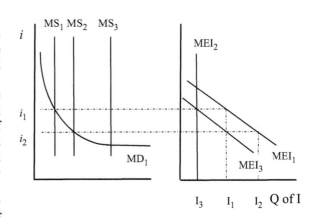

MS3, an increase in the idle balances of speculators will NOT lead to an increase in demand for bonds and so no fall in interest rates. Money cannot influence the real economy in this liquidity trap.

Alternatively, when interest rate elasticity is zero so investment is insensitive to interest rates, as with MEI_2, a decrease in interest rates will not increase investment. Money cannot influence investment. Keynesians would not advocate the use of monetary policy in these cases. A third case entails the MEI shifting to the left to MEI_3 as quickly as interest rates fall. Consistent with a deep recession, economic conditions worsen as quickly as the cost of capital falls. Thus, investment does not increase despite falling interest rates.

Krugman, Gavyn Davies and Tim Congdon extended the notion of a liquidity trap. Krugman's trap is focused on changes in the price level of goods and services. Krugman posited that at zero short rates, unless monetary policy raises the expected rate of inflation, the real rate of interest precludes the full utilisation of resources. With low or negative inflationary expectations, consumers will withhold expenditure.

Davies tied the two together. He suggests a full liquidity trap has three crucial characteristics.
1. short rates should be (effectively) at zero;
2. bond yields should be at their lower limit in the risk/return sense;
3. the real economy should be operating below capacity because real interest rates, though very low, are stuck at levels that are too high to induce sufficient aggregate demand. Underlying inflation rates should therefore be declining.

Note:- the demand for money curve is predicated on a liquidity trap. As bond prices do not automatically have an upper bound, the trap cannot exist with negative nominal rates of interest rates. Does this mean that the money demand curve retains its negative slope at interest rates below zero? Keynes and Fisher assumed yes. But what sort of money? Gavyn Davies argues that if central banks pushed the yields on bank deposits too far into the negative zone, banks and eventually their customers would choose to hold cash instead of the negative yielding deposits. Ultimately, if pushed too far, the entire economy would become a cash-based system. That is, the real constraint on the ability of the central banks to set negative interest rates.

Friedman's Direct Transmission Mechanism

In the diagram below, the direct transmission mechanism entails increasing the Money Supply MS from MS_1 to MS_2. With this additional cash, people find their cash balances are out of kilter with their portfolio so money supply exceeds money demand $MS > MD$. To rebalance the portfolio, people purchase a range of assets, including goods and services. Thus, all asset prices rise. In the real economy, the AD curve shifts to the right.

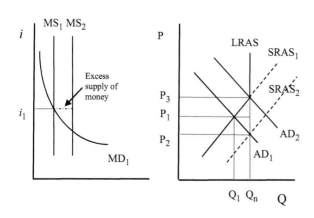

A deflationary gap can be analysed from the perspective of active or passive monetary policy. The economy is operating at Q_1, to the left of Q_n and below trend. In a neo-classical world, with flexible wages and prices the market wage must fall, which reduces the cost of labour and thus the SRAS shifts to the right to $SRAS_2$. Prices fall and, as a consequence, the level of aggregate demand increases. The money supply has not changed but there is movement to Q_n and the price level falls from P_1 to P_2.

With inflexible wages, as in Keynes' world, increasing the money supply could be a solution. The AD curve shifts to the right from AD_1 to AD_2. Price rises from P_1 to P_3 whilst output moves towards Q_n.

The Term Structure of Interest Rates

The yield curve plots the yields of similar-quality bonds against their time maturity periods. In a world of certainty, the curve will reflect only liquidity preferences. As there is a greater likelihood that unforeseen events will undermine the investment, with uncertainty, a risk-averse investor needs to be offered a risk premium for holding a long-term investment, rather than a short.

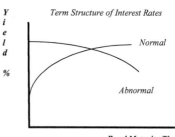

The figure above shows a *normal* term structure with a higher rate offered to those more willing to lock their capital away in a bond with a longer period to maturity. In other words, in equilibrium, holders of long and short dated bonds have equal compensation, accounting for risk.

In the event that interest rates were expected to fall, where short term rates are higher than long, yield curve becomes inverted or 'abnormal.' Longer dated stocks are more exposed to uncertainty. Borrowing on a short term basis when interest rates are about to fall may be cheaper than if you borrow long. Inflation can play a significant role. Market sentiment suggests is a pending economic recession. It implies the yields offered by long-term fixed income bonds will fall in the future.

If inflation is expected in the future, holders of long dated stock must be compensated with higher returns. A steepening curve is associated with rising inflation expectations. Commonly, this comes about due to a tightening labour market and stronger economic activity. Higher policy rates are anticipated. When the yield curve is steep, banks are able to borrow money at lower interest rates and lend at higher interest rates. Deflation implies the opposite. From December 2018-March 2020 the 2-year 10-year Treasuries differential floated around 20bps, the lowest since just before the onset of recession in 2007. It rose anticipating inflation.

Work by Engstrom and Sharpe suggested that the traditional warning signs of recession (2-year to 10-year gap) may not be as powerful as analysis that focuses on shorter term rates. Rather, the yield curve around 3-month and 18-months served as a stronger predictor of recession in the coming year by capturing the market's conviction that the FED would need to cut rates soon in response to a slowdown. 18th March 2019, the 3m-2y yield differential flipped.[7] At the beginning of May 2019 the 2y stood at 2.39% below the 10y @ 2.51% but also below the 3m @ 2.43%. By August around a third of the bond market ($17tn) were trading at negative yields. This corresponded with the inverted US yield curve. In May, the 10-2year spread was back at pre-2019 levels @0.49%, with the 10yr yield at 0.69%.

Over the recent past, economic policy instruments have appeared unfit for purpose. Some governments have resorted to developing unconventional methods for managing the economy. If one goes to the Reserve Bank of India's website, one can find a review of **Central Banks' Unconventional Policy Measures**. It suggests some of the following:-

❑ Quantitative Easing entails central banks buying all sorts of assets from commercial banks (as opposed to only gilts and highly rated paper). This should boost liquidity allowing the commercial banks more scope to lend. If the banks hoard liquidity rather than lending it, then this option will not work.

❑ Direct credit easing: through the purchase of commercial papers, corporate bonds and asset-backed securities the central bank could extend liquidity support to

---

[7] https://www.treasury.gov/resource-center/data-chart-center/interest-rates/Pages/TextView.aspx?data=yieldYear&year=2019

corporates directly. This is a means of avoiding using banks as an intermediary of monetary policy.

❑ Indirect (endogenous) easing entails expanding the size of the central bank's balance sheet by lending to banks at longer maturities, against collateral that includes assets whose markets are temporarily impaired. This option could widen the pool of collaterals that may be accepted by the central bank for refinancing operations.

❑ Forward guidance: in the zero lower bound interest rate era, the signal of a cut of rates was no longer possible. Guidance does not require a target, but that might help manage expectations. Credibility is everything here. Offering guidance which turns out not to be followed or fails to achieve any stated ends would devalue the usefulness of future statements. Guidance may matter less now zero is no longer the lower bound. Indeed, Swiss, Canadian, Singaporean, Swedish and Australian central banks all engaged in unpredictable interest rate policies in the first 4 months of 2015. In March 2018, the BoE was signalling an increase in interest rates. Economists and the market lined up behind that. Then, in the following April and May it changed tone, wrong footing the market, the way forward guidance should not.

❑ Twisting the yield curve entails targeting a certain period to maturity e.g. one associated with mortgages, to alter a key rate in the real economy. The degree of monetary stimulus is marked by the shape of the yield curve. The flatter yield curve, the greater the stimulus. This raises the price of long term bonds strengthening the bank balance sheet that owns them. The BoJ uses yield curve control, setting a target of 0% on 10-year government bond yields. Unfortunately, failing to achieve its 2% inflation target, after heavy printing, is leaving it with few options. Rather than raise inflation expectations, by capping long-term rates, Central Banks could lower them deterring current expenditure.

❑ Negative interest rates on offer at the central bank. This should act as a disincentive for high street lenders to leave their surplus with the central bank. This tack, introduced by the ECB in June 2014, entailed a cut its deposit rate from 0 to –0.10%.

❑ Helicopter money is a gift to all citizens from the central bank. This boosts the money supply. As QE persistently increases the money supply in the way OMO does not, one can see why it's viewed as the peoples' QE. It avoids banks and rich folk. However, to ensure the money is spent, it should be offered in the form of vouchers, with a limited life, so that it cannot be horded.

❑ At the beginning of April, the FED committed to a $500bn municipal debt buying programme. It also funnelled up to $600bn in loans to small to medium-sized firms, via banks.

❑ Concurrently, the BoE offered the Treasury up an unlimited overdraft. This followed helicopter money offered by the US Treasury.

❑ On 30th April 2020, the ECB decided to pay banks between 0.50% and 1% to borrow from its Targeted Long Term Refinancing Operations (TLTRO). This is a €3bn bank subsidy.

QE ARGUMENTS

As QE was tried, tested and amended, a number of explanations of the transmission mechanism emerged.

1. As a variant of OMO, QE improves bank liquidity. This should boost bank lending, putting money in to people's hands, so increase in nominal spending. Charlie Bean stated in 2010 that there was a need to get consumers to save less and spend more, (shifting the AD curve, right). This was achieved in 2017Q1 when the savings ratio at 3.7% was at its lowest annual level since 1963.

2. QE lowers interest rates. By purchasing bond prices across all maturities bond prices rise and yields fall, pushing down interest rates, which, through the indirect transmission mechanism should boost investment. A variant on this is Yield curve control and Operation Twist, where a particular interest rate is targeted, which affects the well-being of mortgagers. By reducing the likelihood of default, this helps the solvency of banks: by reducing the servicing of mortgages, this could boost spending.

3. QE boosts asset prices.
    a. From the direct transmission mechanism, the excess of cash holdings will cause an imbalance in a portfolio. Asset prices will rise as agents to rebalance their portfolio, shifting their asset holding away from and cash to shares, gold, commodities and goods and services. Thus, the AD shifts. The BoE found that the rise in asset prices favoured the top 5% that hold 40% of the UK's personal assets. The richest 20% save ⅓ of their income and contribute 40% of all consumer expenditure. QE is the basis for huge inequalities.
    b. From a permanent income perspective, permanent consumption is based on wealth. An increase in wealth due to a rise in asset prices will lead to an increase in consumption. So asset price increases should raise demand in the economy for goods and services.
    c. As the asset rises in value, the family home provides a greater unit of collateral against which more borrowing can be made.

4. QE lowers returns on investment grade assets. Investors turn to higher yield corporate bonds and equities. So companies can raise record levels of capital at a low cost. Henkel ($500m-2yr) and Sanofi (€1bn-3yr) issued debt at negative yields (-0.05%) in September 2016, the first corporates to do so in Euros. Even if the companies do not invest, this cheap debt improves their chances of survival. Banks also benefit. With fewer failures banks are less exposed to corporate debt defaults. Share buy-backs are driving up stock exchange and CEO remuneration. More worryingly, from a competition perspective QQE was funding Japanese banks taking over regional competitors. This trend is not so welcome.

5. QE is a means of helping banks switch bad assets with good and build up reserves to improve their solvency. QE entails buying up corporate debt, some of which may have a lowish credit rating. This socialises the risk of failure, lowering the cost of borrowing. The IMF estimated that systemically important banks, too

important to fail, received an implicit subsidy of $150-590bn. The subsidy is imputed from the cost of borrowing that the largest banks enjoy that would be bailed-out; specifically, the costs of insuring against default, plus credit rating. The breakdown by country was:

    a.   US $15-70bn, 15bp lower interest rate costs
    b.   Japan $25-110bn 25-60bps
    c.   UK $20-110bn 20-60bps
    d.   Eurozone $90-300bn 60-90bps

    The NY FED estimated that each bond sale for the largest US banks was $60-80m cheaper over smaller ones.

6.   QE lowers the external value of the currency - boosting exports. This is not an explicit policy but has supporting benefits, closing output gaps, increasing inflation and employment. However, Brazil was most vexed about US QE, claiming that the world was in a midst of a currency war. Moreover, it caused major difficulties with the management of the Hong Kong dollar in April 2018 and August 2019. Since Dec 2004 it has operated a currency board, with a peg to the US$ at HK$7.80±5.

7.   An increase in money supply should raise price expectations and encourage consumption today rather than tomorrow. QE affects financial asset prices quickly, but goods and services are sluggish. Janet Yellen doubted whether a policy based purely on shifting expectations could ever work. Long-run inflation expectations become anchored at a particular level only after the actual rate has been stable at a level beforehand. Sadly, as with the MTFS, another expectations dependent theory, expectations rise only if consumers believe in the model.

Alan Blinder and Mark Zandi for the US Centre on Budget and Policy Priorities find that without the fiscal stimulus, QE and the financial policies that resulted in a quickly recapitalised banking system:

- the US economy would have shrunk by 1000bps greater than the 4% recession in the US;
- twice as many people would have lost their jobs, and the unemployment rate would have been 600bps higher than the 10%;
- the federal budget deficit could have reached $2.8tn (20% of GDP);
- the recovery would have been slower, too. By 2011, the policies ensured that output was 1600bps higher than the crisis trend.

The BoE estimated that without QE GDP would be 8% lower and unemployment would have peaked 4% higher (12%). Cumulatively, over 2008-2012, incomes were 20% higher worth £23,000 to each household.

One might argue that the QE orthodoxy misses the main point. Japan lost two decades to stagnant growth and the BoJ still turned to bonds in March/April.

- Greenspan, the former FED chair, suggested a Minsky thesis that a prolonged period of stability is a necessary and sufficient condition for an asset price bubble. Agents become used to a low risk environment, encouraging more reckless behaviour. QE weakens normal market disciplines.

- QE socialises the higher risk non-sovereign bonds, which may push up borrowing costs to other (European) nations.
- Banks lost interest in customer savings.
- Low interest rates, rather than an ageing population, precipitated a pensions' crisis.
- The preservation of *zombie companies* locks resources in to slow growing companies, slowing productivity growth. In the UK, R3 reported the number of zombies (which are not paying the principal on their loans) had fallen from 160,000 in November 2012 to 102,000 in August 2013. Begbies Traynor, using a broader definition, put the number at 432,000. These figures emerged as RBS was criticised for forcing viable companies into receivership. The BoE found that the largest 5 banks were offering forbearance on: 14% of loans to SMEs; 5 to 8% of secured household loans; 28% of leveraged loans; and 35% of commercial property loans. However, not all members of each group take out a loan: the 14% of SME zombie loans apply to only 6% of SMEs.
- Between 2007 and 2015, public investment in the Eurozone fell by around €20bn when €3tn of sovereign debt was issued. In the Eurozone plus the US, total non-finance sector debt increased from 225% of GDP to 250% but with tepid growth in output or wages.

After a decade of QE, Swiss, Swedish, UK, central banks the FED, BoJ and the ECB held $15tn in debt, of which $9tn is sovereign debt. ECB $4.9tn, BoJ $4.53tn, and FED $4.47tn. Of the total sovereign debt of $46tn, these 6 hold 20% of it. In 2008, there was $25tn. This exposes central banks to interest rate rises. 40% of developed nations' sovereign debt is to be refinanced by 2021. In June 2018, the concern was both the FED and the ECB unwinding their balance sheets causing a liquidity crisis. The Treasury needs to sell $2.34tn in bonds by 2020, sucking $1tn out of the system.

Beyond refinancing, Portugal (€7.2bn), Ireland (€15bn) and Italy (€150bn) have a high exposure to Euribor, floating interest rates. There is €150tn worth of debt tied to this floating interest rate. A variant on Libor, it is to be replaced by 2020.

NEGATIVE INTEREST RATES

The BoE's Andrew Haldane suggests currently we have the lowest real interest rates for 5,000 years. Over 2019/20, in March the BoE reduced the repo rate to 0.1%, in September the ECB shifted its deposit rate to -0.5% from its previous -0.4%, whilst Sweden raised its repo rate to 0% from -0.25%.

Negative interest rates on deposits in the bank are a charge on saving. Negative interest rates are a concern on a number of levels. In a sense, negative interest rates have been with us for years. Real rates have been negative without causing unusual outcomes. The financial markets were imperfect and there were heavy regulations over retail borrowing. What is new is that following the Swiss, Swedish, Danish and ECB policy changes, nominal rates of interest rates from January 2016 for debt became negative. Issues:-

❑ In [old] theory, there is a lower bound with a liquidity trap to nominal rates so that a bond purchaser, at that bound, would only make a loss so monetary policy becomes impotent. If buyers believe that interest rates *can* go lower, then they might buy what appears to be an over-priced bond. So is there a liquidity trap any more? Perhaps yes. It was suggested that the Swiss lower bound could close to – 0.75%, but this is not clear.

❑ An interest rate regulates the time-preference of consumption. A positive rate encourages a consumer to forgo current consumption for greater future consumption. Investment is, in effect, future consumption – so saving is converted to investment today for consumption tomorrow. A negative interest signals that today's consumption is too little and this needs to be rebalanced.

❑ Using DCF/NPV criteria, low interest rates should foster longer term projects. From a MEI perspective, the economy should benefit from more investment. An excess of investment in production could be deflationary, driving up output and prices down.

❑ In November, Volksbank Furstenfeldbruck offered an instant access rate of -0.5% on deposits of €1. Three months earlier, Jyske Bank in Denmark, charged -0.6% on deposits and -0.5% on 10-year loans.

❑ With deflation, the real value of loans increases over time.

❑ Before 2008, many current bank accounts entailed charges for their use. Negative rates act as a charge for using the bank to store your money. In effect, it is a *Gesell tax*; a tax on sight deposits. As deposits present an opportunity cost, this puts interest rates into the same category as inflation, so there should be a shift in portfolio structures:-

  o As with inflation, consumers will convert cash into goods. There should be an increase in the velocity of money, V ($MV = PT$).

  o Consumers will prefer holding cash, so there will be an increase in cash holdings.

  o Gavyn Davies argued that if central banks pushed the yields on bank deposits too far into the negative zone, the entire economy would become a cash-based system.

  o Businesses prefer holding assets that hedge against price rises.

❑ Large depositors, such as banks, may prefer paying a *Gesell tax* to other outcomes, particularly the non-repayment of loans. In 2014Q2, the US non-financial sector (corporates) held $2.58tn in cash and money market funds. This was up from $2.3tn in 2009. Fears that are most acute include:-

  o The UK breaking up following an exit from Europe

  o The Ukrainian crisis getting worse – Russian disruption of Brexit and Trump elections

  o There is a financial crisis ahead in either housing or commercial property

❑ Negative rates may be deployed for differing reasons. A lack of lending presents a coordination problem. Some customers are likely to default on existing debt. Lower (negative) rates reduce that risk. To off-set deflation Sweden (repo rate)

and the ECB (deposit rate) use negative rates. But... QE is causing Denmark and Switzerland exchange rate pressures. Negative interest rates discourage investors from buying the DKr and SFr.

❑ However... in a time of deflation the real value of money rises. As interest rates tend to shadow prices, falling prices can off-set negative interest rates.

❑ However... the combination of falling prices and rising exchange rates may mean that buying Swiss debt at negative nominal rates still generates a positive yield. A Polish 3 year bond, on offer in SFr @ –0.213%, would be attractive if the Swiss deposit rate was –0.75%.

❑ An interest rate is both a rationing and a signalling device. The criticism from Capitol Hill was that US forward guidance was unpredictable for financial markets. The demand was for [Taylor] rules-based monetary policy. A bill before the house could enforce this demand. Guidance has moved away from guidance to a pledge.

❑ The setting of a low rate of interest should discourage savings. A German saver was estimated to have lost €500 in interest but a borrower saved $2000 in lower payments – a net benefit.

❑ Negative interest rates could also be seen as a punishment. The banks prospered whilst the rest suffered during the recession that they caused. Now negative interest rates are an ideal tool. Without negative savings rates, the banks must absorb the pain. The pain for a 0.25% reduction in repo rate is 2-3% of bank earnings. In 2018, European banks paid the ECB €7.2bn in deposits.

❑ The Swedish authorities found banks lend less not more.

❑ Lower bond yields reduce the tax payer's liabilities, shifting wealth from global investors to governments keen to reduce their debt ratios. Fitch estimated that in July 2016 across 34 countries with nearly $13.2tn [out of a total of $34tn] debt with a negative yield, annual interest on sovereign debt was reduced by $500bn/yr compared with 2011. So a 10-year bond in 2011 would yield 3.87% in 2011 and 1.17% in 2016 at the median. For Japan this amounts to $95bn/yr and Germany, the UK and the US combined $104bn.

❑ In May, the UK Treasury sold £3.75bn in 3-yr gilts @ an average yield of negative 0.003%. Another record.

But what if borrowing, not saving was the source of funds? Borrowing at low rates would lead to an over, not under investment. One such investment is in corporate debt. It has been reported that the biggest buyers of shares in the US market have been not real investors but companies buying-back their own shares with cheap, borrowed debt. McKinsey estimated that global corporate debt has more than doubled from 26% to 56% of GDP. One by-product of this is over-valued shares. Moreover, around ¼ of dollar denominated corporate bonds were issued by non-US firms. Emerging markets had issued around $4.5tn in dollar denominated debt: an increase of 100% in five years.

Lending institutions, such as those in the leasing sector, upon which Japan's SMEs rely on for liquidity, are squeezed. The Japan Lending Association provided funds equivalent to 7% of Japanese GDP in 2015. For the year to August 2016, volume was down 10.6%, an outcome of the negative interest rate policy but the opposite objective.

Pensions and Penalties
Some major institutions are obliged to buy government debt for reserve purposes, such as banks. But there is a key reason, these bonds are liquid and are preferable to holding cash in the vault or cash with the central bank – which earns a negative return.

McKinsey Global Institute considered the implications of low returns among lenders and borrowers. Net debtors, such as the State and non-financial corporations, have gained whereas net creditors, such as insurance companies, pension providers and households, lose. The Institute estimated that the UK government benefited by £120bn whereas UK households had lost £110bn. Due to low interest payments, profits of non-financial corporations have risen by 20%, *but then black holes in pensions schemes have emerged.* Why? Income in perpetuity – or until you die is related to interest rates. As rates fall, the capital sum that is required to meet the obligations rises, so more capital has to be put aside by the fund managers for this.

The BIS suggests that low long term interest rates may be a function of insurance companies covering their liabilities and the risk of falling yield in the future. They had to buy bonds, lowering yields. Yields have been too low for too long, crucifying pensions.

Final salary schemes are, therefore, a large problem. Blackrock, the fix interest rate bond trader, pointed out that negative interest rates affected savers, particularly those preparing for retirement. A typical 35 year old has to save over 3× as much to have the same retirement income if rates are 2% compared with 5%. Hymans Roberts estimated that total pension deficits of UK companies over the past 15 years have risen from £250bn to about £900bn despite £500bn being injected in to them.

The collapse of Tata Steel shone a light on British Steel's £485m pension deficit. The fund, worth £15bn covers 130,000 members (85,000 retired + 45,000 to retire), would go with the sale of the steel interests. This was the key issue. The Pension Protection Fund, set up to support funds in this position would have its reserves wiped out. It was estimated that if loss of the pension fund was 5% that would amount to the loss £750m, double the previous loss the protection scheme has to deal with. BHS went down with a £591m pension black hole soon after. In June 2017, the Hoover pension scheme went into the Pension Protection Fund. Those under retirement age would receive an immediate 10% cut in their pension pot and those already retired, would receive less. The Hoover scheme has a deficit of about £250m with the scheme's liabilities around £500m (just below BHS's). Hoover Candy stopped producing washing machines in Merthyr Tydfil in 2009, but a head office and a distribution warehouse remained. Of the 7,800 members, 5,319 are pensioners and 2,184 who have deferred their pensions. Pensions' liabilities are now a severe impediment to corporate rescues.

The same lump sum problem applies to NHS medical negligence claims. They present a significant cost (£4.5bn over the past five years). But the lump sums that should provide set incomes for the lifetime of the patient-claimants must increase as the interest rate decreases.

Modern Monetary Theory
The essential elements of MMT can be summarised as follows:
- The fundamental idea of the Modern Monetary Theory (MMT) is that " … a monetarily sovereign country like the US with debts denominated in its own currency and a floating exchange rate cannot default in debt denominated in its own currency. Therefore, ".… the only limit on government spending is inflation". The government budget constraint should be replaced by an inflation constraint.
- A government deficit is necessarily mirrored by an equivalent private sector surplus.
- Monetary policy is relatively ineffective in a slump: fiscal policy is more powerful.
- A government can buy goods and services without the need to collect taxes or issue debt.
- Through money creation, interest costs can be constrained. Indeed, a substantial and persistent budget deficit can be financed at low, if not near-zero, cost.
- Inflation is still caused by demand and cost-push drivers which, through fiscal policy and monetary financing, government set the general price level. This implies that the central government and the central bank are the same and that inflation, should it arise, can readily be controlled by higher taxation and bond issuance to remove excess liquidity.

The budget deficit and public sector indebtedness should be allowed to adjust to the level necessary to secure full employment. In turn it is suggested that this goal should be achieved through a government-sponsored blanket jobs guarantee, which would act as an automatic stabiliser. When private sector jobs were plentiful, government spending on the guarantee would be lower, and vice versa. Alternatively, full employment could be achieved by large-scale spending on infrastructure, financed, if necessary, by the central bank.
- It is a closed-economy model, making no allowance for the possibility of monetary expansion causing the exchange rate to fall rapidly. It really only applies to very large States.
- It overlooks the potential for monetary expansion and an extended period of low interest rates to create the conditions for domestic financial instability
- It deals with demand deficient unemployment only.
- It has wealth distribution issues.
- Greater national debt will place an interest burden on the budget deficit
- It presents a moral hazard for the State, undermining the market as an instrument to impose fiscal rectitude. De facto, making governments such as Argentina's

appear sound. Indeed, MMT is sanguine about the national debt. One would anticipate that a government would be obliged to run a large enough primary budget surplus to stabilise debt growth, at some point. This could involve dramatic tax increases or public expenditure cuts, which are politically unpalatable, if not impossible, to deliver.

EXCHANGE RATES

The implicit idea in textbooks is that most exchange rate dealings relate to economic fundamentals, but De Grauwe suggests that this is a misconception. According to BIS, in 2007, daily trades in FX were worth $3.2trn. This was up by 71% from 2004. International trade did not increase by 71% in 3 years. The breakdown of trades is as follows: spot (for immediate delivery) makes up ⅓; forwards 11% and the rest are swaps. In other words, FX trades are largely OTC (bilateral deals), not based on auction prices. By April 2016, turnover/day of foreign exchange was valued at $5.067tn, down from 2013. The US £ making up almost 44% of trades. London accounts for 43% of the global $6.6tn in currency trades, up from 37% in 2016. The biggest banks, which hold nearly half of worldwide FX trading, earned a combined $16.3bn in revenue from FX trading in 2018. In September, BIS reported that London trades in the Indian rupee stood at $47bn/day, whereas RBI handled $35bn/day, so raising the issue that the RBI would have difficulty controlling its currency.

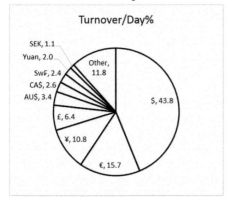

Turnover/Day%

It is also normal for textbooks to talk about two [extreme] forms of exchange rate regime: fixed and floating. But, as the IMF observes, there are a variety of fixed forms:
- Float
- Intermediate – soft peg or managed float (Managed or dirty float – no predefined management rate; Crawling bands - predefined band movements; Crawling peg – predefined movement; Horizontal bands – predefined bands; Adjustable peg – predefined rate)
- Fixed for unknown period
- Hard Peg – currency unions, currency boards, dollarisation.

Exchange Rate Diagrams
The free market forces of demand and supply determine floating Exchange Rates. Since one country's residents, say those of the US, demands the currency of another's on the foreign exchange market, say the UK's, it follows that demand for US$s implies supply of Sterling and supply of £s suggests a need for $s. Assuming costless trading, if the exchange rate is £1 = $2, then a TV in UK priced at £150 sells for $300 in the USA and a US fridge price $400 sells for £200 in UK.

The diagram right reflects the workings of the foreign exchange market for Sterling (£) and US Dollars $. The supply curve slopes upwards as UK residents supply MORE £s to buy MORE US goods when they appear cheaper to them, i.e. when a £ buys more $s. The demand curve for Sterling slopes downwards as US residents will demand £s to buy more British goods when they appear cheaper to them, i.e. when a $ buys more £s. The equilibrium exchange rate occurs where the demand and supply for Sterling is equal, i.e. at $2/£. If the exchange rate was at $1/£, the *Balance of Payments* will be in surplus (excess demand for Sterling on the foreign exchange market of $Q_2 - Q_1$).

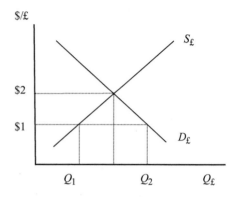

A rise in disposable income among UK residents will increase the demand for US exports, i.e. the supply curve for Sterling on the foreign exchange market shifts to the right (to $S_£^2$). The consequence for the exchange rate is a decrease from £1 = $2 to £1 = $1 in the diagram below.

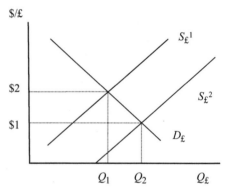

The depreciation in the value of the £ makes imports relatively dearer and exports relatively cheaper. The UK TV sells for $150 in USA. The US fridge sells for £400 in UK. If the £ buys more foreign currency, the £ is said to have appreciated.

Fixed Exchange Rates
A pegged rate is an arrangement whereby the central bank intervenes in the exchange market to peg the exchange rate but still keeps an 'independent' monetary policy. If a country runs a BoP surplus, the central bank has to intervene in the ForEx as before. To neutralize the monetary effects of intervention, the central bank sells an equal quantity of domestic assets (say government bonds), cancelling the effects of the money supply. To maintain an independent monetary policy it may offset the monetary effects of intervention in the exchange market by sterilization operations. The distinction between 'pegged' and 'fixed' rates lies in the adjustment system. A fixed rate is one where intervention in the exchange market is allowed to affect the money supply. If a country runs a BoP surplus, the central bank has to intervene in the Foreign Exchange (ForEx) markets to prevent its currency from appreciating. In exchanging domestic for foreign currency, the increased supply of domestic coinage swells the reserves of the banking system and increases domestic expenditure. This

leads to an increased demand for imports and, hence, correcting the surplus, automatically. Thus, a fixed exchange rate system is a monetary rule that contains a self-adjusting equilibrating mechanism of the BoP.

Convertibility is a unilateral fix. The degree of convertibility is the ease with which a country's currency can be converted into gold or another currency. Non-convertibility implies a barrier to international trade. Government restrictions can often result in a currency with low convertibility. For example, a government with low reserves of hard foreign currency often restricts currency convertibility because the government would not be in a position to intervene in the foreign exchange market (i.e. revalue, devalue) to support their own currency if and when necessary.

The characteristics of a hard currency peg can be illustrated with currency board. Here, there is a higher level of commitment to monetary rectitude than a pegged rate. The characteristics of a currency board are:
* A fixed exchange rate – tied to one other or to a basket;
* Monetary base can expand to no more than 100% of the foreign currency reserves;
* It precludes any lender-of-last-resort facility. The lack of a lender-of-last-resort facility makes the banking sector more vulnerable to a confidence crisis;
* Loss of monetary policy;
* Cannot use the exchange rate for BoP adjustment.

Estonia, Lithuania, Bosnia, and Bulgaria all established currency board-like systems from 1992 to 1997. QE, reducing the interest rate to zero and printing money, is not possible under a currency board regime. If hard-wired to a currency engaged in QE, the economy may suffer grievously. The central bank would have to absorb additional foreign currency, with potentially inflationary consequences. Alternatively, when bonded to an appreciating currency, the impact of higher interest rates etc. could lead to a recession and a potential speculative hot money outflow, which must be neutralised.

The rules of the Hong Kong currency board peg require the Hong Kong Monetary Authority to use its reserves to buy the currency once it hits the lower limit of the HK$7.75 to HK$7.85 band against the US dollar. In April 2018, it slumped as low as HK$7.85. Hong Kong is the world's least affordable housing market. House prices rose nearly 13% over the past year, and 146% over the past decade. About 90% of mortgages in Hong Kong are linked to Hibor, the local interbank rate.

HK shows the links between internal and external changes in the interest rate. Purchasing HK$ would remove some excess liquidity from the financial system (QE from China), lifting local short-term interest rates and making the currency more attractive to hold. Raising interest rates directly would hurt (slow) the property market. In the event, the HKMA raised its base rate by 0.25% to 2%. When this failed to work, it bought HK$51.33bn in the week from the 12th April, the first interception since its inception in December 1984. The currency climbed to 7.8498 and 3m Hibor stood at

1.21% when US Libor was 2.38%. In principle, one should track to other but the gap is related to excess liquidity from Chinese investments, putting pressure on the currency.

Whilst the Yuan was weakening in August 2018, the HK Market Authority intervened several times to shore up the currency. Following the rise in the US repo rate in December, March saw a similar defence, spending $2bn to maintain the rate.

In the diagram right is an analysis. Note that central rate (peg) of 7.8:$ is the same as one HK$ buying @ 0.128 US$. There is than an upper

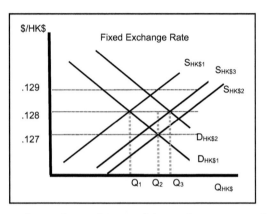

(.129) and lower (.127) rate. The rate slumped to .127, possibly on better rates of return in the US. To increase demand (demand curve right from $D_{HK\$1}$ to $D_{HK\$2}$) first interest rates were raised and then the authority bought currency. Note that because interest rates rose, the supply curve should shift left. Mortgage costs should diminish disposable income, reducing the demand for imports. Thus, if these policies moved the currency back to peg, equilibrium would be at Q_3 where $S_{HK\$3}$ intersects with $D_{HK\$2}$. Tracking the events in the US Hong Kong's central bank cut its benchmark interest rate on 1st August in its first policy easing since late 2008. Till then HK financial market and currency had not been affected by the recent social unrest in the city. In July, the Central Bank held $448.5bn of assets in its foreign exchange fund alone as of July, representing roughly seven times the currency in circulation. Again there was a speculative attack in mid August but that came to nought.

Dollarisation/ Currency Union are like those of a currency board, but by taking another country's currency, the domestic central bank cannot print money. Examples include Ecuador ($), Kosovo and Montenegro (€) (without permission). Scotland could be in this position.

Fischer (2001) suggested that, with open, small economies, an adjustable peg as an exchange rate regime choice is not sustainable. A shift to a harder peg is the trend. Prophetically, Fischer notes that, when borrowing in a foreign currency, lulled by a stable regime, investors reduce their perceptions of risk. When the crisis does come it is exceptionally damaging for the banking system. Poeck et al. (2007) divide currency crises into three groups:-
1. weak fundamentals based on excessive expansion of credit. Speculation of a devaluation follows a fall in interest rates and an outflow of reserves;
2. self-fulfilling expectations with multiple equilibria. Central banks fulfil the expectations of speculators and devalue, following a loss of confidence. There is

no one equilibrium exchange rate. The current one is abandoned when the costs of maintaining it outweigh the costs of deserting it;

3.   beyond weak fundamentals, a weak banking sector and poor financial regulation leading to moral hazard and over-indebtedness abroad.

Importantly, when internal objectives outweigh external the central bank has an incentive to devalue.

Venezuela

In January 2011, the Venezuelan Bolivar was devalued. Venezuela had three exchange rates.

1.   The DIPRO rate of the Bolivar was devalued from 2.15 to 2.6 to the Dollar. This rate was reserved for necessities like foods and medicines.

2.   The Oil rate was pegged at 4.3Bvrs:$ for non-essentials.

3.   The parallel or black market rate which was over 6Bvrs:$ but would be managed officially by the central bank.

In February 2013, the official fixed exchange rate of 4.3 bolívars to the $ was

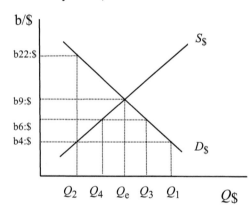

repegged to 6.3 bolívars. It still might be over-valued with an estimated 9 bolivars: $ as an 'equilibrium' exchange rate and 22.36 bolivars on the informal market. We can explore these numbers in the diagram, below. The diagram is constructed with the US$ not the bolívar as its base. Therefore, the initial position has it that the US is in surplus to Venezuela at 4 bolívars to the $ of $Q_1 - Q_2$. A devaluation of the bolívar amounts to a revaluation of the dollar to 6 bolívars to the $. This reduces the surplus to $Q_3 - Q_4$. Operating at equilibrium would require a higher revaluation of 9 bolívars to the $. With the exchange rate at 4 bolívars to the $ there would be excess demand. This could result in a black market in dollars. Under these circumstances, the rate of exchange could rise to 22 bolívars to the $.

Capital controls could be an alternative, or used in combination. Assume that the target exchange rate is 4 bolívars to the $. To ensure there is no net outflow of funds, Venezuela should restrict the demand for Dollars to the supply. This entails only allowing Venezuelan to acquire Q_2 Dollars. In effect, this shifts the demand curve for Dollars to the left $D_{\$1}$ to $D_{\$2}$. This results in balance of payments equilibrium, but the currency is not convertible.

The combination could result in the diagram left where the new exchange rate with currency restrictions addresses some of the problems, but a black market exchange rate

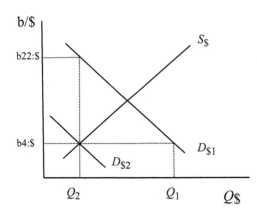

persisted. On 18 February 2016, the bolívar was devalued from 6.3 Bvrs to 10 Bvrs. The inflation rate was 2,616% in 2017, over 2% a day. The consequences are evident in the exchange rate. In January 2018, the heavily subsidized DIPOR rate of 10Bvrs:$ was scrapped and the central bank relaunched an exchange system known as DICOM, which most recently sold dollars at 3,345Bvs: $. The central bank said the first auction of the DICOM system yielded an exchange rate of 30,987.5Bvrs:€ (around 25,000Bvrs:$). The black market rate stood at 228,000Bvrs:$.

In June 2018, inflation was at 128.4% (annualised 46,305%). In July 2018, the market rate of 119,900 Bvrs, was not close to the black market rate of 4mBvrs:$. At the end of July, the President, Nicolas Maduro announced plans to delete five zeros from the bolívar, two more than planned in March. Countries facing hyperinflation have done this in the past. On August 30th, 1924, Germany removed 12 zeros creating the new Reichsmark. On January 1st 2005, Turkish Lira lost six zeros. On February 2nd 2009, the Zimbabwean dollar was redenominated for the third time in three years equivalent to removing 25 zeros from the note.

Argentina
In mid-June 2018 with the currency @ 28.45peso: $
- the central bank of Argentina began raising the RRR from 20% to 25% to reduce the money stock by up 100bnpeso (£2.7bn).
- The central bank also sold $175bn in an unusual auction of reserves.
- The government sold $4bn in bonds on the week before @ up to 32.92% in peso terms.
- The central bank lowered the cap on banks' foreign currency holdings from 10% to 5% of total assets.
- Asked for a $50bn IMF loan

Price inflation in March 2019 was 54.7%. Central Bank set out the following policies:
- Seeking to reduce the monetary base by an additional 10%
- Extending its target for zero growth in the monetary base until December 2019
- Reducing its currency band from 2% to 1.75%/month
- Reducing the amount of dollars the central bank can buy if the peso falls below the currency band floor from $75m to $50m/day
- Expanding the limit Leliq banks can hold

At the end of the month the central bank offered Leliq notes @ 68.237% to boost demand for the currency again. President Mauricio Macri imposed a price fix on 60 essential' products for at least six months, and public service prices steady for the rest of the year. These include cooking oils, flour, yogurts, jams, biscuits and Yerba mate tea. There were also separate measures to help keep domestic meat prices low. However, the peso was hitting all-time lows of 43.97:$. In April 2019, the Bank announced that the Leliq rate wound not drop below 62.5%.

Markets and Politics
July usually sees a peak in demand for local currency in Argentina due to the collection of bonuses and expenses linked to the southern hemisphere winter vacation. In July, Argentina's Central Bank reduced its interest rate floor on its benchmark Leliq notes from 62.5% to 58%. It also reduced the reserve ratio by 300bps.

On August 12th 2019 things changed. A massive upset by opposition candidate Alberto Fernandez in the primary election led, on the following day, to the peso collapsing by 30.3% to 65:$ Argentina's interbank lending rate rose to 86% from 61%. The central bank used $50m million in its own reserves, for the first time since September 2018, to intervene in the foreign exchange market and defend the peso in the face of a massive sell-off. Moreover, credit default swap prices from data provider IHS Markit showed five-year credit default swaps (CDS) marked at 2,116 basis points. At that level, the probability of a default within five years is estimated to be 75%.

To reduce capital flight in the past it imposed a tax of 30% on spending in Dollars externally. In December, it was signalled that this and higher export taxes on farm products would be introduced. As a result, Argentina's black market peso fell 7.93% to 72.50: $ in one day. Importantly the official rate was 59.75:$, which was held steady by strict capital controls imposed in September. The next day, the central bank cuts benchmark interest rate from 63% to 58% and a further drop followed to 53% at the end of December. Suffering from low investment, -1.7% in Q3, high inflation and rising poverty levels it saw unemployment hit 9.7% a recent high in Q3. Young people were especially hard hit by unemployment, with young women at a rate of 24%.

At the end of 2019 its debt stood at $323bn. In February, it postponed a $1.47bn principal payment on the country's AF20 bond until Sept. 30th. This followed the decision to restructure its debt issued in foreign currency. The peso-denominated AF20 is linked to Argentina's foreign exchange rate, and was issued under Argentine law. To avoid scheduled debt repayments of $20bn on 2020Q2, a decree, was passed in March to permit a restructuring of $68.8bn in foreign law bonds. The aim was to avoid a damaging sovereign default at the end of March. That said, Argentina's central bank lowered the benchmark interest rate to 38% from 40% in early March, the eighth cut since the middle of December.

In April, it halted a large part of $7bn in dollar denominated debt payments but covered by local law due in May until 2021. The bigger picture entails $22bn foreign currency capital payments and more than $10bn interest foreign currency payments in 2020 plus it has $70bn in foreign-law bonds. To meet bond payment agricultural export are key. Concurrently, S&P Global Ratings downgraded Argentina to selective default (SD) from CCC-; Fitch downgraded Argentina's long-term foreign currency rating to "Restricted Default" from CC; and Moody's to CA from CAA2. In May, it missed a $503m interest payment in foreign currency which was originally due on April 22 – the ninth default. It had spent $44bn of the IMF's loan.

To add to woes, Argentina's main river artery, the Parana River, was at an 11-year low in April, forcing exporters to load less merchandise on ships. A cargo ships would load to 31 rather than 34 feet deep normally. Measured in tonnes, those 3 feet result in a reduction of 7,500t of cargo on a Panamax ship or 5,400t on a Handymax. So more ships and crews were needed when Corona restrictions reduced the number of crews.

Condoms
As the costs of living bite, Argentineans see contraception as an optional expense. Sales of condoms and birth control pills tumbled. The first 9 months of 2019 saw condom sales down 8% compared with 2018 on a price on a price increase of 36%. Sales of birth control pill sales were also down - 6% for the year; around 144,000 women who stopped taking contraceptives each month.

Argentina's auto sales for 2020 were likely to be around 220,000 units, down from 460,000 in 2019. Taxes represent around 55% of the retail cost of cars. However, with two prices, one can identify the informal market exchange rate. A Ford Ka's list price was 822,870 pesos, or around $12,100 using an official rate. If bought in dollars the price drops to $7,300. So the official rate of 68p:$ was 60% of the unofficial @ 112p:$.

The Capital Account
Although we pay great attention to goods and services, when discussing a balance of payments, in actual fact, for economies like ours, capital flows are far greater in value than their current account counterparts. Capital is captured by two accounts:
- Capital account: acquisition and disposal of fixed assets, e.g. land, remittances and EU transfers
- Financial account (which was the capital account until 1998): acquisition and disposal of other financial assets

In the diagram below there is a representation of how a common exchange rate affects the current and the capital accounts.
The balance of payments on the current account is in equilibrium at E_1, while the capital account is only in balance when the exchange rate is at E_3. With only one exchange rate for the economy, the price of the currency will gravitate to E_2. At this rate, the current account is in deficit $(q_2 - q_1) = q_3$ and the capital account is in surplus $(q_5 - q_4) = q_3$. In 2015Q1, China ran a balance of payments deficit of $80bn whilst enjoying a surplus on the current account of $80bn. There was an exit of $179bn in capital.

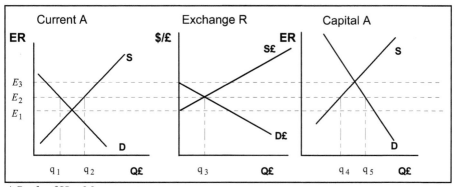

A Rush of Hot Money
If there is an increase in the demand for portfolio investments, (there is a rush of hot money into the economy) the demand curve in the capital account shifts to the right, in the diagram below. This drives the D£ schedule upwards. The result is a rise in the equilibrium exchange rate from E_2 to E_4. There will be a larger surplus on the capital and a greater deficit on the current account. This rush could be related to interest rate increases in the domestic market.

The Traditional Exchange Rate Models
The 'traditional', flow-oriented approach focuses on the current account and trade. The exchange rate affects, and is affected by, the relative competitiveness of the internationally traded goods and services. This can be seen in terms of the assets and liabilities denominated in foreign currency, or of the competitiveness of exports and imports. Even non-international traders would be affected, indirectly, through costs of materials purchased from importers. Export-oriented firms benefit from a fall, and importing ones from a rise, in the exchange rate.

The Portfolio Approach

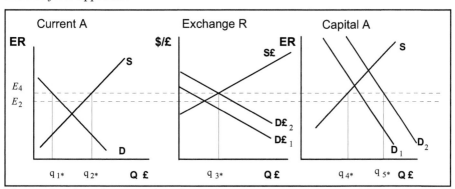

The stock-oriented approach reflects the operations of the portfolio manager. The manager is concerned about returns and risk. Risk is reduced through diversification, within and across asset classes and within and across countries. The exchange rate is a mediator between domestic and international markets for bonds and stocks. Expectations of future incomes from these assets are affected by relative currency values. Following a fall in the share price, such that a company is undervalued, foreign investors will switch to domestic currency to purchase the under-priced shares, causing an inflow of funds. Thus, there should be a negative relationship between stock prices and exchange rates.

Large speculative flows follow, if not lead, exchange rate changes. A devaluation increases nominal GDP, pushing up the demand for money and interest rates, leading to an inflow of capital. Before a devaluation, speculation would precipitate large outflows. This encourages residents to move their (savings) capital abroad to retain some of its value. A devaluation pushes up the price of imports with a consequential rise in costs of some exports. There is a decline in real income. The costs of servicing debt denominated in other currencies to the Sovereign and others increases (such as a mortgage in Poland & Hungary in Swiss Francs). The value of that debt denominated in the local currency falls in foreign currency terms, lowering the value of investments of international portfolio investors. To invest further in assets denominated in the local currency, the portfolio investor will expect greater returns.

Long-run Trade Deficit

At the end of 2016 the UK faced a 5.9% current account deficit, the greatest level since 1948. It is also experiencing a drop on external investments that it is paying to foreign investors in the country. The ONS explained that this is due to rates of return being better in the UK than elsewhere. The decline in FDI credits since 2011 has been entirely driven by a fall in the rate of return UK investors achieved on their overseas investments. In contrast, increases in

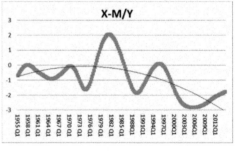

FDI debits have been due to increased investment. This suggests that the current account deficit is increasing because the UK economy offers better rates of return than others. Thus, Carney argued that the UK was relying on the kindness of strangers (overseas investors). However, an alternative view is that, much like Japan, the UK can dispose of foreign assets. Between 2012 and 2016, there was a net outflow of foreign investment of £82bn. However, UK investors divested £526bn in foreign assets. As UK investors hold overseas assets worth 420% of GDP the UK can continue on its current path.

The diagram above shows the net exports divided by GDP filtered to remove the cyclical/erratic elements. The long-run appears worrisome with a general decline from the 1980s despite the UK's holding of overseas assets. A widening external deficit also makes it harder to close the fiscal deficit, since the domestic private sector (households and/or companies) must run larger deficits to compensate.

ERMII
With the creation of the single European currency, the Euro, there needed to be a successor to ERM to prepare new accession countries for entry to the single currency. The accession country should not disrupt economic stability within the single market. As such, a convergence criterion on exchange rate stability requires participation in ERMII.

Participation in ERMII is voluntary but all Member States of the European Union, except Denmark and the United Kingdom, are required to adopt the Euro. This would apply to a detached Scotland. Before it can qualify to adopt the euro, a country must participate in ERMII without severe tensions for at least two years. The exchange rate of a non-Euro area Member State is fixed against the Euro and is only allowed to fluctuate within set limits (±15%). In theory, interventions are coordinated by the ECB and the central bank of the non-euro area Member State. The non-Euro area Member States can opt for a narrower band. Denmark operates a band of ±2.25%.

Beyond the 2-year membership, convergence criteria are required to be met. They are:-
- Price stability: Not more than 150bps above the rate of the three best performing Member States as measured by the CPI;
- Sound and Sustainable public finances: Deficit ratio not more than 3%; debt ratio not more than 60%;
- Long-term interest rate: Not more than 200bps above the rate of the three best performing Member States in terms of price stability.

Some have fulfilled the requirements recently. Divided by currency regime, the table above provides a guide to countries.

Euro			ERMII	Floating	
Austria	Germany	Malta	Denmark	*EU:*	*EU:*
Belgium	Greece	Netherlands	±2.25%.	Bulgaria[8]	Sweden
Cyprus	Ireland	Portugal		Croatia	*EEA:*
Estonia	Italy	Slovakia		Czech Rep.	Iceland
Finland	Latvia	Slovenia		Hungary	Norway
France	Lithuania	Spain		Poland	*EFTA:*
	Luxembourg			Romania	Switzerland

Croatia announced in November that it would aim for joining the Euro in 2024. In March, it claimed it would stick to this deadline. Although, Croatia achieved a balanced budget, its debt ratio was 70%. Given what the rest of the world was engaging in fiscal and monetary loosening, public debt was expected to rise. It had announced support a package worth 30bn kuna. Currency uncertainty is a problem.

---

[8] Currency Board - Reuters OCTOBER 31, 2019 Factbox: Foreign exchange regimes around the world

Around 75% of savings are held in Euros. Bulgaria also announced during the pandemic that it would apply for membership of the ERM-II and the EU banking union simultaneously. What should be advantageous is that there is a currency board peg to the €, so the ERM conditions should be met already. Support/recovery costs are important. Membership should allow Sofia access to ECB financing. Countries outside will have to take on debt at high interest rates.

A devaluation is losing its potency.
We teach that a devaluation can correct a balance of payments. Really, this concerns the current account. The requirement of the Marshall-Lerner condition relates to price elasticity of demand. As the exchange rate changes relative prices, goods should be price sensitive. The change in exports and imports should be positive. QE/QQE presents another set of results. British QE led to a 25% decline in Sterling's value but the current account failed to improve. Japan, the former great exporting powerhouse, seems to be facing the same problem. The World Bank, after reviewing 46 countries, concluded that a devaluation is only half as effective at boosting exports as it might have been 20 years ago. Why?

- For Japan, many of its great industrial companies are based overseas. The falling Yen helped Toyota's profits. Although 60% are built overseas, of the remaining 40% of vehicles built, over half are for export. For a depreciation of one Yen, operating profit would rise by 2%. Honda, which produces 80% of its vehicles overseas does not benefit as much. Sony, which produces ¾ overseas and pays its suppliers of its games and digital camera divisions in $, loses ¥3bn per depreciation of one Yen.

- Supply chains are global with parts made in units, so a devaluation leads to the cost of imports increasing as well as exports being boosted. Over a third of exported goods are assembled with components from other third party countries. An Apple phone, assembled by Foxconn, would see a rise in the costs of it components possibly off-setting the cost advantage a devaluation might offer Apple phones in the US. To address this, 'real value added' profit is the new focus. One can contrast China and Japan. Japan's supply chain is interwoven with China's. With their QQE a 17% depreciation over a year is associated with, in the quarter to June 2015, the largest drop in exports in five years. By contrast, as China moves up the value-added chain, the import intensity of exports would decline.

- An alternative view is that, rather than boost output, prices are adjusted. Given the exclusivity of the product might be tarnished by greater volume, companies might prefer moving up-market. Phillippe Martin of Sciences Po finds that French multinationals prefer pocketing the profit rather than upping the volume. In a sense, a branded good should not be price sensitive. Non-price competition may be the basis of rivalry. By implication, the law of one price, which relies on homogeneity of product and zero transport costs, would not apply.

Purchasing Power Parity

In principle, an exchange rate should reflect the cost of the same product in both countries. A car in the US costing $15,000 should be priced at £10,000 in the UK if the exchange rate of $1.5: £ is an accurate measure of relative prices. Of course, if this is a car built in the US, there should be a difference related to transport costs. But this would be the only explanation of difference. In a transport cost free perfect model, arbitrage would drive the price for the same good to be identical – the law of one price – for all goods. So exchange rates should then reflect what a given sum of money (possibly gold) would purchase in either country. There are two versions of PPP, absolute and relative.

❑   Absolute PPP entails the above; the equalization of goods purchased with the same amount of funds;

❑   Relative PPP posits that *changes* in the exchange rate reflect *changes* in relative costs – inflation. A relatively high rate of inflation would lead to a corresponding depreciation of the exchange rate.

The assessment of this model has presented problems. The price indices would include prices of traded and non-traded goods, so not an accurate measure of changes in relative prices of traded goods. Relative Unit Labour Costs (RULC) would be an interesting alternative. This would give some idea of the wage cost per hour. Of course, not all workers are equally productive in that hour. Some workers are more productive and have access to superior capital. Also, climate may make certain activities difficult. Pricing goods in hours of labour to produce them would be a further alternative.

CHANGING VEHICLES

In 2004, it was argued that the difficulties of replicating human perception, such as executing a turn against oncoming traffic, involves so many factors that it was hard to imagine discovering the set of rules that can replicate a driver's behaviour. By 2010, Google announced that it had modified several Toyota Priuses to be fully autonomous. In 2013, the phrase 'self-driving car' was nowhere to be found in documents published by the US Dept. of Transportation. Today the FT is full of this phrase. The business model is also changing Electric cars built by other producers may turn car manufacture into a low-margin business. Competitive advantage may come through suppliers and new foci. After a century of stability there are great global trends in the car industry: *electrification; autonomous driving; and car sharing and renting.*

Gapper in the FT in December 2016 was asking why own a self-driving car at all. If a car does the driving (so Top Gear is irrelevant) and is available when you want it, why own? An Uber taxi costs $250/mile to hire. Ford estimate that driverless taxis will cost $1/mile. Without the thrill of driving ownership is likely to decline. A city dweller may only use their car for 3% of the time but the financing and depreciation continue inexorably. Rented vehicles can be on the road for a higher proportion of time. The role of marques is likely to change also. Why care about the car you rent?

Sharing

Car builders were looking to renting – taxi or minibus services are the future. Ford estimate that each of minibus vehicle will displace 25 cars in China and 11 in the US. In May 2017, Ford, looking at a new business model, advocating taking cars off the road, emphasised moving away from car owners and switching to sharing. Ford purchased Chariot for £50m in 2016. It then announced a minibus shuttle service across London in 2017 and 2018 it announced Argo will be a robo-taxi firm operating at scale by 2021, transporting goods and people. Maven has been launched by GM, which has purchased a taxi-booking firm (Lyft) for $500m.

Daimler owns taxi apps MyTaxi and Hailo. With other facilities and in alliance with Bosch it aimed to focus on shared fleet. Rather than taxis, BMW focused on owners renting out their own BMW vehicles. These strategies merged with the creation of a joint venture covering 5 major areas (sharing, on-demand mobility, parking services, electronic charging, on-demand ordering and payment component of the business). They recognise the threat that car sharing is to them. The merger combined Car2go (D) and DriveNow and ReachNow (BMW). In December, BMW and Dailmer *scrapped* their US car-sharing operation. They will continue in Europe. GM's Malvern car-sharing unit was shut down and Chariot was sold by Ford. In general, McKinsey estimates that car sharing could be worth $30bn by 2030 seems not to be turning into profit opportunities.

Electrification

International Energy Agency estimate that in 2017 there were 2m electric cars on the road. This would rise to 50m by 2025 and 300m by 2040 – around 20% of cars vehicles. This would curtail oil demand by just 2%. Not all car companies are going the same way. Volvo, in July, pledged to end the production of combustion engines by 2019 and Daimler is building a platform for the EQ by 2022 for electric vehicles only. BMW are developing powertrains that can insert hybrid, combustion, and electric engines.

A shocking direction

Detailed production plans for North America indicate that Ford and GM will make 5.2m SUVs and pickup trucks in 2026, but only about 320,000 electric vehicles. Petrol-SUVs have a higher profit margin than mostly smaller, expensive-to-develop electric vehicles. Indeed, they make more profit on each luxury SUV - such as GM's $80,000 Cadillac Escalade or Ford's $76,000 Lincoln Navigator - than they do on a dozen compact cars. In the US, Ford replaced the Focus compact sedan (31 miles/gallon) with the Ford Escape compact SUV (26 miles/g), whose starting price is $6,000 higher. One could see this as reflecting the collapse of oil prices, pointing toward cheap petrol for the foreseeable future. Moreover, the US Environmental Protection Agency rules encourage more roomy and powerful cars. With lobbying from Detroit, cars have to meet tougher emissions and mileage targets than light trucks. This latter a category includes pickups and many so-called crossover vehicles that look like SUVs but have the mechanical underpinnings of cars. By extending the new generation Cadillac Escalade by 8 square foot it increases the amount of CO_2 the car can emit by 2% to 3% and still complying with regulations. The IEA suggested that if SUV demand continues at a similar pace seen in the last decade, they would add 2m barrels/day oil consumption by 2040, offsetting the savings from nearly 150m electric cars.

Batteries are a problem. They limit the distance one can travel; they are expensive; and must be replaced. Progress at making batteries more powerful occurred at a rate of

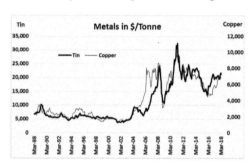

15%/yr for a decade and has reduced the cost to $150-250/kwh. Lithium battery components are dependent on China. In anode, cathode, electrolyte solution and separator supply China has increased its market share to 50-77% by around 10 percentage points between 2014 and 2016. Goldman Sachs forecasts that China will increase its market share of world electric car production from 45% in 2016 to 60% in 2030. China intends on making rare earths the equivalent of oil to the Arabs. In March 2018, it signed an agreement with Glencore to supply 50,000 tonnes of Cobalt over 3 years. This represents half the world's output in 2017. It appears that they could control the raw material and be strong in its use. South Crofty was the last of hundreds of Cornish tin mines to close in 1998. The price of tin continued to fall to a low of $3,730.80/tonne in February 2002. Things have changed. In two years to 2018, price has risen 25% to $21,000. Tin can be used in electric batteries. Also, such mines contain deposits of lithium. Mining is expanding in developed countries. For example, lithium at the Zinnwald project in Southern Saxony, and Kaustinen, in Finland. A nickel mine in Sotkamo, Finland and in Serbia jadarite (boron and lithium). In Cornwall, there is investment in copper and tin mines and tin, tungsten and copper near Plymouth. South Crofty was expected to be reopened 2019.

Autonomous Driving
There are different levels of autonomy.
0. No automation – human does the driving
1. Car able to take limited control of the steering or speed e.g. cruise control
2. Car able to take control of the steering and speed but the driver must monitor the road at all times
3. Driver can take their eyes of the road but must be able to retake control if needed
4. The car is de facto the driver but for poor conditions e.g. snow or country roads the driver must be able to retake control
5. The car drives itself

Cars without pedals and steering wheels will be on the road. California approved new rules that allow for level 5 vehicles in April 2018. This will encourage car manufacturers to relocate to where the beasts of Silicon Valley are already ensconced. The Dept. of Motor Vehicles wants an enforcement interaction plan. What responsibilities will the companies have if the car is involved in an accident should be outlined.

Many cars already have level 1 autonomy. Mercedes and Tesla have level 2 capability in some vehicles. Audi unveiled an A8 in July 2017 with level 3 capability. It will operate at low speeds (<60kph) and only if the car can sense white lines and guardrails. The system must judge when the human should revanche control, which is an area of weakness. How to achieve this, and will the human be alert enough to deal with what is a non-standard situation in 10 seconds, are at issue. It may be better to skip level 3 and move to 5. Daimler is aiming for level 5 vehicles, whereas BMW is designing vehicle with wheels and pedals with level 3-4 capability.

In July 2018, Baidu announced that it would be mass producing a self-drive bus. Without a driver's seat, steering wheel or pedals it has level-4 autonomy. It runs on electric power and can travel up to 100km after a two-hour charge, at up to 70km/h. Softbank is to buy 10 of these Apolongs buses for 'demonstration tests' within Japan by early 2019.

The First Fatality
In March 2018, the first fatality blamed on autonomous cars occurred in Arizona when a 49-year-old woman was hit by a car and killed as she crossed a street. A human monitor was behind the wheel. It turned out he was pratting with his phone. In the near-term, buses have a greater chance of public acceptance than self-drive cars. Car and truck manufacturers seemed to have backed away from level 5 autonomy. Cars need 3-dimensional maps that are continuously updated and accurate to a centimetre. GPS is not precise enough for self-driving cars so for car systems data must be shared among the vehicle eco system. Those on the road provide updates for others. The amount of information collected by a car by its Light Detecting and Ranging (LIDAR) sensors in a day is over a terabyte. This cannot be sent through the internet efficiently. As yet there is no agreement among map companies on standards and data sharing, so this information is proprietorial.

The maps are needed to reduce the amount of work that the autonomous software has to do to recognise the world around it. As with animals and movement, the software could focus on differences between known and perceived. So that the stored 'memory' could tell the car what should be there, which the car measures against the perceived, including the ephemeral pedestrians and cyclists. This though is predicated on recognition. Snowflakes can confuse scanners and snow banks and drifts can alter the appearance of objects. What software do you write for skidding or spinning? So winter in much of the rich world is a challenge.

MARKET FAILURE-EXTERNALITIES

Markets allocate resources efficiently when the benefit from the marginal activity = its extra cost i.e. MB = MC. However, this presumes that there are no spillovers that affect third parties; clear property rights; perfect competition; and people are the best judges of their own well-being.

Externalities – Short-run
Social costs and benefits emerge from the exchange process. An externality occurs when a cost or benefit from an activity or transaction impacts on parties not involved in that activity or transaction. The market mechanism may have produced at the most efficient point of production so that private MB = MC but do social MB = MC? In other words, do these externalities leads to a market failure – the over or under production/consumption of the good in question?

The cost of diesel is set to rise (see elasticity and shipping), but the falling demand for diesel cars means that this is already a headache for car manufacturers. They fell foul of a nitrogen oxide emission requirement. But diesel is less of a carbon emitter than petrol. So, as diesel is phased out, the 2021 requirement of 95g/km of CO_2 looms large. The fine of €95/g×no. of cars could impose a cost of €30bn, so by promoting petrol, EU manufacturers are going the wrong way. You might expect that with modern materials that the car was getting lighter. In 2018, the average car weighted 1,392kgs, 122kg heavier than 20 years previously. This is, in part, a wealth thing. A sports utility vehicle is relatively more popular. A Range Rover weighs 2,300kg. Smaller cars such as the Golf (1,335kg) are heavier than they could be because of the safety features that we expect. Also, we want more 'performance' – which means a heavier engine. In 2017 CO_2 g/km were on average 118.5g and in 2018 121g. UBS expected car company earnings for 2021 to be €7.4bn (14%) lower because of the cost of meeting the carbon target. Peugeot is most exposed (25% lower) with VW (13%) Renault (10%) Daimler (9%) and BMW (7%) being better off. Electric cars also have a weight problem – the battery. A Tesla X has one weighing 2,300kg – the same weight as a Range Rover. The performance of an electric car falls by a fifth if 300kg is added to a 950kg car. The cost of installing a small car with battery and electric motor is €2500-4000, so small cheap cars will be squeezed out.

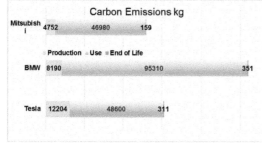

Carbon Emissions kg
Mitsubishi 4752   46980   159
Production Use End of Life
BMW 8190   95310   351
Tesla 12204   48600   311

Electric Dreams
According to Trancik Lab at MIT, the Tesla Model SP100D, a battery-electric vehicle, emits 48,600kg of CO_2 over its 270,000km road life. This is around half of the BMW 750i xDrive and broadly similar to the Mitsubishi Mirage, both of which

have internal combustion engines. However, when higher production emissions are taken into account the Tesla emits 226g/km but the petrol engine Mirage is notably less at 192. The concern is that larger electric vehicles are not that green. Rare earths are dirty and carbon-heavy in their production. Indeed, by 2030 the Mirage could be banned in Europe whilst the Tesla won't be. For the electric car it is the battery that causes green concerns. A top of the range vehicle will need 60kg of lithium and 10kg of cobalt. Moreover, the full life cycle assessment should take into account the generation of electricity itself. It could be coal or wind powered. An e-Golf is estimated to produce 9,700kg of carbon over its lifetime: when powered by renewable sources, there could be a 61% reduction over the standard Golf. If powered by EU electricity, it is only a 26% reduction.

Shipping Problems
From 1st January 2020 the threshold of sulphur emissions from shipping dropped from 3.5% a 0.5%. One large container ship emits more sulphur dioxide than 50m diesel cars. The International Maritime Organisation prohibited 94,000 ships from burning untreated high sulphur fuel oil (HSFO). This leaves three options available to shippers:
1. Abatement - Install scrubbers (exhaust gas cleaner systems that extract the sulphur as the HSFO is burned). Scrubbers take 6-9 months to install. From an industry supply perspective, the best possible outcome is around 1200 are installed before the 2020 deadline (out of the +60,000 needed).
2. Switch to liquid natural gas (LNG) propulsion systems. Given the capital expenditure requirement and uncertainty around enforcement of the regulation, plus volatility in the LNG markets over the next two years and availability at ports, this is unlikely.
3. Switch fuel intake to low sulphur fuel oil (which is equivalent to distillate). This is the most likely outcome.
The base global demand for distillate (diesel, kerosene, heavy and light gas oil) is around 30m b/day. The bunker (ship engine) fuel market accounts for around 5.5m b/d, with 70% (4mb/day) accounted for by around 70,000 ferries, cruise/container ships, dry bulk transport and oil tankers. These ships consume over 50% of the total global fuel oil demand.

Fuel oil is obtained during petroleum distillation, and has traditionally been the bottom of the barrel, high sulphur by-product formed along with gasoline and distillate by refiners. Given crude availability is skewed to light crude, refiners' supply of distillate is inelastic; they are already operating near maximum utilisation rates. In response to the shift, a growing proportion of the global shipping fleet now burns fuel closer in profile to the diesel used in cars. Pyrenees, an Australian crude, in January was selling for almost $95/b, way above Brent crude @ $65. It is heavy thick oil that is low in sulphur.

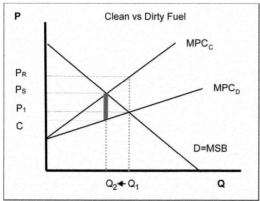

Let's examine this adapting a standard diagram. In the diagram left, the demand for sea-transportation shipping across a standard distance D = MSB (for the sake of ease). The marginal costs of that shipping distance is MPC_D. This is the cost using *dirty* fuel. The quantity of shipping is Q_1. However, as there are negative externalities produced this is an inefficient level of output for society. Sulphur is spewed into the atmosphere. The current charter fee P_1 is too low. If forced to use a clean fuel, the cost of shipping would rise to P_R. At this higher price, is would be uneconomic to ship so much. The socially efficient level of shipping is Q_2 where MSB=MSC_C. The price of shipping rises to P_S. Failure to comply should result in a fine >P_S – C (larger than the thick(red) line).

As indicated above, these high and low sulphur oil derivatives were complements in supply; now they are substitutes. Middle distillate demand covers diesel and jet fuel. As such, other forms of transportation will see an increase in costs. According to the IATA, in 2018 the global airline industry's net profit was $32bn. The fuel bill was around $180bn accounting for around 23.5% of operating expenses at $73/b Brent. A notable increase in this could push some to the wall. Industries dependent on airlines, such as tourism will also be adversely affected, particularly as this tends to be price sensitive (high price elasticity). The Select Committee on Climate Change reported in May 2019 that Britain could exceed its CO_2 aviation target for 2028-32 by 20%. A Pigovian passenger tax of £26/seat would hurt the shorter intra-UK/European routes.

Impact[9]
Fuel costs make up approximately 70-80% of total transport costs so as shippers moderate their speed to economise on fuel, perishable goods (like agricultural produce) cannot be transported so far and manufacturers may alter production facilities as geographical proximity becomes more important, reducing shipping from Q_1 to Q_2. In May 2019, a speed limit was proposed. Taking 24 days to cross the pacific rather than 20 increases the number of cargo ships needed by 20%. Relative prices are as follows: With Brent crude at $65 on 1st January Rotterdam 3.5%-HSFO oil price was $28.9 and the more expensive LSFO $77.8/b. In May 2020, Brent was $34.5, with the 3.5% $27.4 and 1%-LSFO @$34.5. The expected tightness in the diesel market did not materialise as refiners proved adept at blending lower-sulphur fuel mixes to boost

---

[9] FT 15 4 19 Cleaner shipping will push up the cost of flying and driving, by Dizard

supplies. Some ship owners were keen to keep using high-sulphur fuel oil, either because they had installed sulphur-stripping scrubbers on their vessels, or because they were concerned that the new fuel blends might damage their engines. Carnival Corporation, the world's biggest cruise operator, invested more than $500m in retrofitting most of its ships with scrubbers. As refiners produced less high-sulphur fuel oil, an unexpected scramble for barrels ensued, sending prices spiking higher. The result was that diesel's premium over its dirtier rival, rather than expanding, fell by almost a third in January. While ship operators can make back the costs of the devices within a few years, a growing number of ports are looking at banning their use, so the scrubber solution may die.

Diesel cars are being squeezed out of the market already, so automobile manufacturers may actually see a bump in demand for electric cars. In February 2019, the EU agreed to CO_2 emissions from new trucks and buses by 30% by a 2030. Rail transportation is not so easy. Rail transported 16.95bn tonne-km of freight in 2017/18 equating to 10% of freight surface transport. But then, as with cars, there is a commitment for diesel trains to be phased out in the UK.

Again substitutes in supply, the power generation market will benefit, and coal lose. As HSFO contains around 50% more energy per unit than coal, it will be switched to be a fuel for power generation, competing with coal in emerging markets (HSFO emits less CO_2 than coal). Schroders estimated that HSFO prices would need to decline to around $100/tonne to be competitive with coal fired power stations with coal @ $50/t coal. This requires a significant fall from a spot of $254/t in May.

There is research into alternatives. An alternative zero-carbon fuel, Ammonia, has almost twice as much energy as liquid hydrogen by weight and has nine times the energy density of lithium-ion batteries. Ammonia can be liquefied quite easily, has a higher volumetric energy density than liquid hydrogen, and it can be burnt in an internal combustion engine.

Internalising a Negative Externality, Literally
Pollution has a knock on effect on labour productivity. Chang, Zivin, Gross and Neidell found call centre staff working for the same company in different Chinese cities were 5-6% less productive on polluted days. Moreover, Kings College researchers reported in November pollution can increase lung cancer by 10% and heart stroke by 6%.

MARKET FAILURE-DEMERIT GOODS

Demerit activities are those that are over consumed by consumers. Whatever gambling responsibly is is a moot point. In April 2019, Fixed Odds Betting Terminals stakes dropped from £100 to £2. It was scheduled to come in in October 2019 by the government, but under pressure from parliament including Sports minister Tracey Crouch resigning in protest, the date was brought forward. Fixed-odds betting terminals generated £1.8bn in revenue a year for the betting industry and taxes of £400m for the government.

Demerit Marketing
The insurance industry is a remarkable instrument of market driven good. Global reinsurers are stepping up their warnings to life insurer clients about the potential risks of vaping. Reinsurers insure the insurers. They give broad advice to insurers, rather than specific policy or pricing recommendations, but can potentially refuse to provide reinsurance or can raise premiums if their guidance is ignored. Swiss Re and Hannover RE, which already advised life insurers to treat vapers like smokers, has asked them to be particularly cautious about insuring people aged under 25 following a jump in lung injuries in the US. The new advice focus on young vapers and the vaping of liquids containing tetrahydrocannabinol. SCOR, a French reinsurer, in October, advised that e-cigarettes contain nicotine which may have toxic effects, including on brain development in teenagers and young adults.

The premiums for a 20-year policy for a 35-year old offering £100,000 of life cover and £100,000 of critical illness cover would be around £11.89/month for a non-smoker/non-vaper. A smoker/vaper would pay £20.56 for the same cover. Reviti, a new insurer was out of line in offering a discount of up to 15% for vapers in Britain. Customers who quit tobacco and nicotine altogether got a discount of up to 50%. Interestingly, it is owned by cigarette and e-cigarette firm Philip Morris. But then Philip Morris is seeking to shift its image as a purveyor of cancer-sticks to new smoking alternatives as youthful. In May 2019, a Reuters investigation that found Philip Morris had used young on-line personalities, including a 21-year-old woman in Russia, to promote IQOS, a 'reduced risk' heated-tobacco device. The company invested $6bn in developing 'smoke-free' products, such as IQOS, hoping to earn about 40% of its revenue (or $20bn) from these products by 2025.

Researchers at Stanford University suggested that PMorris is seeking to undermine public smoking laws and encourage dual use of cigarettes and alternative devices. Many users will continue smoking outdoors, but turn to e-cigarettes or IQOS where they are permitted indoors. Such switching can deepen nicotine addiction and make cessation less probable. PMorris has partnerships with restaurants, bars and salons in the Czech Republic, Ukraine, Romania and Japan, that designate themselves as 'IQOS friendly' spaces, where cigarettes are banned but the IQOS device is allowed.

Price Minimum
In December 2017, the UK Supreme Court accepted the Scottish Government's right to impose a minimum of 50p a unit on alcoholic beverages. The court accepted that there would be market would be subject to distortions but the policy was a proportionate means of achieving a legitimate aim. The 2016 UK guidelines recommend no more than 14 alcoholic units a week (six pints of beer or seven glasses of wine). A Cambridge University study in the Lancet of 600,000 drinkers estimated that having 5-10; 10-15; and over 18 drinks/wk shortens life expectancy by 6 months;

between 1 & 2 years; and 4-5yrs respectively. Also, every 12.5 units above the guidelines increases the probability of: a stroke by 14%; fatal hypertensive disease by 24%; heart failure by 9%; and a fatal aortic aneurysm by 15%.

The industry, obviously keen to argue for free trade, suggested that this contravened EU Law and would have no effect on drinking problems. It would affect ordinary drinkers, not the alcoholics. Given that cider can cost as little as 18p/unit this strikes one as misleading. Anyway, the ONS found that 80% of rich (those earning >£40,000) workers had had alcohol the week before whereas

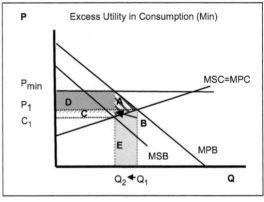

the proportion was only 50% among lorry drivers receptionists and labourers. In the diagram right, a price minimum P_{min} could force consumption down from Q_1 to Q_2 but, the welfare outcomes are different to a tax. Consumer surplus would fall by triangle A + box D. Producer surplus would fall by triangle B + box C. There would also be a decline in expenditure, which is the same as the reduction in costs (area E). From the producer's perspective, this is at the expense of output and jobs. Areas A+B+E are lost, but the supermarket gains areas C+D in higher profit. Thus, if $[Q_2 \times P_{min}] > [P_1 \times Q_1]$, the supermarket is better off.

A Sweetened Pill Swallowed Partly

As part of a healthy balanced diet, NHS recommend an adult's *reference intakes* (RIs) for a day are: Energy: 8,400 kJ/2,000kcal; total fat: 70g; saturates: 20g; carbohydrate: 260g; total sugars: 90g; protein: 50g; and salt: 6g. The Behavioural Insight Team found that people under-report their calorie intake by up to 50% affecting policy initiatives. One benefit of poorer health is that people do not live as long. The PwC estimate that the shortfall in Defined Benefits pension schemes, valued at £530bn, could be £310bn smaller. For example, a previous estimate of a 40 year old living to 90 was revised down to living to 84.

In April 2016, Mars took the unusual step of advising to its customers that some of its products should only be consumed *weekly*, not *everyday*. As part of its ambition to create and promote healthier food choices, it wanted to reduce the consumption of high salt, sugar or fat content produce such as Dolmio's carbonara, lasagne sauces, pesto, and macaroni oven kits, and Uncle Ben's oriental sauces.

The fizzy drinks industry is illustrative of an amoral approach to marketing. The sugar tax announced in the April 2016 budget prompted the Soft Drinks Association to describe it as 'the misguided campaign on sugar.' This would include Coco-Cola,

Britvic and Suntory. Secretly, they have been taking steps. 50% of the sugar intake of the average US citizen comes from fizzy, energy and sports drinks, plus tea.

Depending on how much extra sugar has been added, bottled drinks had 18p or 24p/ ltr tax added in April 2018. When George Osborne announced the sugar tax in 2016 the expected revenue was about £500m/yr. By November 2017, the anticipated figure had dropped to £275m/yr. Again, firms responded with reduced sugar recipe. Irn Bru stopped making the original full-sugar version. AG Barr, the brand owner, expected 99% of its drinks range, including other brands, to be below the threshold by the time it came into force. Suntory had reduced the sugar content of Ribena and Lucozade by 50%. Britvic, owners of Robinson's, J2O and Fruit Shoot, has pursued this policy since 2013. By the November 2018, the tax raised £153.8m imposed 7 month previously.

Mexico has high rates of obesity and sugar consumption. Over 70% of the population is overweight with more than 70% of the added sugar in the diet derived from sugar-sweetened drinks. A sugar tax was introduced in 2014. The University of North Carolina and the Mexican Instituto Nacional de Salud Pública (National Institute of Public Health) found that a 1 peso (4p)tax / ltr of sugary drink, led to a decline in consumption by 18.8ml/person in 2014 and 29.3ml in 2015. Purchases of other untaxed drinks went up on average by 2% over the two years. Euromonitor reported that a 33¢/ltr tax introduced in Berkeley, California reduced sweetened beverage consumption by 21% and increased water consumption by 63%. In comparison, other cities in the US reported a 4% increase in SSB consumption, and only 19% increase in water consumption in that time. That said, the Mexico tax raised £880m/yr; the French, £263m, Belgian £87m; and the Finish £79m. Since the beginning of 2018 when Norway's tax on sweets and sugary drinks rose dramatically, Norwegians make a day trip to Sweden to get their sugar fix. All sweetened drinks are now taxed at about 43p/litre. Also, all sweets and chocolate, chewing gum and sweet biscuits are now taxed at £3.34/kg.

The idea that consumers should be making these choices is also flawed. In February 2019, Nestle decided to withdraw is Milkybar Wowsomes, which used ⅔ the amount of sugar, after just 2 years into its lifecycle. In the same month, Unilever announced that by 2021, it would stop marketing and advertising foods and beverages to children under the age of 12 in traditional media, and below 13 via social media channels. They also claimed that it would not use any influencers, celebrities or social media stars who primarily appeal to children under the age of 12.

Below is a social welfare diagram. The marginal social cost (MSC) of manufacturing sugary drinks is the same as the marginal private costs (MPC) (we'll ignore the cost of bottle disposal, say – but see plastics and coffee). However, the costs to the individual (and to society) from drinking are not fully borne by the consumer. Additional costs, such as time off work, poorer well-being, and time in hospital receiving treatment for diabetes are borne by both the individual (and society). There are, thus, two elements that are blended together: the over consumption by individuals; and the impact on society's medical and other services that over indulgence brings.

As a point of exploration, the following entails considering the marginal social benefits merely as the socially defined appropriate level of sugary drink consumption, not that defined by individuals. Thus, the over consumption can be viewed as excess utility.

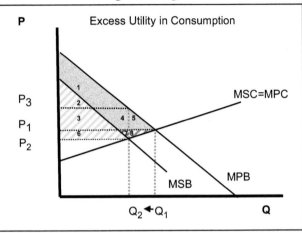

Individuals consume the drinks up to point Q_1 where the cost of the drink (P_1) provides that level of marginal utility. A lower level of consumption is socially desirable (Q_2). This is where the extra cost of producing a unit of sugary drink reflects the full net benefit to the consumers, including the demerit of weight, a shorter life etc..

Welfare can be judged from the excess consumer and producer surplus. Assuming no negative externality in production, total revenue is $Q_1 \times P_1$ and consumer surplus comprises areas 1+2+3+4+5. However, if the level of consumption was more socially acceptable, there would be a lower price and quantity. Then, total revenue would be $Q_2 \times P_2$ and consumer surplus would be areas 2+3+6, a clearly smaller total area and, hence, fewer resources allocated to drink's production. The well-being accounting is not straight-forward. Society must benefit from the correction in the assessment of utility. As the triangles do not overlap perfectly, we end up with the measure of the excess as 1+4+5–6. However, producer surplus falls because of the reduced consumption by 6+7+8. Thus, as measured by individuals, there is a net fall in well-being of 1+4+5+7+8.

A Tax in a Coffee Cup
Because of their plastic lining, some 2.5bn coffee cups are thrown away annually in the UK, almost none of which are recycled. Consistent with a Pigouvian solution the Environmental Audit Committee (EAC) had proposed a charge of 25p for disposable coffee cups. Starbucks started charging 5p for disposable coffee cups in 35 London stores as part of a trial in January 2018. Waitrose, over several months from April 2018 year stopped using (52m/yr) disposable coffee cups. The government was hoping for a more Coasian solution. If they found some way of reducing cup use coffee vendors could sell more coffee. A solution is for the consumer to bear some of the recycling cost – reuse old cups. Pret a Manger (50p) Costa Coffee (50p) and Starbucks

(25p) were already there, offering discounts for using reusable cups. An independent coffee chain Boston Tea Party (BTP) found that only 5% of customers took up 25p discount for its reusable cup scheme. It stopped supplying disposable cups and saw sales drop by £250,000 over 10 months to April 2019.

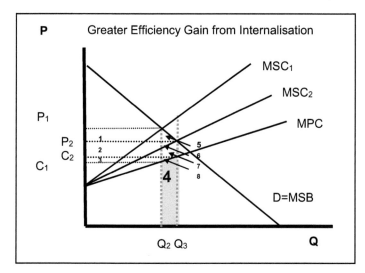

In effect, the coffee vendor and consumer share the benefits of reducing the tax burden. The vendor sells fewer cups per litre of coffee sold and the consumer consumes more coffee per £1 spent on coffee. The outcome is that more coffee is sold than Q_2. In the diagram right for the sake of ease assume that the cost of coffee cups is zero. As before there is still the cost of disposal inherent in MSC_1 but now, assume that that cost can be halved as everyone reuses a cup once. So that the new MSC curve is MSC_2. The Pigouvian tax is P_1-C_1. By reusing, more coffee is consumed than before $Q_3 > Q_2$. There is a rise in costs of = 4+7+8. Rise in benefits = 4+5+6+7+8. Therefore, the higher Coasian output to leads to a net increase of 5+6+7+8. The new price is P_2. Lower than the Pigouvian tax price. However, recycling costs remain. The Coasian tax is P_2-C_2. This raises revenue of areas 2+5+6+7. So with the greater coffee consumption, society is better off by 5+8.

Externalities and Public Opinion
If David Attenborough says there is a problem; there is a problem. BBC documentary Blue Planet II raised consumer understanding of the issue, with 10.3m viewers. Following this, new targets hit the headlines. KPMG banned plastic cups. Using 3m/yr that cost £60,000 it is providing reusable water bottles. Diageo announced in that it would phase out the use of plastic straws and stirrers from all its offices, events, promotions, advertising and marketing globally – and is advocating the same for its partners and customers. Iceland found when it surveyed 5,000 people 80% were in favour of the retailer getting rid of plastic. It went with public opinion with its own brand products. Pizza Express, Morrisons, Waitrose, and McDonalds followed suit in June 2018.

Unilever's 'Sustainable Living' brands accounted for 60% of the company's growth in 2016, and they grew more than 50% faster than the rest of the business. Bulldog

Skincare for Men has developed sugarcane packaging as a replacement for plastic. Not only does this get rid of the issue of plastic waste, but sugarcane saves carbon dioxide, rather than releasing it into the atmosphere. Bulldog's marketing research suggests that in skincare, from a commercial perspective, by opting to buy their products consumers were rewarding companies that take a positive stand.

Shops with over 250 employees were required to impose a plastic bag charge of 5p levy in England in October 2015 Wales (2011), Scotland (2014) and Northern Ireland (2013). Before the levy the average consumer used 140 bags/yr (7.64bn in 2014). This dropped to 25. The outcome of a small charge resulted in a notable reduction in consumption. Having phased out the 5p carrier bags in the past year in England, Wales and Scotland, Morrisons began selling paper shopping bags also aside plastic reusable bags – both types for 20p.

Markit Economic Research 17/08/2015
The Markit Eurozone Purchasing Managers' Index has been compiled by Markit's economics team since 1998 surveying around 5,000 manufacturing and services private sector companies, tracking variables such as output, new orders, stock levels, employment and prices. The index can be used to estimate GDP change on a quarterly basis

PMI	GDPΔ%	PMI	GDPΔ%
40	-1.2	52	0.2
42	-1.0	54	0.5
44	-0.7	56	0.7
46	-0.5	58	0.9
48	-0.3	60	1.2
50	0.0		

GDP (quarterly %Δ) $= -5.93 + 0.118$ PMI
(adjusted $R^2 = 0.725$)

A PMI would be interpreted as below
$0.324 = -5.93 + 0.118 \times 53$. In other words, an increase of around 0.3% on a quarterly basis or 1.2% on an annual basis. A PMI of 50.0 is indicative of GDP being unchanged on the previous quarter. Conducted the week commencing 16th March, the PMI for the UK pointed to the economy shrinking at a quarterly rate of 1.5-2.0%. This is in line with the worst point of the 2008-09 recession. The index fell from 53 in February to 37.1, with the Service sector falling from 53.2 to 35.7. They were better than the Eurozone figures of 51.6 to 31.4, with services nose-diving to 28.4 from 52.6. Thus $-1.55 = -5.93 + 0.118 \times 37.1$

Reserve Bank of India estimated the following:
http://www.rbi.org.in/scripts/AnnualReportPublications.aspx?Id=896

The Export Demand Function for India: Some Inferences on the Impact of the Global Recession on India Box II.32
An estimate of India's exports for the period 1980-81 to 2007-08 reveals a long-run elasticity of demand for India's exports with respect to world GDP. RBI uses the following abbreviations:
X = Quantity index of India's exports, YW = World GDP at constant prices in US$ terms, RXP = ratio of India's export price (unit value index of India's exports deflated

by the Rupee-US$ nominal exchange rate) to world export price (unit value index of world exports in US$ terms). ln = natural log.

The dependent variable is quantity (of exports), which is a function of income, and relative price. As RBI used natural logarithms, the expression can directly assess elasticities. The expression is

$$ln\ X = -56.96 + 3.73\ ln\ YW - 1.94\ ln\ RXP + 0.81\ AR(1)$$
$$(-7.72)\quad (8.43)\qquad (-1.78)\qquad\qquad (7.28)$$
$$R^2 = 0.99\quad DW = 1.65\qquad SEE = 0.07$$

Interpretation:- High R^2 indicates a robust model, but the DW is low (need dof and a critical value to judge). The t-ratios are in brackets. We have not got a critical value, but let us use the notional one of 2. This suggests that exports are influenced by income but not prices. The income elasticity of 3.73 would indicate that it exports luxury goods. The −1.9 suggests India exports price sensitive goods (*but* − 1.78 suggests that value is not significantly different from zero).